HOW TO DEVELOP POWER AND PERSONALITY IN SPEAKING

HOW TO DEVELOP POWER AND PERSONALITY IN SPEAKING

by

GRENVILLE KLEISER

With an Introduction by

LEWIS O. BRASTOW, D.D.

GYAN

Published by

GYAN

Gyan Publishing House
5, Ansari Road
Daryaganj, New Delhi-110002
Phone: 011-47034999, 9811692060
E-mail: books@gyanbooks.com

Distribution Network
gyanbooks.com
India, USA, Canada, UK, Australia, France

ISBN : 978-81-212-6039-8 (PB)
First Published, 1910

2nd Impression 2021

Printed at: Gyan Press, Delhi.

How to Develop Power and Personality in Speaking
Author: Grenville Kleiser

HOW TO DEVELOP POWER AND PERSONALITY IN SPEAKING

By

GRENVILLE KLEISER

Distinguished Speech Specialist. Author of "How to Speak in Public," "Humorous Hits and How to Hold an Audience," and compiler and editor of "The World's Great Sermons"

With an Introduction by

LEWIS O. BRASTOW, D.D.

Professor Emeritus of Practical Theology in Yale University

PREFACE

EVERY man seeks power. It may be social, financial, or political power, physical, mental, or spiritual power, according to the ideal he sets before him. The highest and most enduring power is that which comes from the development of personal character.

The purpose of this book is to give practical suggestions and exercises for building the body, the voice, and the vocabulary, for training the memory and imagination, and for the general development of power and personality in the speaker.

The author's work as instructor in public speaking has brought him into intimate touch with the needs of men of widely varied type and temperament. He has observed in many instances the lack of development in these two essentials to true success—power and personality—and it is his hope that this book will help many men to realize more fully their highest ideals.

In conjunction with this work the author has compiled, in ten small volumes, "The World's Great Sermons," which will be found useful in solving many problems of right living.

Appreciative acknowledgment is made to authors and publishers for kind permission to use copyrighted material.

GRENVILLE KLEISER.

New York City,
December, 1908.

INTRODUCTION

WE have here an elucidation that is thoroughly sane of the art of expression by one who has made himself master of his task by careful study and training as a teacher of students of preaching. Professor Kleiser is quite right in his opinion that ministers "have not yet come to realize to any appreciable extent the value of thorough training in the art of expression." The writer is able to confirm this judgment by many years of experience as a teacher of homiletics. There is doubtless a well-grounded prejudice against certain methods of teaching "elocution" so called that have prevailed in time past. But intelligent preachers and students of the art of preaching should know, and in fact do know, that such methods are obsolescent and that modern methods of teaching the art of expression are rational and normal.

The task that every public speaker has to master is the task of handling himself. No man can accomplish that task without thorough training in the art of expression, and every student of his art should be eager to avail himself of the best that can be done for him in securing such thorough and facile handling of himself. "What we need," says Emerson, "is vent." But this depends on the kind of vent.

Untrained vent, like that of a wild locomotive that has lost control of its forces and has left the rails, is of little avail. Training in a normal method of expression will not fail to have a reactionary effect upon the activities of the mind as well as upon the emotions, the imagination and the will. Such training enables one to coordinate the products of the mind with the emotional and ethical activities.

What a man says is not the speaker's entire problem, and in and for itself alone is after all not the supreme interest. The literary and artistic form of thought is part of its very life, and the form which speech takes in vocal utterance and in the manifestation of other forces of the physical personality is proportionately important. A preacher's delivery is the transmission of his message through the potencies of his personality. It is the expression of himself, and at its best it must be the trained self. It is the speaker's method of uttering to best advantage the physical, mental, emotional and moral forces of his personal being. The free normal expression and interpretation of great truth is a genuine inspiration which every preacher should know. It is not a credit to any man's intelligence, and much less to his moral purpose, that he treats with contempt so important an art as that which would train his personality as the organ of religion and would equip him for the expression of its great realities with dignity, grace and strength. The dramatist spares himself no toil in the culture of self-expression. His success depends upon it.

Preaching is an art, but it is a moral art, and on moral grounds the preacher should train himself assiduously and laboriously in the exercise of it.

Professor Kleiser has done well to direct attention once more, and in so forceful, attractive and practical a manner, to the importance of the art of which he is at once the master and the servant. It is to be hoped that through this volume he may secure new incentive to the study of this art, and that he may find the realization of his most ardent desires.

LEWIS O. BRASTOW.

Yale University,
New Haven, Conn., 1908.

CONTENTS

PART ONE—POWER AND PERSONALITY IN SPEAKING

PART TWO—SELECTIONS FOR STUDY AND PRACTISE

INDEX OF AUTHORS

PART I

POWER AND PERSONALITY IN SPEAKING

CHAPTER I

POWER AND PERSONALITY IN SPEAKING

The public speaker and the preacher have much in common. The difference lies mainly in their message. Both are concerned with the problem of convincing and persuading men. To achieve this result there must be brought to bear the highest possible training in thought and expression.

In the best sense, a public speaker should be a man of sterling character, of lofty purpose, of trained ability, and, like the preacher, he should be prepared, if need be, to offer himself a living sacrifice in the cause of truth. "Let no man who is a sneak try to be an orator," said Beecher, and he might have added, Let no man aspire to distinction in public speaking, whether in pulpit, on platform, or elsewhere, unless he be willing to spend his days and nights in developing all the resources of his mind, voice, and body.

The lawyer can learn much from the sincerity, sympathy, and persuasiveness of the preacher; the preacher in turn may take a valuable lesson from the concise, direct, and convincing style of the lawyer; while the average public speaker may learn from both the value of truth and earnestness as effective elements in speech.

Assuming that the preacher, thoroughly trained in voice and manner, having the highest truth to proclaim, and uttering it from a position of authority, is the ideal public speaker, may we not here find the fundamental elements of success for those who would speak with truth and effectiveness upon other occasions?

Two essential elements in successful preaching are truth and personality. By truth here is meant God's revelation. The truth of the preacher is the Bible truth. Not exclusively, for the Bible will conduct him beyond the Bible, to the heart, to history, and to the book of nature, but the ultimate authority for him is the Bible as the revealed truth of God. Three things are involved in this matter of truth—receiving, adapting, and giving. The preacher will first find and appropriate the truth to himself. He will adapt it in such a way as to make it available for his practical work as a teacher. He will adopt the best means in his power of giving that truth to others.

No one thing will add so much to a man's power in speaking as the conscious possession of truth. As Cardinal Newman says, "What is so powerful an incentive to preaching as the sure belief that it is the preaching of the truth?" The speaker knows he stands upon a solid rock, and this assurance produces the highest type of self-confidence.

It is the work of the preacher to interpret the truth, not to create it. That he may search out the right kind of truth he should have a clear and definite purpose ever before him. Phillips Brooks says, in speaking of the minister: "He must receive the truth as one who is to teach it. He can not, he must not study as if the truth he sought were purely for his own culture or enrichment. This will bring, first, a deeper and more solemn sense of responsibility in the search for truth; second, a desire to find the human side of every truth, the point at which every speculation touches humanity; and, third, a breadth which comes from the constant presence in the mind of the fact that truth has various aspects and presents itself in many ways to different people, according to their needs and characters."[1]

It will be seen, then, that no two men will convey their message exactly alike. They will speak out of the fulness of their own hearts and experiences. Each man has a grasp of partial truth, but no man has the whole truth. As Professor James says, the truth is too great for any one actual mind. Each man will give what he has to give.

The importance of truth is nowhere emphasized more than in the Bible. "The *truth* of the Lord endureth forever."—*Psalm* cxvii., 2. "Thy law is the *truth.*"—*Psalm* cxix., 142. "All thy commandments are *truth.*"—*Psalm* cxix., 151. "He that walketh uprightly, and worketh righteousness, and speaketh the *truth* in his heart."—*Psalm* xv., 2. "All the paths of the Lord are mercy and *truth* unto such as keep his covenant and his testimonies." —*Psalm* xxv., 10. "His *truth* shall be thy shield and buckler."—*Psalm* xci., 4. "The lip of *truth* shall be established forever."—*Proverbs* xii., 19. "And ye shall know the *truth*, and the *truth* shall make you free."—*John* viii., 32. "Jesus saith unto him, I am the way, the *truth*, and the life: no man cometh unto the Father, but by me."—*John* xiv., 6. "Sanctify them through thy *truth*: thy word is *truth.*"—*John* xvii., 17. "For this cause came I into the world, that I should bear witness unto the *truth.* Every one that is of the *truth* heareth my voice."—*John* xviii., 37. "But speaking the *truth* in love, may grow up into him in all things, which is the head, even Christ."—*Ephesians* iv., 15. "For the fruit of the Spirit is in all

[1] Phillips Brooks, *Yale Lectures on Preaching.*

goodness and righteousness and *truth*."—*Ephesians* v., 9. "Stand therefore, having your loins girt about with *truth*, and having on the breastplate of righteousness."—*Ephesians* vi., 14. "And it is the Spirit that beareth witness, because the Spirit is *truth*."—*I John*, v., 6.

The knowledge and consciousness of this truth will do much toward making a man eloquent in speech. "There is a calm and earnest trust in God's ordinance," says Austin Phelps, "that truth shall do its work in the salvation of men, which every preacher needs to make him what the world calls a natural orator. Possest of such a trust, all preachers may be natural orators. That trust creates a spirit of repose in the use of God's instrument. It makes a preacher feel that he can afford to preach the truth naturally. He need not exaggerate it; he need not distort it; he need not deck it with meretricious ornament; he need not mince it, nor inflate it, nor paint it. He has only to speak it in a spirit of reverence and love, and let it do its work. It will do its work. He may safely repose in it. In the very heat and turmoil of the world's hostility to his message, he may wrap himself in the spirit of a child's faith. That shall be to him and to his life's work like the mantle of a prophet. He may *know* in his inmost soul that his words are the wisdom of God and the power of God."

But truth alone is not sufficient, else we might leave the sermon to the printed page. What is needed is the message and the man, or truth conveyed through personality. The qualities of a truly great personality are many. Among them are faith, personal piety, unselfishness, magnetism, sociability, culture of mind and heart, and devotion to humanity. Paul's personality speaks even from the printed page because of his unquenchable love for men. The personal side of the preacher is strikingly emphasized by Beecher in his *Yale Lectures:* "Make religion attractive by the goodness that men see in you; be so sweet, so sparkling, so buoyant, so cheerful, hopeful, courageous, conscientious and yet not stubborn, so perfectly benevolent and yet not mawkish or sentimental; blossoming in everything that is good, a rebuke to everything that is mean or little—make such men of yourselves that everybody who looks upon you may say, 'That is a royal good fellow; he has the spirit that I should like to lean upon in time of trouble, or to be a companion with at all times.' Build up such a manhood that it shall be winning to men."

One great object of preaching, like other forms of public speaking, is persuasion. The final test is whether men *act*. They are convinced of the truth through the intellect; they are persuaded to act upon the truth through the heart. How this can best be done is one of the problems of successful preaching.

In his lecture on *The Secrets of Effective Preaching*[1] the Rev. J. H. Jowett says: "Months ago I determined that there should be more of the tender lover in my pulpit speech, more of the wooing note of the Apostle Paul, more of the gentleness and tender constraint of my Lord." He advocates less scolding and more pleading, less driving and more wooing in pulpit delivery. It is this tenderness of speech, the truth spoken in love, that wins men. Doctor Jowett further suggests that the preacher should question himself thus: "Do I feel sin to be loathsome? Am I possest of a tender sensitiveness, that can discern even the faintest movings in the hearts of my people, and which will reveal

[1] *The Secrets of Effective Preaching*, delivered before the Free Church Congress, Cardiff, March, 1901. Hodder & Stoughton.

to me their inclinations long before they receive any outward expression? And, Lord Jesus, have I been a wooer, a lover, and are any in Thy kingdom because they were just enticed into it by the tender persuasiveness of my life and speech? And have I linked the proclamation of duties to the love of Calvary? And has my teaching had New Testament perspective and proportion, and have I evinced delight in my own message?"

The affectionate spirit in preaching is what is most needed. This will impart beauty and feeling to the spoken word. It will give zeal and sincerity to the message. Thus will the whole man speak when possest of the truth and a genuine love for men. Schleiermacher possest this "persuasive, penetrating, kindling effusion of feeling" in his preaching, and little do we wonder when we read these fervent words he wrote to his father: "From my heart I do wish that God's blessing may be upon my sermons, so that they may be sources of true edification and speak to the heart, as, I trust, they will ever come from the heart. To you I need not say how deeply I am moved at the thought of being numbered among those to whom so important an office is entrusted, nor need I assure you that I do not now, and never shall, look upon it merely as a means of livelihood."

It is said of Cardinal Newman that the tones of his voice seemed as if they were something more than his own. His musical voice had such a rare charm for his hearers that they did not miss the entire absence of gesture. His body and soul glowed with suppress emotion as he entered more deeply into his subject. He is vividly described by Principal Shairp as having this peculiarity in delivery: "Each sentence was spoken rapidly, but with great clearness of intonation, and then, at the close of every sentence, there was a pause that lasted for several seconds. Then another rapidly but clearly spoken sentence, followed by another pause, till a wonderful spell took hold of the hearer. The look and bearing of the preacher were as of one who dwelt apart, and who, tho he knew his age well, did not live in his age. From his seclusion of study, and abstinence, and prayer; from habitual dwelling in the unseen, he seemed to come forth that one day of the week to speak to others of the things he had seen and known in secret. As he spake, how the old truths became new! how they came home with a meaning never felt before! The subtlest of truths were dropt out as by the way in a sentence or two of the most transparent Saxon. What delicacy of style, yet what calm power! how gentle yet how strong! how simple yet how suggestive! how homely yet how refined! how penetrating yet how tender-hearted! And the tone of voice in which all this was spoken sounded to you like a fine strain of unearthly music."[1]

Probably no American preacher is more closely studied than the late Phillips Brooks. He exemplified in his own life and preaching the force of a consecrated personality, which he so earnestly advocated to others. He claimed that the qualities most to be desired in the sermon—"clearness, logicalness, vivacity, earnestness, sweetness, and light"—should first be in the preacher himself, else they would not find their natural place in his message. Sincerity, courage, joy in one's work, purity and personal uprightness, he emphasized in his counsel to others and fully demonstrated in his own life. With his broad and genial optimism he

---

[1] Quoted by Alexander Whyte, in Newman's *An Appreciation in Two Lectures*. Longmans, 1903.

said: "The world has not heard its best preaching yet. If there is more of God's truth for men to know, and if it is possible for the men who utter it to become more pure and godly, then, with both of its elements more complete than they have ever been before, preaching must some day be a complete power." Regarding Phillips Brooks himself, what higher tribute and recommendation can be offered to his honored name than these words of Doctor Brastow? "Any man who would know better what it is to be a helpful, pastoral preacher, a real preacher, full, simple, earnest, unconventional, the preacher of an imaginative, suggestive, and ethical mind, who cares chiefly to make the truth effective, who is bent upon getting it at work in the minds and hearts of men, who would fuse and fire the truth with the energies of a manly human soul, may well give himself with diligence to Phillips Brooks."[1]

The ultimate purpose of all true preaching is the salvation of men. The work of the Christian minister is the preaching of Christ and of Christianity as the one religion based on love. If his heart and tongue be not on fire with holy zeal in proclaiming this greatest of all gifts to mankind, he can not and will not succeed. "Whenever a minister forgets," says Lyman Abbott, "the splendid message of pardon, peace, and power based on faith in Jesus Christ as God manifest in the flesh, whenever for this message he substitutes literary lectures, critical essays, sociological disquisitions, theological controversies, or even ethical interpretations of the universal conscience, whenever, in other words, he ceases to be a Christian preacher and becomes a lyceum or seminary lecturer, he divests himself

---

[1] *Representative Modern Preachers*, by Lewis O. Brastow, D.D., Professor of Practical Theology in Yale University. The Macmillan Company, 1904.

of that which in all ages of the world has been the power of the Christian ministry, and will be its power so long as men have sins to be forgiven, temptations to conquer, and sorrows to be assuaged.''[1]

A young man asked an old minister who had heard him preach: ''What do you think of my sermon?'' ''A very poor sermon, indeed,'' said he. ''It took me a long time to prepare it,'' said the astonished young man. ''Ay, no doubt of it.'' ''Why, did you not think my explanation of the text a very good one?'' ''Oh, yes,'' said the old preacher, ''very good, indeed.'' ''Well, then, why do you say it is a poor sermon? Were not the metaphors appropriate, and the arguments conclusive?'' ''Yes, they were very good as far as that goes, but still it was a very poor sermon.'' ''Will you tell me why you think it was a poor sermon?'' ''Because,'' said he, ''there was no Christ in it.'' Said the young man: ''Christ was not in the text; we are not to be preaching Christ always; we must preach what is in the text.'' The old minister said: ''Don't you know, young man, that from every town and every village and every little hamlet in England, wherever it may be, there is a road to London? So from every text of Scripture there is a road to the metropolis of the Scriptures, that is, Christ. And, my dear brother, your business is, when you get to a text, to say, 'Now what is the road to Christ?' and then preach a sermon, running along the road toward the great metropolis—Christ. And I have never yet found a text that had not got a road to Christ in it, and if ever I do find one that has not got a road to Christ in it, I will make one; I will go over hedge and ditch,

[1] *The Christian Ministry*, Lyman Abbott, quoted by Rev. Arthur S. Hoyt, in *The Work of Preaching*. The Macmillan Company, 1905.

but I would get at my Master, for the sermon can not do any good unless there is a savor of Christ in it."

The essential elements, then, of successful preaching, and of any public speaking worth while, are truth and personality. The Christian preacher is at once an interpreter, a herald, a teacher, a counselor, an evangelist, an ambassador. His is the supreme message of life. His authority is the word of God, his religion is that of love, his inexhaustible theme is Christ. Such a work demands the highest development of all his physical and mental powers, and an unswerving consecration of heart and soul to the cause of his Master.

CHAPTER II

HOW TO DEVELOP PHYSICAL POWER

It is as important for the public speaker to develop his body as to develop his mind. As the medium of expression it should be kept at the highest attainable point. Many of our most gifted speakers, especially clergymen, break down from lack of physical vigor, often just at the time when their best work should be done. A strong mind in a strong body should be the aim of every public man.

Joseph Parker gave as his prescription for what he called "a great effort" in preaching a Turkish bath twice a week for three weeks, exercise on the hills every morning at daylight, a plunge in the sea in summer, and a vigorous run on the beach. "Then," said he, "there will be freshness in your breath, a ringing tone in your voice, and a substance in your muscle not soon exhausted. You will not enter the pulpit as a clammy, flabby old man with a heckling voice and a wandering eye, but as a giant ready for a giant's task."

A man should give a reasonable amount of time daily to his physical development. He should put to himself each night a series of questions to test his faithfulness in this respect. He may ask: Have I exercised my body sufficiently this day? Have I chosen the most nourishing food? Have I breathed deeply and abundantly of fresh air? Have I spent any time in the sun? Have I given proper attention to bathing? Have I rested and relaxed at proper intervals? Have I been unduly hurried or excited? Have I washed out my system with generous drafts of pure drinking water? It would be advisable to write down a list of such questions in a note-book and keep a record for at least a month.

Demosthenes, in order to strengthen his lungs, used to repeat as many verses as he could in succession, climbing a hill. Gladstone chopped down trees for physical pastime. Spurgeon interested himself in geology in order to spend as much time as possible in the open air. Henry Ward Beecher gave particular attention to physical training, diet, and relaxation. Webster owed much of his greatness as a speaker to his commanding physique.

"Freshness of feeling," says Dr. Kennard, "will be preserved by maintaining a *healthy appetite and digestion.* Dyspepsia and the worries that wait upon its leaden steps are terribly aging. Care for the hygienics and athletics of his entire nature will reward him openly. He must not only work faithfully, but play regularly; must not only gird with mighty tension, but relax and rest at frequent intervals and give himself abundant sleep. Even the all-enduring camel must have his burden unloosed at night, but many a preacher never lays aside his heavy pack; he carries his church burdens the whole twenty-four hours and the whole twelve months through, and is writing sermons and settling disputes and raising church debts in his dreams. Is it any wonder that his soul grows seedy, and that he becomes mentally round-shouldered and decrepit?"[1]

The first great requisite for the public speaker physically is a well-developed chest. This may be rapidly brought about by deep breathing exercises in the open air, and by

[1] *Psychic Power in Preaching*, J. Spencer Kennard, D.D.

combined breathing and physical exercises at home. After expanding the lungs somewhat fully, the chest should be gently tapped with the palms of the hands. It is helpful to rub the chest vigorously with salt and water, finishing with a rough towel. Habitually carry the chest high and full without undue straining.

The abdominal and waist muscles should be developed in a similar way. In taking a full breath, endeavor to expand the entire circle of the waist, then in exhaling allow the same muscles to contract. Inhale and exhale suddenly several times, while expanding and contracting the abdominal muscles.

During these exercises the breath may be taken through the mouth and nose, but in repose use the nose exclusively. Through diligent practise deep breathing should become an unconscious habit. Many of our most successful pulpit and platform speakers attribute their power of endurance to deep breathing and the proper use of the abdominal muscles.

The entire surface of the body should be washed at least once a day. No arbitrary rules can be laid down for every one. Whether the bath be cold or warm, tub or sponge, must be left to the discretion and convenience of the individual. In a general way, however, it may be said that the best time for a hot bath is at night, and for a cold bath in the morning. After the bath the body should be thoroughly dried with a towel, finishing off with a hand-rubbing. If this is followed with light gymnastics, it will prevent one from taking cold. In any event the circulation should be stimulated. Whenever possible the exercises that follow should be practised in the open air, or near an open window. It should be remembered that deep breathing is the very foundation of good health.

COMBINED DEEP BREATHING, RELAXATION, AND PHYSICAL EXERCISES

The advantage of these exercises is that they combine three in one, giving the greatest possible results in the time expended. They should commend themselves particularly to the busy man.

1. **The arms.** Thoroughly relax the arms at the sides, and while inhaling deeply raise them slowly until the hands meet as high as possible above the head. Clasp the hands tightly, hold the breath, make the upper chest and arms tense or rigid, then after a few moments gently relax, dropping the arms to the sides while exhaling evenly, slowly, and deeply. When the arms are properly tensed they will tremble.

2. **The chest.** Stand erect, chest active, arms stretched out in front with palms together. Swing the arms suddenly to the back, at the same time deeply inhaling and rising on the toes. Each time gently relax. The movement should be rapid and animated. Keep in mind that you are developing your chest.

3. **The legs.** Inhale deeply, fold the arms across the chest, then raise the body up and down on the toes ten times without touching the heels to the floor. Hold the breath throughout the exercise and avoid jerkiness in the movements.

4. **The thighs.** Inhale deeply, fold the arms, and while balancing yourself on the balls of the feet sink to a sitting position, up and down, six times. Inhale as you go down, exhale as you come up.

5. **The abdomen.** Lie flat on your back. Raise the heels from the floor and bring the knees back toward the

chest while deeply inhaling. Then thrust the legs out suddenly without touching the floor. Repeat in moderation.

6. **The legs relaxed.** Stand behind a chair to support yourself. Swing the right leg back and forth several times thoroughly relaxed. Repeat with the left leg. Avoid unnecessary movements of the rest of the body.

7. **The upper chest.** Inhale deeply, fully expanding the chest, and while holding the breath raise the shoulders up and down six times. Exhale very slowly.

8. **The waist and abdomen.** Stand erect, hands over head, palms front. Without bending the knees bend forward from the waist until the tips of the fingers touch the floor, at the same time inhaling a full breath. As you resume your upright position gently exhale and relax. In the first part of this movement tense the muscles of the legs and abdomen.

9. **Stationary running.** Begin a stationary running movement, very slowly at first, throwing the heels well up at back. Inhale and exhale very evenly through the nose and at regular intervals. Gradually increase the rapidity of the movement.

10. **Walking on all fours.** Walk about the room on all fours, breathing quietly and evenly. This will develop many of the muscles of the body and is particularly good for reducing superfluous flesh around the abdomen.

This exercise may be varied by raising the legs straight up above the head and allowing them to drop slowly down again. Also by raising the body to a sitting position and bending forward as far as possible towards the toes. Practise these exercises very deliberately while breathing naturally and deeply.

CHAPTER III

HOW TO DEVELOP THE SPEAKING VOICE

A well-trained voice is an instrument of great power in a public speaker. As the principal medium through which the preacher reaches his people it is worthy of the highest cultivation. Few men are gifted by nature with voices equal to all ordinary requirements, and in most cases it is a matter of long, earnest and systematic practise. Every man who speaks in public should acquire the power to use his voice in continued effort without weariness. A well-equipped speaker will know how to make his voice reach the furthermost auditor without noticeable effort. He will learn to unconsciously vary his voice in infinite ways to suit his varied thought. He will, in short, through painstaking practise, develop his voice and bring it under the control of his will so as to make it respond to any demand he makes upon it.

The first aim in voice culture should be to secure a pure quality of tone. That is to say, every particle of breath that is given out should be converted into voice. This quality of voice is more agreeable to listen to than any other, it carries a greater distance, and is less strain upon the speaker himself. Pure tone is the natural and appropriate expression of pure thought, and the harmonious adjustment of all the vocal parts. In the exercises that follow, the mouth should be well open, and the breath applied to the vocal organs at first gently and continuously.

The larynx should be *steadied*, but all rigidity of the throat muscles must be avoided. There should not be the slightest waste of breath. The ear of the student should be bent upon his voice that he may become in time his own best critic. Practise very softly at first, and persistently aim to produce a free, flowing, pure stream of voice.

PURITY OF TONE

1. **Smoothness of tone.** Stand easily erect, with chin level, the arms dropt loosely at the sides. Inhale through the mouth as if yawning, deeply but moderately, throwing out the abdomen and the upper chest. Place the lips in the position of *ah* as in the word father, and commence a singing tone on this vowel, aiming at softness and smoothness. While the tone is in progress observe closely whether any breath is escaping unvocalized, and if so, endeavor to hold it back in the lungs or "reservoir." Remember that in order to acquire steadiness and smoothness of voice, you must learn to apply to the vocal cords *just the amount of breath required* for a given tone; no more, no less. While the tone is in progress the mind should be constantly at work in a persistent effort to improve the quality of the voice.

Carefully observe the following: Open the mouth wide enough to let the tone out freely and softly; groove the tongue to give the mouth more of a funnel shape; depress the root of the tongue and raise the soft palate to give increased space at the back of the throat; and aim throughout the practise to turn every particle of breath into clear pure tone. Altho the voice should be quite soft in this exercise, it should be full and deep; that is to say, it should seem to come from the depths of the chest and not from the throat. The larynx should be *steadied,* but there should be no rigidity of the vocal apparatus. Liberate the throat muscles by thoroughly relaxing all the parts, and let the voice flow from the mouth freely.

Concentrate the mind, from time to time, on the muscles of the abdomen, so that all strain and effort will be there. Do not forget to keep the tone soft, steady, smooth, and deep. Keep the mouth wide open without undue exaggeration. Adhere strictly to one pitch at a time, but take all the various pitches in turn. The voice grows through use. At first take those keys that sound to you the best, and work up and down from them by degrees. Avoid extremes of pitch until there has been considerable practise on the middle keys.

Having secured a reasonably pure tone, aim next to direct the voice toward the hard palate—the hard bony arch just above the upper teeth. From this part of the mouth cavity the voice gets much of its "ringing" quality. Learn to attack the tone as soon as the mouth is opened. This exercise if faithfully practised each day for a few minutes, as prescribed, will enable you to get control of your voice, to get it properly "placed," and finally to secure a pure quality of tone. Practise moderately, in warm fresh air. Occasionally stand before a looking-glass during the exercise to observe your mouth and throat. Five minutes' practise is ample at the beginning.

2. **Freedom of tone.** Inhale as before, fully and deeply, open the mouth wide as in *ah,* but before actually commencing the tone, fix in your mind the pure quality of voice you wish to produce and *hear it mentally.* Then let the voice flow forth freely and smoothly, without any effort at the throat, all strain concentrated at the abdominal

muscles, using these to back your tone up and to steady it. Remember—and this can not be too often repeated—you are to sing *through* the throat and not from it, that the tone is to seem to come from the very depths of the body, and that all effort must be from the abdominal muscles.

Time the duration of this tone from day to day, and endeavor to increase it. After a little practise there should be no difficulty in holding it half a minute or more.

3. **Economy of breath.** Inhale deeply, exhale softly on *ah*, stopping the tone short every few seconds, holding it and mentally counting four, then continuing and stopping at like intervals. This is to be done on a single breath and with open mouth. Aim to make the attack and close each time sharp and clear, but without added force. Apply the breath, but do not push it. Be careful not to squeeze the tone. Practise on all the pitches in succession.

4. **Projection of tone.** Inhale deeply, and exhale on singing *oo* as in boot. The shape of the lips in producing this vowel has a tendency to help the tone forward. Care should be taken, however, not to unnecessarily purse or pinch the lips. The lips should protrude as in whistling, but with a suggestion of relaxation. During this exercise it will prove helpful to send the tone forward to some imaginary person or object.

5. **Roundness of tone.** Inhale deeply, and exhale on singing *o* as in old. The shape of the lips and mouth cavity in producing this sound suggests its character of roundness. It is a particularly valuable exercise for developing vocal purity and fulness. It should be noted that the vowel *o* has a distinctively rich quality, and this should be encouraged throughout this exercise.

Again inhale fully and deeply, but this time keep the

chest high and active during the singing of the vowel, making the entire movement from the abdomen.

6. **Blending of tone.** Inhale deeply, and exhale on singing *oo, o,* and *ah,* blending them into one continuous stream of voice. The transitions from one vowel to the other should be very gradual. In this exercise the tone will seem to go forward of its own accord, and the student should assist this tendency.

7. **Shock of the glottis.** This exercise is to be practised with care and very moderately at first. Strike the voice softly but clearly on the element *hup,* taking a breath between each stroke. Keep to one pitch at a time, without the slightest variation. After a few strokes have been made in bright, clear tone, change to other pitches until the entire scale has been covered. This is a valuable exercise for clarifying the voice. As in previous exercises, the breath must not be heard.

Repeat this exercise in the elements *he, ha, haw, hah, ho,* and *hoo.* Take one element at a time and master it before proceeding to the next. Practise very slowly at first, but as facility is gained the speed may be increased.

EXAMPLES FOR PRACTISE IN PURE TONE

The following extracts contain a large number of open liquid sounds, and will be found useful in securing pure quality of voice. They should be read aloud, standing, with special regard to this quality, while endeavoring to apply the results of the previous exercises. To distinguish pure quality of tone may at first be difficult, but the student should persevere until the ear is trained to discern the slightest waste of breath during voice production.

1. I wandered by the brookside,
  I wandered by the mill;
I could not hear the brook flow,
  The noisy wheel was still;
There was no burr of grasshopper,
  No chirp of any bird,
But the beating of my own heart
  Was all the sound I heard.

I sat beneath the elm-tree
  And watched the long, long shade,
And as it grew still longer
  I did not feel afraid;
For I listened for a footfall,
  I listened for a word,
But the beating of my own heart
  Was all the sound I heard.

He came not—no, he came not;
  The night came on alone;
The little stars set, one by one,
  Each on his golden throne;
The evening wind passed by my cheek,
  The leaves above were stirred,
But the beating of my own heart
  Was all the sound I heard.

Fast silent tears were flowing,
  When something stood behind;
A hand was on my shoulder:
  I knew its touch was kind.
It drew me nearer, nearer;
  We did not speak one word,
For the beating of our own hearts
  Was all the sound we heard.

"The Brookside." RICHARD MONCKTON MILNES.

2. Blow, blow, thou winter wind,
Thou art not so unkind
As man's ingratitude;
Thy tooth is not so keen
Because thou art not seen,
Although thy breath be rude.
Heigh-ho! sing heigh-ho! unto the green holly:
Most friendship is feigning, most loving mere folly:
Then, heigh-ho! the holly!
This life is most jollly.

Freeze, freeze, thou bitter sky,
Thou dost not bite so nigh
As benefits forgot:
Though thou the waters warp,
Thy sting is not so sharp
As friend remember'd not.
Heigh-ho! sing heigh-ho! unto the green holly:
Most friendship is feigning, most loving mere folly:
Then, heigh-ho! the holly!
This life is most jolly.

"As You Like It." SHAKESPEARE.

3. Our bugles sang truce, for the night-clouds had lower'd,
And the sentinel stars set their watch in the sky;
And thousands had sunk on the ground overpower'd,
The weary to sleep, and the wounded to die.

When reposing that night on my pallet of straw
By the wolf-scaring fagot that guarded the slain,
At the dead of the night a sweet Vision I saw;
And thrice ere the morning I dreamt it again.

Methought from the battle-field's dreadful array
Far, far, I had roam'd on a desolate track:
'Twas autumn—and sunshine arose on the way
To the home of my fathers, that welcomed me back.

I flew to the pleasant fields traversed so oft
  In life's morning march, when my bosom was young,
I heard my own mountain-goats bleating aloft,
  And knew the sweet strain that the corn-reapers sung.

Then pledged we the wine-cup, and fondly I swore
  From my home and my weeping friends never to part;
My little one kiss'd me a thousand times o'er,
  And my wife sobb'd aloud in her fulness of heart.

"Stay—stay with us!—rest!—thou art weary and worn!"—
  And fain was their war-broken soldier to stay;—
But sorrow return'd with the dawning of morn,
  And the voice in my dreaming ear melted away.

"The Soldier's Dream." THOMAS CAMPBELL.

4. Abou Ben Adhem (may his tribe increase!)
Awoke one night from a deep dream of peace,
And saw, within the twilight in the room,
Making it rich, like a lily in bloom,
An angel writing in a book of gold.
Exceeding peace had made Ben Adhem bold,
And to the presence in the room he said,—
"What writest thou?"—The vision raised its head,
And with a look made of all sweet accord,
Answer'd, "The names of those who love the Lord."
"And is mine one?" said Abou. "Nay, not so,"
Replied the angel. Abou spoke more low,
But cheerily still; and said, "I pray thee, then,
Write me as one who loves his fellow men."

The angel wrote, and vanish'd. The next night
It came again with a great wakening light,
And show'd the names whom love of God had blest,
And lo! Ben Adhem's name led all the rest!

"Abou Ben Adhem and the Angel." LEIGH HUNT.

5. Full many a glorious morning have I seen
Flatter the mountain-tops with sovereign eye,
Kissing with golden face the meadows green;
Gilding pale streams with heavenly alchemy,
Anon permit the basest clouds to ride
With ugly rack on his celestial face,
And from the forlorn world his visage hide,
Stealing unseen to west with this disgrace:
Even so my sun one early morn did shine
With all-triumphant splendor on my brow;
But, out, alack! he was but one hour mine,
The region cloud hath mask'd him from me now.
    Yet him for this my love no whit disdaineth;
    Suns of the world may stain, when heaven's sun staineth.

Why didst thou promise such a beauteous day,
And make me travel forth without my cloak,
To let base clouds o'ertake me in my way,
Hiding thy bravery in their rotten smoke?
'Tis not enough that through the cloud thou break,
To dry the rain on my storm-beaten face,
For no man well of such a salve can speak
That heals the wound and cures not the disgrace:
Nor can thy shame give physic to my grief;
Tho thou repent, yet I have still the loss:
The offender's sorrow lends but weak relief
To him that bears the strong offense's cross.
    Ah! but those tears are pearl, which thy love sheds,
    And they are rich and ransom all ill deeds.

No more be grieved at that which thou hast done:
Roses have thorns, and silver fountains mud;
Clouds and eclipses stain both moon and sun,
And loathsome canker lives in sweetest bud.
All men make faults, and even I in this,
Authorizing thy trespass with compare,
Myself corrupting, salving thy amiss,
Excusing thy sins more than thy sins are:

For to thy sensual fault I bring in sense—
Thy adverse party is thy advocate—
And 'gainst myself a lawful plea commence:
Such civil war is in my love and hate,
  That I an accessary needs must be
  To that sweet thief which sourly robs from me.

"Sonnets." SHAKESPEARE.

6. Let us pass directly into the soul's history, and catch from what transpires in its first indications the sign or promise of what it is to become. In its beginning it is a mere seed of possibility. All the infant faculties are folded up, at first, and scarcely a sign of power is visible in it. But a doom of growth is in it, and the hidden momentum of an endless power is driving it on. And a falling body will not gather momentum in its fall more naturally and certainly than it will gather force in the necessary struggle of its endless life now begun. We may think little of the increase; it is a matter of course, and why should we take note of it? But if no increase or development appears, if the faculties all sleep as at the first, we take sad note of that and draw, how reluctantly, the conclusion that our child is an idiot, and not a proper man! And what a chasm is there between the idiot and the man! One a being unprogressive, a being who is not a power; the other a careering force, started on its way to eternity, a principle of might and majesty begun to be unfolded, and to be progressively unfolded forever. Intelligence, reason, conscience, observation, choice, memory, enthusiasm, all the fires of his inborn eternity are kindling to a glow, and, looking on him as a force immortal, just beginning to reveal the symptoms of what he shall be, we call him man. Only a few years ago he lay in his cradle, a barely breathing principle of life, but in that life were gathered up, as in a germ or seed, all these godlike powers that are now so conspicuous in the volume of his personal growth. In a sense, all that is in him now was in him then, as the power of an endless life, and still the sublime progression of his power is only begun. He conquers now the sea and its

storms. He climbs the heavens and searches out the mysteries of the stars. He harnesses the lightning. He bids the rocks dissolve, and summons the secret atoms to give up their names and laws. He subdues the face of the world, and compels the forces of the waters and the fires to be his servants. He makes laws, hurls empires down upon empires in the fields of war, speaks words that can not die, sings to distant realms and peoples across vast ages of time; in a word, he executes all that is included in history, showing his tremendous energy in almost everything that stirs the silence and changes the conditions of the world. Everything is transformed by him even up to the stars. Not all the winds, and storms, and earthquakes, and seas, and seasons of the world have done as much to revolutionize the world as he, the power of an endless life, has done since the day he came forth upon it, and received, as he is most truly declared to have done, dominion over it.

And yet we have, in the power thus developed, nothing more than a mere hint or initial sign of what is to be the real stature of his personality in the process of his everlasting development. We exist here only in the small, that God may have us in a state of flexibility, and bend or fashion us, at the best advantage, to the model of His own great life and character. And most of us, therefore, have scarcely a conception of the exceeding weight of glory to be comprehended in our existence. If we take, for example, the faculty of memory, how very obvious is it that as we pass eternally on we shall have more and more to remember, and finally shall have gathered in more into this great storehouse of the soul than is now contained in all the libraries of the world. And there is not one of our faculties that has not, in its volume, a similar power of expansion. Indeed, if it were not so, the memory would finally overflow and drown all our other faculties, and the spirits, instead of being powers, would virtually cease to be anything more than registers of the past.

But we are not obliged to take our conclusion by inference. We can see for ourselves that the associations of the mind, which are a great part of its riches, must be increasing in number and variety forever, stimulating thought by multiplying its suggestives, and beautifying thought by weaving into it the colors of sentiment, endlessly varied.

The imagination is gathering in its images and kindling its eternal fires in the same manner. Having passed through many trains of worlds, mixing with scenes, societies, orders of intelligence and powers of beatitude—just that which made the apostle in Patmos into a poet, by the visions of a single day—it is impossible that every soul should not finally become filled with a glorious and powerful imagery, and be waked to a wonderfully creative energy.

By the supposition it is another incident of this power of endless life, that, passing down the eternal galleries of fact and event, it must be forever having new cognitions and accumulating new premises. By its own contacts it will, at some future time, have touched even whole worlds and felt them through and made premises of all there is in them. It will know God by experiences correspondingly enlarged, and itself by a consciousness correspondently illuminated. Having gathered in, at last, such worlds of premise, it is difficult for us now to conceive the vigor into which a soul may come, or the volume it may exhibit, the wonderful depth and scope of its judgments, its rapidity and certainty and the vastness of its generalizations. It passes over more and more, and that necessarily, from the condition of a creature gathering up premises into the condition of God, creating out of premises; for if it is not actually set to the creation of worlds, its very thoughts will be a discoursing in world-problems and theories equally vast in their complications.

In the same manner, the executive energy of the will, the volume of the benevolent affections, and all the active powers, will be showing, more and more impressively, what it is to be a power of endless life. They that have been swift in doing God's will and fulfilling his mighty errands, will acquire a marvelous address and energy in the use of their powers. They that have taken worlds into their love will have a love correspondently capacious, whereupon also it will be seen that their will is settled in firmness, and raised in majesty, according to the vastness of impulse there is in the love behind it. They that have great thoughts, too, will be able to manage great causes, and they that are lubricated eternally in the joys that feed their activity, will never tire. What force, then, must be finally developed in what now appears to be the tenuous and fickle impulse, and the merely frictional activity of a human soul.

"The Power of an Endless Life." HORACE BUSHNELL.

FLEXIBILITY OF TONE

1. **Speaking vowels.** Recite aloud, in clear speaking tones, *e, a, aw, ah, o,* and *oo,* first with rising inflection, then falling inflection. Next combine the two, making a circumflex inflection. Apply the breath to the vocal cords in just the right quantity. The tone should be bright and smooth.

2. **Alternating high and low.** Repeat the last exercise, in alternate high and low pitches. Do not move the head. Avoid extremes of pitch at first.

3. **Alternating loud and soft.** Repeat the vowels as before, in alternate loud and soft voice. The loud tones should not be too loud, and the soft tones should be free from breathiness. Keep the head and body still.

4. **Varied inflection.** On the elements *le, la, law, lah, lo, loo,* practise first on a rising, then a falling inflection. The length of the inflection should vary from short, very short, long, and very long. All the keys of the speaking voice should be used, from high to low, and from loud to soft.

5. **Counting.** In pure, clear-cut voice, count from one to ten in one breath. Repeat in various pitches and inflections. Then count to twenty in one breath, to thirty, and longer if possible, but all *in one breath.*

EXAMPLES FOR PRACTISE IN FLEXIBILITY

These are to be recited aloud with all possible variety in keeping with the thought. There is up and down in thought, as well as gentleness and force. To bring out these appropriate elements is the work of the student in rendering the following examples. First analyze the extract silently to get a general idea of its meaning. Mentally picture each thought as vividly as possible.

1. From early childhood, even as hath been said,
From his sixth year, he had been sent abroad
In summer to tend herds: such was his task
Thenceforward till the later day of youth.
Oh, then, what soul was his, when, on the tops
Of the high mountains, he beheld the sun
Rise up, and bathe the world in light! He look'd—
Ocean and earth, the solid frame of earth
And ocean's liquid mass, beneath him lay
In gladness and deep joy. The clouds were touched,
And in their silent faces did he read
Unutterable love. Sound needed none,
Nor any voice of joy; his spirit drank
The spectacle; sensation, soul, and form
All melted into him; they swallowed up
His animal being; in them did he live,
And by them did he live, they were his life.
In such access of mind, in such high hour
Of visitation from the living God,
Thought was not; in enjoyment it expired.
No thanks he breath'd, he proffer'd no request;
Rapt into still communion that transcends
the imperfect offices of prayer and praise,
His mind was a thanksgiving to the Power
That made him; it was blessedness and love!

"The Excursion." WILLIAM WORDSWORTH.

2. Soft heath this elevated spot supplied,
With resting-place of mossy stone; and there
We sate reclined, admiring quietly
The frame and general aspect of the scene;
And each not seldom eager to make known
His own discoveries; or to favorite points
Directing notice, merely from a wish
T' impart a joy, imperfect while unshared.
That rapturous moment ne'er shall I forget
When these particular interests were effaced
From every mind! Already had the sun,
Sinking with less than ordinary state,
Attained his western bound; but rays of light—
Now suddenly diverging from the orb,
Retired behind the mountain tops or veiled
By the dense air—shot upward to the crown
Of the blue firmament—aloft—and wide;
And multitudes of little floating clouds,
Pierced through their thin ethereal mold, ere we,
Who saw, of change were conscious, had become
Vivid as fire—clouds separately poised,
Innumerable multitude of forms
Scattered through half the circle of the sky;
And giving back, and shedding each on each,
With prodigal communion, the bright hues
Which from the unapparent fount of glory
They had imbibed, and ceased not to receive.
That which the heavens displayed, the liquid deep
Repeated; but with unity sublime!

While from the grassy mountain's open side
We gazed, in silence hushed, with eyes intent
On the refulgent spectacle, diffused
Through earth, sky, water, and all visible space,
The Priest, in holy transport, thus exclaim'd:—
"Eternal Spirit! Universal God!
Power inaccessible to human thought
Save by degrees and steps which Thou hast deign'd:—

To furnish; for this image of Thyself,
To the infirmity of mortal sense
Vouchsafed; this local, transitory type
Of Thy paternal splendors, and the pomp
Of those who fill Thy courts in highest heaven,
The radiant cherubim;—accept the thanks
Which we, Thy humble creatures, here convened,
Presume to offer; we, who from the breast
Of the frail earth, permitted to behold
The faint reflections only of Thy face,
Are yet exalted, and in soul adore!
Such as they are who in Thy presence stand,
Unsullied, incorruptible, and drink
Imperishable majesty stream'd forth
From Thy empyreal throne, the elect of earth
Shall be—divested at the appointed hour
Of all dishonor—cleansed from mortal stain.
Accomplish, then, their number; and conclude
Time's weary course! Or, if, by Thy decree,
The consummation that will come by stealth
Be yet far distant, let Thy Word prevail,
Oh! let Thy Word prevail, to take away
The sting of human nature. Spread the law,
As it is written in Thy holy book,
Throughout all lands; let every nation hear
The high behest, and every heart obey!"

"The Excursion." WILLIAM WORDSWORTH.

3. For mark well, even in the course of a single night, changes may take place in human things without your being consulted which entirely alter your position; and each one who, instead of concerning himself with the common good, and regarding himself as a part of the great whole, has limited his interest to some narrow circle, perhaps opposed to the private interest of some one else; every one has a soul which, with all its desires and joys, its treasures and possessions, may in a night be required of him! And the more keenly the strife has been carried on, the less sure can human wisdom be of any

firm ground or of any certain issue; the more foolish would it be to undertake to answer the question, Whose shall those things be which thou hast provided, or hast wished to provide? But where instead of strife and wrangling, instead of self-seeking and covetousness, that rule of life and feeling guides men which makes them rich in God; in that God who makes His sun shine on the evil and on the good, and sends rain on the just and on the unjust; in that God before whom all are equal, His fatherly love going forth to all; whose wise decrees are indeed hidden from us, so that we can never for one short moment lift the veil that conceals them, but whose laws and will are clearly revealed and should be written on the hearts of those who confess the name of His Son;—among such people there is an end of this folly; each of them is willing that his soul should be called away at any moment; and such men know whose the things shall be which they have provided.

"True Harvest Joy." F. E. SCHLEIERMACHER.

4. Have you ever seen a poor girl at midnight sitting down on a doorstep crying? Somebody passes by, and says, "Why do you sit here?" "I have no house, sir. I have no home." "Where is your father?" "My father's dead, sir." "Where is your mother?" "I have no mother, sir." "Have you no friends?" "No friends at all." "Have you no house?" "No; I have none. I am houseless." And she shivers in the chill air, and gathers her poor ragged shawl around her, and cries again, "I have no house—I have no home." Would you not pity her? Would you blame her for her tears? Ah! there are some of you that have houseless souls here this morning. It is something to have a houseless body; but to think of a houseless soul! Methinks I see you in eternity sitting on the doorstep of heaven. An angel says, "What! have you no house to live in?" "No house," says the poor soul. "Have you no father?" "No; God is not my Father, and there is none beside Him." "Have you no mother?" "No, the Church is not my mother; I never sought her ways, nor loved Jesus. I have neither father nor mother." "Have you no house, then?" "No; I am a houseless soul."

"Spurgeon's Illustrative Anecdotes." LOUIS ALBERT BANKS.

6. Once more unto the breach, dear friends, once more;
Or close the wall up with our English dead!
In peace, there's nothing so becomes a man,
As modest stillness and humility:
But when the blast of war blows in our ears,
Then imitate the action of the tiger;
Stiffen the sinews, summon up the blood,
Disguise fair nature with hard favor'd rage,
Then lend the eye a terrible aspect;
Let it pry through the portage of the head,
Like the brass cannon; let the brow o'erwhelm it,
As fearfully as doth a galled rock
O'erhang and jutty his confounded[1] base
Swill'd[2] with the wild and wasteful ocean.
Now set the teeth, and stretch the nostril wide;
Hold hard the breath, and bend up every spirit
To his full height.—On, on, you noblest English!
Whose blood is fet from fathers of war-proof,
Fathers that, like so many Alexanders,
Have, in these parts, from morn till even fought,
And sheathed their swords for lack of argument.
Dishonor not your mothers: now attest,
That those whom you called fathers did beget you:
Be copy now to men of grosser blood,
And teach them how to war! And you, good yeomen,
Whose limbs were made in England, show us here
The mettle of your pasture; let us swear
That you are worth your breeding, which I doubt not;
For there is none of you so mean and base,
That hath not noble luster in your eyes.
I see you stand like greyhounds in the slips,
Straining upon the start. The game's afoot;
Follow your spirit: and, upon this charge,
Cry—God for Harry! England! and Saint George!

"Henry V. to His Troops." SHAKESPEARE.

---

[1] *Confounded.*—Vexed or troubled.
[2] *Swill'd.*—Used for *washed much.*

6. In this refulgent summer, it has been a luxury to draw the breath of life. The grass grows, the buds burst, the meadow is spotted with fire and gold in the tint of flowers. The air is full of birds, and sweet with the breath of the pine, the balm of Gilead, and the new hay. Night brings no gloom to the heart with its welcome shade. Through the transparent darkness the stars pour their almost spiritual rays. Man under them seems a young child, and his huge globe a toy. The cool night bathes the world as with a river, and prepares his eyes again for the crimson dawn. The mystery of nature was never displayed more happily. The corn and the wine have been freely dealt to all creatures, and the never-broken silence with which the old bounty goes forward has not yielded yet one word of explanation. One is constrained to respect the perfection of this world in which our senses converse. How wide; how rich; what invitation from every property it gives to every faculty of man! In its fruitful soils; in its navigable sea; in its mountains of metal and stone; in its forests of all woods; in its animals; in its chemical ingredients; in the powers and path of light, heat, attraction, and life, it is well worth the pith and heart of great men to subdue and enjoy it. The planters, the mechanics, the inventors, the astronomers, the builders of cities, and the captains history delights to honor.

But when the mind opens and reveals the laws which traverse the universe and make things what they are, then shrinks the great world at once into a mere illustration and fable of this mind. What am I? and What is? asks the human spirit with a curiosity new-kindled, but never to be quenched. Behold these outrunning laws, which our imperfect apprehension can see tend this way and that, but not come to full circle. Behold these infinite relations, so like, so unlike; many, yet one. I would study, I would know, I would admire forever. These works of thought have been the entertainments of the human spirit in all ages.

A more secret, sweet, and overpowering beauty appears to man when his heart and mind open to the sentiment of virtue. Then he is instructed in what is above him. He learns that his being is without bound; that to the good, to the perfect, he is born, low as he now lies in evil and weakness. That which he venerates is still his own, tho he has not realized it yet. *He ought.* He knows the sense of that grand word, tho his analysis fails entirely to render account of it. When in innocency or when by intellectual preception he attains to say,—"I love the Right; Truth is beautiful within and without forevermore. Virtue, I am thine; save me; use me; thee will I serve, day and night, in great, in small, that I may be not virtuous, but virtue";—then is the end of the creation answered, and God is well pleased.

The sentiment of virtue is a reverence and delight in the presence of certain divine laws. It perceives that this homely game of life we play, covers, under what seem foolish details, principles that astonish. The child amidst his baubles is learning the action of light, motion, gravity, muscular force; and in the game of human life, love, fear, justice, appetite, man, and God, interact. These laws refuse to be adequately stated. They will not be written out on paper, or spoken by the tongue. They elude our persevering thought; yet we read them hourly in each other's faces, in each other's actions, in our own remorse. The moral traits which are all globed into every virtuous act and thought—in speech we must sever, and describe or suggest by painful enumeration of many particulars. Yet, as this sentiment is the essence of all religion, let me guide your eye to the precise objects of the sentiment, by an enumeration of some of those classes of facts in which this element is conspicuous.

The intuition of the moral sentiment is an insight of the perfection of the laws of the soul. These laws execute themselves. They are out of time, out of space, and not subject to circumstance. Thus in the soul of man there is a justice whose retributions are instant and entire. He who does a good deed is instantly ennobled. He who does a mean deed is by the action itself contracted. He who puts off impurity, thereby puts on purity. If a man is at heart just, then in so far is he God; the safety of God, the immortality of God, the majesty of God, do enter into that man with justice. If a man dissemble, deceive, he deceives himself, and goes out of acquaintance with his own being. A man in the view of absolute goodness, adores, with total humility. Every step so downward, is a step upward. The man who renounces himself, comes to himself. See how this rapid intrinsic energy worketh everywhere, righting wrongs, correcting appearances, and bringing up facts to a harmony with thoughts. Its operation in life, though slow to the senses, is at last as sure as in the soul. By it a man is made the Providence to himself, dispensing good to his goodness, and evil to his sin. Character is always known. Thefts never enrich; alms never impoverish; murder will speak out of stone walls. The least admixture of a lie—for example, the taint of vanity, the least attempt to make a good impression, a favorable appearance—will instantly vitiate the effect. But speak the truth, and all nature and all spirits help you with unexpected furtherance. Speak the truth, and all things alive or brute are vouchers, and the very roots of the grass underground there do seem to stir and move to bear you witness. See again the perfection of the Law as it applies itself to the affections, and becomes the law of society. As we are, so we associate. The good, by affinity, seek the good; the vile, by affinity, the vile.

These facts have always suggested to man the sublime creed that the world is not the product of manifold power, but of one will, of one mind; and that one mind is everywhere active, in each ray of the star, in each wavelet of the pool; and whatever opposes that will is everywhere balked and baffled, because things are made so, and not otherwise. Good is positive. Evil is merely privative, not absolute: it is like cold, which is the privation of heat. All evil is so much death or nonentity. Benevolence is absolute and real. So much benevolence as a man hath, so much life hath he. For all things proceed out of this same spirit, which is differently named love, justice, temperance, in its different applications, just as the ocean receives different names on the several shores which it washes. All things proceed out of the same spirit, and all things conspire with it. Whilst a man seeks good ends, he is strong by the whole strength of nature. In so far as he roves from these ends, he bereaves himself of power, of auxiliaries; his being shrinks out of all remote channels, he becomes less and less, a mote, a point, until absolute badness is absolute death.

The perception of this law of laws awakens in the mind a sentiment which we call the religious sentiment, and which makes our highest happiness. Wonderful is its power to charm and to command. It is a mountain air. It is the embalmer of the world. It is myrrh and storax, and chlorin and rosemary. It makes the sky and the hills sublime, and the silent song of the stars is it. By it is the universe made safe and habitable, not by science or power. Thought may work cold and intransitive in things, and find no end or unity; but the dawn of the sentiment of virtue on the heart gives and is the assurance that Law is sovereign over all natures; and the worlds, time, space, eternity, do seem to break out into joy.

This sentiment is divine and deifying. It is the beatitude of man. It makes him illimitable. Through it, the soul first knows itself. It corrects the capital mistake of the infant man, who seeks to be great by following the great, and hopes to derive advantages *from another*, by showing the fountain of all good to be in himself, and that he, equally with every man, is an inlet into the steps of Reason. When he says, "I thought"; when love warms him; when he chooses, warned on high, the good and great deed; then, deep melodies wander through his soul from Supreme Wisdom. Then he can worship, and be enlarged by his worship; for he can never go behind this sentiment. In the sublimest flights of the soul, rectitude is never surmounted, love is never outgrown.

"The Divinity School Address." RALPH WALDO EMERSON.

ROUNDNESS AND RESONANCE OF TONE

The orotund voice is the simple pure tone rounded out into greater fulness. The word comes from *rotundus*, meaning round. It is produced mainly by an increased resonance of the chest and mouth cavities, and a more vigorous action of the abdominal muscles. It always has the character of fulness, but is not necessarily a loud tone. Neither is it an "assumed" voice, but should result from expanded thought and increased intensity of feeling. Its force varies in degree with the thought being exprest. It may be effusive or flowing, expulsive or rushing, explosive or bursting.

It is used in language of great dignity and power, in intense and ponderous thought, and in grandeur and sublimity. It is also used in public prayer, and in certain Bible and hymn reading. Coupled with the simple conversational style of speaking, it greatly enlarges the public speaker's possibilities of expression. It gives variety and appropriateness to the spoken word. An ordinary colloquial style of speaking, when long continued, becomes tame and uninteresting to an audience; but when all the gradations of soft, medium, and full orotund voice are added, the speaker is conscious of vastly increased scope and power.

It will be found helpful in the following exercises to keep the chest high and active throughout. The abdomen may expand and contract fully without letting the chest down from its full active position. If the student will also *think* depth and roundness during the exercises, it will assist in securing the desired qualities.

A resonant voice avails itself of all the various parts of the throat and chest that can contribute vibration. Like the strings of a violin or the stem of a tuning-fork, the voice needs some kind of solid body to give it character. This is imparted principally by the resonance chambers; viz., by the cavities of the mouth and throat, by the chest, and by the facial resonators.

1. **Facial resonance.** The face immediately surrounding the mouth and extending into the cheek bones can be employed to advantage in producing resonance. Inhale

a full deep breath, and begin a low *humming* sound on the element *maw*. Project the lips but do not part them, as the element is to be thought rather than exprest. The trembling sensation felt at the lips in producing this sound should be helped as much as possible until it extends up the face. This vibratory effect will be made to spread the more rapidly if the student thinks of circles while practising, of water rising from a fountain, or some other suggestive thought. While the humming is in progress keep to one tone at a time, but in turn change to other pitches. Aim to increase the vibrations and use considerable force in doing so. No harm can possibly come to the throat or voice through this exercise, so it may be practised with impunity.

2. **Open resonance.** Repeat the last exercise, but gradually open the mouth so that the element *maw* will pour forth in free liquid quality. There will be a tendency to lose the facial resonance as the mouth is opened, but this must be resisted. Open the mouth very gradually and endeavor to maintain the same degree of resonance throughout.

3. **Throat resonance.** Gently sing the vowel *e*, endeavoring to bring into vibration all the parts around the back of the mouth, particularly the soft palate and root of the tongue. As this vowel has a natural tendency to be throaty, great care should be taken to avoid rigidity and squeezing the tone.

4. **Chest resonance.** Inhale a full deep breath, and while singing the vowel *o* hold the chest high and rigid throughout the exercise. Think of the chest as a sounding-board and make it vibrate as much as possible. Repeat this vowel in the speaking voice, with rising and falling in-

flection, following the directions given for the singing tone. As the tone is in progress think of roundness and fulness of voice. Hold in mind some lofty thought, or think of immensity, power, and majesty.

EXAMPLES FOR PRACTISE IN RESONANCE

1. My Lords, I do not mean to go further than just to remind your Lordships of this,—that Mr. Hastings' government was one whole system of oppression, of robbery of individuals, of spoliation of the public, and of supersession of the whole system of the English government, in order to vest in the worst of all the natives all the power that could possibly exist in any government; in order to defeat the ends which all governments ought, in common, to have in view. In the name of the Commons of England, I charge all this villainy upon Warren Hastings, in this last moment of my application to you.

Therefore, it is with confidence that, ordered by the Commons of Great Britain, I impeach Warren Hastings of high crimes and misdemeanors.

I impeach him in the name of the Commons of Great Britain in Parliament assembled, whose parliamentary trust he has betrayed.

I impeach him in the name of the Commons of Great Britain, whose national character he has dishonored.

I impeach him in the name of the people of India, whose laws, rights, and liberties he has subverted, whose property he has destroyed, whose country he has laid waste and desolate.

I impeach him in the name and by virtue of those eternal laws of justice which he has violated.

I impeach him in the name of human nature itself, which he has cruelly outraged, injured, and opprest, in both sexes, in every age, rank, situation, and condition in life.

EDMUND BURKE.

"The Impeachment of Warren Hastings."

2. Upon the principle on which the attorney-general prays sentence upon my client—God have mercy upon us! Instead of standing before Him in judgment with the hopes and consolations of Christians, we must call upon the mountains to cover us; for which of us can present, for omniscient examination, a pure, unspotted, and faultless course? But I humbly expect that the benevolent Author of our being will judge us as I have been pointing out for your example. Holding up the great volume of our lives in His hands, and regarding the general scope of them—if He discovers benevolence, charity and good will to man beating in the heart, where He alone can look; if He finds that our conduct, tho often forced out of the path by our infirmities, has been in general well-directed, His all-searching eye will assuredly never pursue us into those little corners of our lives, much less will His justice select them for punishment without the general context of our existence, by which faults may be sometimes found to have grown out of virtues, and very many of our heaviest offenses to have been grafted by human imperfection upon the best and kindest of our affections. No, gentlemen, believe me, this is not the course of divine justice, or there is no truth in the gospels of heaven. If the general tenor of a man's conduct be such as I have represented it, he may walk through the shadow of death, with all his faults about him, with as much cheerfulness as in the common paths of life; because he knows that, instead of a stern accuser to expose before the Author of his nature those frail passages which, like the scored matter in the book before you, checker the volume of the brightest and best-spent life, His mercy will obscure them from the eye of His purity, and our repentance will blot them out forever.

"The Freedom of the Press." LORD ERSKINE.

3. When Freedom from her mountain height
   Unfurled her standard to the air,
She tore the azure robe of night,
   And set the stars of glory there;
She mingled with its gorgeous dyes
The milky baldric of the skies,

And striped its pure, celestial white
With streakings of the morning light;
Then from his mansion in the sun
She called her eagle-bearer down,
And gave into his mighty hand
The symbol of her chosen land.

Majestic monarch of the cloud!
  Who rear'st aloft thy regal form,
To hear the tempest-trumpings loud,
And see the lightning lances driven,
  When strive the warriors of the storm,
And rolls the thunder-drum of heaven;
Child of the sun! to thee 'tis given
  To guard the banner of the free,
To hover in the sulfur smoke,
To ward away the battle-stroke,
And bid its blendings shine afar,
Like rainbows on the cloud of war,
  The harbingers of victory!

Flag of the brave! thy folds shall fly,
The sign of hope and triumph high,
When speaks the signal trumpet tone,
And the long line comes gleaming on;
Ere yet the life-blood, warm and wet,
Has dimmed the glistening bayonet,
Each soldier eye shall brightly turn
To where thy sky-born glories burn,
And, as his springing steps advance,
Catch war and vengeance from the glance
And when the cannon-mouthings loud
Heave in wild wreaths the battle-shroud,
And gory sabers rise and fall,
Like shoots of flame on midnight's pall;
Then shall thy meteor-glances glow,
  And cowering foes shall sink beneath
Each gallant arm that strikes below
  That lovely messenger of death.

Flag of the seas! on ocean wave
Thy stars shall glitter o'er the brave;
When death, careering on the gale,
Sweeps darkly round the bellied sail,
And freighted waves rush wildly back
Before the broadside's reeling rack,
Each dying wanderer of the sea
Shall look at once to heaven and thee,
And smile to see thy splendors fly
In triumph o'er his closing eye.

Flag of the free heart's hope and home,
  By angel hands to valor given;
Thy stars have lit the welkin dome,
  And all thy hues were born in heaven.
For ever float that standard sheet!
  Where breathes the foe but falls before us,
With Freedom's soil beneath our feet,
  And Freedom's banner streaming o'er us?

"The American Flag." JOSEPH RODMAN DRAKE.

BRILLIANCY OF TONE

1. **"Bell" exercise.** Inhale deeply and fully; compress the air against the closed lips until they burst open on the word *bell*. Immediately place the tongue against the roof of the mouth to utter the sound of *l*, and hold the sound as long as possible, allowing it to die away very gradually in force. Avoid breathiness and violence in the explosion. Remember that the motive power should come from the abdominal muscles, and on no account from the throat. Practise this exercise rather gently at first, but later it can be done with increased sharpness and force.

2. **"Bell" resonance.** This is similar to the last exercise, but an effort is made to increase the vibration of the voice while dwelling on the letter *l*. This can be done by making

the voice tremble and by manipulating the tongue slightly. Aim also to bring the head resonance more particularly into play.

3. "Bell" varied. Repeat the first exercise in great variety. Take first the middle pitches of the voice, then the upper and lower keys. Practise considerably on the very low pitches, aiming at clearness. Strike the word *bell* several times in quick succession. Imitate the striking of a bell, by clear-cut blows, by swells of the voice, and other effects as they suggest themselves.

EXAMPLES FOR PRACTISE IN BRILLIANCY

1. Hear the sledges with the bells—silver bells—
What a world of merriment their melody foretells!
How they tinkle, tinkle, tinkle, in the icy air of night!
While the stars that oversprinkle
All the heavens, seem to tinkle with a crystalline delight;
Keeping time, time, time, in a sort of Runic rhyme,
To the tintinnabulation that so musically wells
From the bells, bells, bells, bells, bells, bells, bells—
From the jingling and the tinkling of the bells.
Hear the mellow wedding-bells, golden bells!
What a world of happiness their harmony foretells!
Through the balmy air of night how they ring out their delight!
From the molten-golden notes, and all in tune,
What a liquid ditty floats
To the turtle-dove that listens, while she gloats on the moon!
Oh, from out the sounding cells,
What a gush of euphony voluminously wells!
How it swells! how it dwells
On the Future! how it tells of the rapture that impels
To the swinging and the ringing of the bells, bells, bells—
Of the bells, bells, bells, bells, bells, bells, bells—
To the rhyming and the chiming of the bells!

Hear the loud alarum bells—brazen bells!
What a tale of terror, now, their turbulency tells!
In the startled ear of night
How they scream out their affright!
Too much horrified to speak,
They can only shriek, shriek, out of tune,
In a clamorous appealing to the mercy of the fire,
In a mad expostulation with the deaf and frantic fire
Leaping higher, higher, with a desperate desire,
And a resolute endeavor, now—now to sit or never,
By the side of the pale-faced moon. Oh, the bells, bells, bells!
What a tale their terror tells of despair!
How they clang, and clash, and roar! What a horror they outpour
On the bosom of the palpitating air!
Yet the air, it fully knows,
By the twanging and the clanging,
How the danger ebbs and flows; yet the ear distinctly tells
In the jangling and the wrangling,
How the danger sinks and swells,
By the sinking or the swelling in the anger of the bells—of the bells—
Of the bells, bells, bells, bells, bells, bells, bells—
In the clamor and the clangor of the bells!
Hear the tolling of the bells—iron bells!
What a world of solemn thought their monody compels!
In the silence of the night,
How we shiver with affright
At the melancholy menace of their tone!
For every sound that floats
From the rust within their throats is a groan.
And the people—ah, the people—
They that dwell up in the steeple, all alone,
And who tolling, tolling, tolling, in that muffled monotone,
Feel a glory in so rolling on the human heart a stone—
They are neither man nor woman—
They are neither brute nor human—they are Ghouls:

And their king it is who tolls;
And he rolls, rolls, rolls, rolls a pæan from the bells!
And his merry bosom swells with the pæan of the bells!
And he dances and he yells;
Keeping time, time, time, in a sort of Runic rhyme,
To the pæan of the bells—of the bells:
Keeping time, time, time, in a sort of Runic rhyme,
To the throbbing of the bells—of the bells, bells, bells,
To the sobbing of the bells; keeping time, time, time,
As he knells, knells, knells, in a happy Runic rhyme,
To the rolling of the bells—of the bells, bells, bells—
To the tolling of the bells, bells, bells, bells—
Bells, bells, bells—
To the moaning and the groaning of the bells.

"The Bells." EDGAR ALLAN POE.

2. Thus saying, from her side the fatal key,
Sad instrument of all our wo, she took;
And, toward the gate rolling her bestial train,
Forthwith the huge portcullis high up-drew,
Which, but herself, not all the Stygian powers
Could once have moved; then in the keyhole turns
The intricate wards, and every bolt and bar
Of massy iron or solid rock with ease
Unfastens. On a sudden open fly,
With impetuous recoil and jarring sound,
The infernal doors, and on their hinges grate
Harsh thunder, that the lowest bottom shook
Of Erebus. She opened; but to shut
Excelled her power; the gates wide open stood,
That with extended wings a bannered host,
Under spread ensigns marching, might pass through
With horse and chariots ranked in loose array;
So wide they stood, and like a furnace-mouth
Cast forth redounding smoke and ruddy flame.

"Discord." JOHN MILTON.

3. The multitude of Angels, with a shout
Loud as from numbers without number, sweet
As from blest voices, uttering joy—Heaven rung
With jubilee, and loud hosannas filled
The eternal regions. Lowly reverent
Toward either throne they bow, and to the ground
With solemn adoration down they cast
Their crowns, inwove with amaranth and gold—
Immortal amaranth, a flower which once
In Paradise, fast by the Tree of Life,
Began to bloom, but, soon for Man's offense,
To Heaven removed where first it grew, there grows
And flowers aloft, shading the Fount of Life,
And where the River of Bliss through midst of Heaven
Rolls o'er Elysian flowers her amber stream!
With these, that never fade, the Spirits elect
Bind their resplendent locks, inwreathed with beams.
Now in loose garlands thick thrown off, the bright
Pavement, that like a sea of jasper shone,
Impurpled with celestial roses smiled.
Then, crowned again, their golden harps they took—
Harps ever tuned, that glittering by their side
Like quivers hung; and with preamble sweet
Of charming symphony they introduce
Their sacred song, and waken raptures high:
No voice exempt, no voice but well could join
Melodious part; such concord is in Heaven.

"Concord." JOHN MILTON.

4. From Harmony, from heavenly Harmony
This universal frame began:
When Nature underneath a heap
Of jarring atoms lay
And could not heave her head,
The tuneful voice was heard from high,
Arise, ye more than dead!
Then cold and hot and moist and dry
In order to their stations leap,
And Music's power obey.

From Harmony, from heavenly Harmony
This universal frame began:
From Harmony to Harmony
Through all the compass of the notes it ran,
The diapason closing full in Man.

What passion can not Music raise and quell?
When Jubal struck the chorded shell
His listening brethren stood around,
And, wondering, on their faces fell
To worship that celestial sound.
Less than a God they thought there could not dwell
Within the hollow of that shell
That spoke so sweetly and so well.
What passion can not Music raise and quell?

The trumpet's loud clangor
Excites us to arms,
With shrill notes of anger
And mortal alarms.
The double double double beat
Of the thundering drum
Cries "Hark! the foes come;
Charge, charge, 'tis too late to retreat!"

The soft complaining flute
In dying notes discovers
The woes of hopeless lovers,
Whose dirge is whisper'd by the warbling lute.

Sharp violins proclaim
Their jealous pangs and desperation,
Fury, frantic indignation,
Depth of pains, and height of passion
For the fair disdainful dame.

But oh! what art can teach,
What human voice can reach
  The sacred organ's praise?
Notes inspiring holy love,
  Notes that wing their heavenly ways
To mend the choirs above.

Orpheus could lead the savage race,
And trees uprooted left their place
Sequacious of the lyre:
But bright Cecilia raised the wonder higher
  When to her organ vocal breath was given
An Angel heard, and straight appear'd—
  Mistaking Earth for Heaven!

As from the power of sacred lays
  The spheres began to move,
And sung the great Creator's praise
  To all the blest above;
So when the last and dreadful hour
This crumbling pageant shall devour,
The trumpet shall be heard on high,
The dead shall live, the living die,
And Music shall untune the sky.

"Song for Saint Cecilia's Day." JOHN DRYDEN.

5. Near yonder copse, where once the garden smiled,
And still where many a garden flower grows wild.
There, where a few torn shrubs the place disclose,
The village preacher's modest mansion rose.
A man he was to all the country dear,
And passing rich with forty pounds a year;
Remote from towns he ran his godly race,
Nor e'er had changed, nor wished to change his place;
Unskilful he to fawn, or seek for power
By doctrines fashioned to the varying hour;
Far other aims his heart had learned to prize—
More bent to raise the wretched than to rise.

His house was known to all the vagrant train;
He chid their wanderings, but relieved their pain.
The long-remembered beggar was his guest,
Whose beard, descending, swept his aged breast;
The ruined spendthrift, now no longer proud,
Claimed kindred there, and had his claims allowed;
The broken soldier, kindly bade to stay,
Sate by his fire, and talked the night away—
Wept o'er his wounds, or, tales of sorrow done,
Shouldered his crutch, and showed how fields were won.
Pleased with his guests, the good man learned to glow,
And quite forgot their vices in their wo;
Careless their merits or their faults to scan,
His pity gave, ere charity began.

Thus to relieve the wretched was his pride,
And e'en his failings leaned to virtue's side;
But in his duty, prompt at every call,
He watched and wept, he prayed and felt for all;
And, as a bird each fond endearment tries
To tempt its new-fledged offspring to the skies,
He tried each art, reproved each dull delay,
Allured to brighter worlds, and led the way.

Beside the bed where parting life was laid,
And sorrow, guilt, and pain, by turns dismayed,
The reverend champion stood. At his control
Despair and anguish fled the struggling soul;
Comfort came down the trembling wretch to raise,
And his last faltering accents whispered praise.

At church, with meek and unaffected grace,
His looks adorned the venerable place;
Truth from his lips prevailed with double sway,
And fools, who came to scoff, remained to pray.
The service past, around the pious man,
With ready zeal, each honest rustic ran;
E'en children followed, with endearing wile,
And plucked his gown, to share the good man's smile.

His ready smile a parent's warmth exprest;
Their welfare pleased him, and their cares distrest;
To them his heart, his love, his griefs were given—
But all his serious thoughts had rest in heaven.
As some tall cliff that lifts its awful form,
Swells from the vale, and midway leaves the storm,
Tho round its breast the rolling clouds are spread,
Eternal sunshine settles on its head.
And e'en the story ran that he could gauge.
In arguing, too, the parson owned his skill,
For, e'en tho vanquished, he could argue still;
While words of learned length and thundering sound
Amazed the gazing rustics ranged around;
And still they gazed, and still the wonder grew,
That one small head could carry all he knew.

OLIVER GOLDSMITH.
"The Village Preacher," in "The Deserted Village."

VOLUME OF TONE

Adequate volume of voice is necessary in order that the public speaker, when occasion demands, should be able to fulfil all requirements. A voice suited to conversation may be wholly unsatisfactory when used in a large hall. How many men, addressing an audience probably for the first time, have been startled and embarrassed by the thinness and strangeness of their own voice.

Proper development of volume of tone, together with a little experience in public speaking, should enable an average person to readily adapt his voice to any ordinary auditorium. His aim should be to be easily heard in all parts of a hall, without undue elevation of pitch or noticeable physical effort.

Volume of voice does not necessarily mean loudness but

rather fulness of tone. Its character is that of depth, roundness, and adequateness. It suggests power in reserve. It therefore inspires confidence both in the speaker and the hearer. As the voice grows through use, volume is to be acquired by practising daily exercises such as are here suggested. In all such practise there should be physical earnestness if the best results are to be secured. Half-hearted, lackadaisical efforts in any pursuit accomplish little. The student should bring his will to bear upon his work. Enthusiasm in the practise of voice exercises will naturally communicate itself to the speaker's public efforts.

It was the custom of Henry Ward Beecher to exercise his voice daily in the open air, exploding it upon all the vowel sounds. As a result of this practise, extending over a period of three years, he developed a voice remarkable for its power and flexibility.

The following combinations should be practised aloud, in clear-cut tone. with abrupt movement of the abdominal muscles:

Be	ba	baw	bah	bo	boo
De	da	daw	dah	do	doo
Fe	fa	faw	fah	fo	foo
Ge	ga	gaw	gah	go	goo
He	ha	haw	hah	ho	hoo
Je	ja	jaw	jah	jo	joo
Ke	ka	kaw	kah	ko	koo
Le	la	law	lah	lo	loo
Me	ma	maw	mah	mo	moo
Pe	pa	paw	pah	po	poo
Re	ra	raw	rah	ro	roo
Se	sa	saw	sah	so	soo
Te	ta	taw	tah	to	too
Ve	va	vaw	vah	vo	voo
We	wa	waw	wah	wo	woo

Ble	bla	blaw	blah	blo	bloo
Bre	bra	braw	brah	bro	broo
Che	cha	chaw	chah	cho	choo
Dre	dra	draw	drah	dro	droo
Dwe	dwa	dwaw	dwah	dwo	dwoo
Fle	fla	flaw	flah	flo	floo
Fre	fra	fraw	frah	fro	froo
Gle	gla	glaw	glah	glo	gloo
Gre	gra	graw	grah	gro	groo
Kle	kla	klaw	klah	klo	kloo
Kre	kra	kraw	krah	kro	kroo
Ple	pla	plaw	plah	plo	ploo
Pre	pra	praw	prah	pro	proo
Sle	sla	slaw	slah	slo	sloo
Sme	sma	smaw	smah	smo	smoo
Spe	spa	spaw	spah	spo	spoo
Sqe	sqa	sqaw	sqah	sqo	sqoo
Ske	ska	skaw	skah	sko	skoo
She	sha	shaw	shah	sho	shoo
Ste	sta	staw	stah	sto	stoo
Swe	swa	swaw	swah	swo	swoo
Tre	tra	traw	trah	tro	troo
The	tha	thaw	thah	tho	thoo
Twe	twa	twaw	twah	two	twoo
Whe	wha	whaw	whah	who	whoo

KEY OF SOUNDS: *e* as in heal; *a* in hail; *aw* in haul; *ah* in hot; *o* in hole; *oo* in boot.

EXAMPLES FOR PRACTISE IN VOLUME

1. There is a pleasure in the pathless woods,
   There is a rapture on the lonely shore,
There is society, where none intrudes,
   By the deep sea, and music in its roar.
   I love not man the less, but Nature more,
From these our interviews, in which I steal
   From all I may be, or have been before,
To mingle with the universe and feel
What I can ne'er express, yet can not all conceal.

Roll on, thou deep and dark blue Ocean—roll!
  Ten thousand fleets sweep over thee in vain,
Man marks the earth with ruin—his control
  Stops with the shore;—upon the watery plain
  The wrecks are all thy deed, nor doth remain
A shadow of man's ravage, save his own,
  When for a moment, like a drop of rain,
He sinks into thy depths with bubbling groan,
Without a grave, unknelled, uncoffined, and unknown.

The armaments which thunderstrike the walls
  Of rock-built cities, bidding nations quake,
And monarchs tremble in their capitals;
  The oak leviathans, whose huge ribs make
  Their clay creator the vain title take
Of lord of thee, and arbiter of war—
  These are thy toys, and, as the snowy flake,
They melt into thy yeast of waves, which mar
Alike the Armada's pride, or spoils of Trafalgar.

Thy shores are empires, changed in all save thee—
  Assyria, Greece, Rome, Carthage,—what are they?
Thy waters wasted them while they were free,
  And many a tyrant since; their shores obey
  The stranger, slave, or savage; their decay
Has dried up realms to deserts:—not so thou,
  Unchangeable, save to thy wild waves' play—
Time writes no wrinkle on thine azure brow—
Such as creation's dawn beheld, thou rollest now.

Thou glorious mirror, where the Almighty's form
  Glasses itself in tempests; in all time,
Calm or convulsed—in breeze or gale or storm,
  Icing the pole, or in the torrid clime
  Dark heaving;—boundless, endless, and sublime—
The image of Eternity—the throne
  Of the Invisible; even from out thy slime
The monsters of the deep are made; each zone
Obeys thee: thou goest forth, dread, fathomless, alone.

And I have loved thee, Ocean! and my joy
Of youthful sports was on thy breast to be
Borne, like thy bubbles, onward: from a boy
I wantoned with thy breakers—they to me
Were a delight; and if the freshening sea
Made them a terror,—'twas a pleasing fear;
For I was, as it were, a child of thee,
And trusted to thy billows far and near,
And laid my hand upon thy mane—as I do here.
"Apostrophe to the Ocean."—"Childe Harold." BYRON.

Lesson talk. This selection should be read throughout in round, full-toned voice. Avoid mere loudness. Here and there the voice should swell in keeping with the thought. Try to picture in the imagination just what you are describing. Fit your voice to the thought. The general rate should be deliberate, but the pausing should be frequent and varied. Do not necessarily pause at the end of a line. Carefully analyze the meaning of each phrase, and pause according to the thought, not according to the lines nor even the grammatical punctuation. Look up in your dictionary the pronunciation of every doubtful word. Are you sure of these: Nature, ne'er, blue, ruin, depths, leviathans, Armada, Trafalgar, Assyria, realms, azure, torrid, wantoned, terror?

2. Hast thou a charm to stay the morning-star
In his steep course? So long he seems to pause
On thy bald, awful head, O sovereign Blanc!
The Arvé and Arveiron at thy base
Rave ceaselessly; but thou, most awful Form!
Risest from forth thy silent sea of pines,
How silently! Around thee and above
Deep is the air and dark, substantial, black,

An ebon mass: methinks thou piercest it,
As with a wedge! But when I look again,
It is thine own calm home, thy crystal shrine,
Thy habitation from eternity!

O dread and silent Mount! I gazed upon thee,
Till thou, still present to the bodily sense,
Didst vanish from my thought: entranced in prayer,
I worship'd the Invisible alone.

Yet, like some sweet beguiling melody,
So sweet, we know not we are listening to it,
Thou, the meanwhile, wast blending with my thought.
Yea, with my life and life's own secret joy:
Till the dilating Soul, enrapt, transfused,
Into the mighty vision passing, there,
As in her natural form, swell'd vast to Heaven!

Awake, my soul! Not only passive praise
Thou owest! Not alone these swelling tears,
Mute thanks and secret ecstasy! Awake,
Voice of sweet song! Awake, my heart, awake!
Green vales and icy cliffs, all join my Hymn.

Thou first and chief, sole Sovereign of the Vale!
O struggling with the darkness all the night,
And visited all night by troops of stars,
Or when they climb the sky or when they sink:
Companion of the morning-star at dawn,
Thyself Earth's rosy star, and of the dawn
Co-herald: wake, O wake, and utter praise!
Who sank thy sunless pillars deep in Earth?
Who fill'd thy countenance with rosy light?
Who made thee parent of perpetual streams?

And you, ye five wild torrents fiercely glad!
Who call'd you forth from night and utter death,
From dark and icy caverns call'd you forth,

Down those precipitous, black, jagged rocks,
For ever shatter'd and the same for ever?
Who gave you your invulnerable life,
Your strength, your speed, your fury, and your joy,
Unceasing thunder and eternal foam?
And who commanded (and the silence came)
Here let the billows stiffen, and have rest?

Ye Ice-falls! ye that from the mountain's brow
Adown enormous ravines slope amain—
Torrents, methinks, that heard a mighty voice,
And stopt at once amid their maddest plunge!
Motionless torrents! silent cataracts!
Who made you glorious as the gates of Heaven
Beneath the keen full moon? Who bade the sun
Clothe you with rainbows? Who, with living flowers
Of loveliest blue, spread garlands at your feet?—
God! let the torrents, like a shout of nations,
Answer! and let the ice-plains echo, God!
God! sing, ye meadow-streams, with gladsome voice!
Ye pine groves, with your soft and soul-like sounds!
And they, too, have a voice, yon piles of snow,
And in their perilous fall shall thunder, God!

Ye living flowers that skirt the eternal frost!
Ye wild goats sporting round the eagle's nest!
Ye eagles, playmates of the mountain-storm!
Ye lightnings, the dread arrows of the clouds!
Ye signs and wonders of the elements!
Utter forth God, and fill the hills with praise!

Thou, too, hoar Mount! with thy sky-pointing peaks,
Oft from whose feet the avalanche, unheard,
Shoots downward, glittering through the pure serene,
Into the depth of clouds that veil thy breast—
Thou, too, again, stupendous Mountain! thou
That as I raise my head, awhile bow'd low
In adoration, upward from thy base

Slow traveling with dim eyes suffused with tears,
Solemnly seemest, like a vapory cloud,
To rise before me—Rise, O ever rise!
Rise like a cloud of incense, from the Earth!
Thou kingly Spirit throned among the hills,
Thou dread ambassador from Earth to Heaven,
Great Hierarch! tell thou the silent sky,
And tell the stars, and tell yon rising sun,
Earth, with her thousand voices, praises GOD.

"Hymn to Mount Blanc." SAMUEL TAYLOR COLERIDGE.

Lesson talk. This selection demands great variety in expression—changes of pitch, force and inflection. It offers a particularly good exercise for breaking up monotony. Note the musical effect in many of the sound-combinations —as in "some sweet beguiling melody," "voice of sweet song," "soft and soul-like sounds," etc.—and try to bring this musical effect out in your voice. Not only picture the various thoughts, but try to *realize* them at the moment of expression. The rate is slow and measured, but animated in feeling. Be sure of the pronunciation of these: Sovereign, Arvé, Arveiron, ebon, dilating, ecstasy, countenance, perpetual, precipitous, jagged, invulnerable, avalanche, stupendous, mountain, suffused, hierarch.

3. What patriotic purpose is to be accomplished by this expunging? Is it to appease the wrath, and to heal the wounded pride of the Chief Magistrate? If he really be the hero that his friends represent him, he must despise all mean condescension, all groveling sycophancy, all self-degradation and self-abasement. He would reject with scorn and contempt, as unworthy of his fame, your black scratches, and your baby lines in the fair records of his country. Black lines! Black lines! Sir, I hope the secretary of the Senate will preserve the pen with which he may inscribe them, and present it to that Senator of the majority whom he may select, as a proud trophy, to be

transmitted to his descendants. And hereafter, when we shall lose the forms of our free institutions—all that now remain to us—some future American monarch, in gratitude to those by whose means he has been enabled, upon the ruins of civil liberty, to erect a throne, and to commemorate especially this expunging resolution, may institute a new order of knighthood, and confer on it the appropriate name of The Knight of the Black Lines.

But why should I detain the Senate, or needlessly waste my breath in future exertions? The decree has gone forth. It is one of urgency, too. The deed is to be done—that foul deed, like the blood-stained hands of the guilty Macbeth, all ocean's waters will never wash out. Proceed, then, to the noble work which lies before you, and like other skilful executioners, do it quickly. And when you have perpetrated it, go home to the people, and tell them what glorious honors you have achieved for our common country. Tell them that you have extinguished one of the brightest and purest lights that ever burned at the altar of civil liberty. Tell them that you have silenced one of the noblest batteries that ever thundered in defense of the Constitution, and bravely spiked the cannon. Tell them that henceforth, no matter what daring or outrageous act any President may perform, you have forever hermetically sealed the mouth of the Senate. Tell them that he may fearlessly assume what power he pleases, snatch from its lawful custody the public purse, command a military detachment to enter the hall of the Capitol, overawe Congress, trample down the Constitution, and raze every bulwark of freedom; but that the Senate must stand mute, in silent submission, and not dare to raise its opposing voice; that it must wait until a House of Representatives, humbled and subdued like itself, and a majority of it composed of the partizans of the President, shall prefer articles of impeachment. Tell them, finally, that you have restored the glorious doctrine of passive obedience and non-resistance; and if the people do not pour out their indignation and imprecation, I have yet to learn the character of American freemen.

"The Expunging Resolution." HENRY CLAY.

CHAPTER IV

HOW TO BUILD A VOCABULARY

A large and varied vocabulary is indispensable to the public speaker. With ten thousand words at his command he should be able to express himself with greater precision and effectiveness than with half that number. To increase his stock of words the speaker must cultivate an intense interest in them. He should form the habit of closely scrutinizing their meaning. He must know their intrinsic value as well as their outward effect. A peremptory challenge should be given to every word he does not thoroughly understand and its meaning studied in the dictionary.

Thoughts and words are intimately related, one being merely the expression or symbol of the other. Some authorities maintain that all thought to be clearly defined in the mind must appear there in so many words. It is true that there are many persons who, while reading silently, must say over each word in the mind in order to thoroughly understand and enjoy what they are reading.

It is difficult to overestimate the power of words. With them we command, we supplicate, we defy, we convince, we condemn, we conciliate. There are many dangerous and deadly "masked words" which everybody uses without understanding them, words colored by a man's own fancy, but which in turn mislead and poison him like so many "unjust stewards." To this class belong words of equivocation, exaggeration and sarcasm. The public speaker's business is to find out the human meanings in words. He will do well, therefore, to heed the advice of Ruskin when he says:

"I tell you earnestly and authoritatively (I *know* I am right in this) you must get into the habit of looking intently at words, assuring yourself of their meaning, syllable by syllable—nay, letter by letter. For tho it is only by reason of the apposition of letters in the function of signs to sounds that the study of books is called 'literature,' and that a man versed in it is called, by the consent of nations, a man of letters instead of a man of books or of words, you may yet connect with that accidental nomenclature this real fact, that you might read all the books in the British Museum (if you could live long enough) and remain an utterly 'illiterate,' uneducated person; but that if you read ten pages of a good book, letter by letter—that is to say, with real accuracy—you are forevermore in some measure an educated person. The entire difference between education and non-education (as regards the merely intellectual part of it) consists in this accuracy."

The study of words, if properly pursued, will prove a fascinating and beneficial exercise. There is an intrinsic pleasure in using the word that precisely expresses one's meaning. Such power and facility gives added self-confidence. It is told of Webster that once while addressing an audience he had difficulty in finding just the word he wanted. He discarded one after another until five or six had been disposed of, when suddenly he found the word he had been so earnestly seeking, and as he gave expression to it the audience, who had mentally followed his anxious search, burst out into spontaneous applause.

The possibility and potency of words is described by

James Martineau, himself a master of word-painting: "Power they certainly have. They are alive with sweetness, with terror, with pity. They have eyes to look at you with strangeness or with response. They are even creative, and can wrap a world in darkness for us or flood it with light. But in all this they are not signs of the weakness of humanity; they are the very crown and blossom of its supreme strength; and the poet whom this faith possesses will, to the end of time, be master of the critic whom it deserts. The whole inner life of men molds the forms of language and is molded by them in turn; and as surely pines when they are rudely treated as the plant whose vessels you bruise or try to replace with artificial tubes. The grouping of thought, the musical scale of feeling, the shading and harmonies of color in the spectrum of imagination, have all been building, as it were, the molecules of speech into their service; and if you heedlessly alter its dispositions, pulverize its crystals, fix its elastic media, and turn its transparent into opaque, you not only disturb expression, you dislodge the very things to be exprest. And in proportion as the idea or sentiment thus turned adrift is less of a mere personal characteristic, and has been gathering and shaping its elements from ages of various affection and experience, does it become less possible to replace it by any equivalents, or dispense with its function by any act of the will."

Preference should be given whenever possible to the short, simple Anglo-Saxon word. The study is not to resolve itself into mere "word-hunting" and a desire to dress one's thoughts in sesquipedalian language. It should be remembered that a large and ponderous vocabulary may be a hindrance rather than a help to expression. Edmund

Burke frequently discloses this fault in his laborious and excessive precision. A multiplicity of words may so darken the windows of thought as to completely obscure all intellectual light. The charm of the Gettysburg address lies chiefly in its simplicity of language, the proper expression of simplicity of thought. Lincoln very early in life formed the "dictionary habit," and to this may be attributed his remarkable skill in the use of words.

Note how the short word is employed to advantage in the following:

Think not that strength lies in the big round word,
  Or that the brief and plain must needs be weak.
To whom can this be true who once has heard
  The cry for help, the tongue that all men speak,
When want, or wo, or fear is in the throat,
  So that each word gasped out is like a shriek
Prest from the sore heart, or a strange wild note
  Sung by some fay or fiend? There is a strength
Which dies if stretched too far or spun too fine,
  Which has more height than breadth, more depth than length.
Let but this force of thought and speech be mine,
  And he that will may take the sleek, fat phrase,
Which glows and burns not, tho it gleam and shine,—
  Light, but no heat—a flash, but not a blaze!
Nor is it mere strength that the short word boasts;
  It serves of more than fight or storm to tell,
The roar of waves that clash on rock-bound coasts,
  The crash of tall trees when the wild winds swell,
The roar of guns, the groans of men that die
  On blood-stained fields. It has a voice as well
For them that far off on their sick-beds lie;
  For them that weep, for them that mourn the dead;
For them that laugh, and dance, and clap the hand;
  To joy's quick step, as well as grief's slow tread,

The sweet, plain words we learned at first keep time,
  And, tho the theme be sad, or gay, or grand,
With each, with all, these may be made to chime,
  In thought, or speech, or song, in prose or rime.

ADDISON ALEXANDER.

In his practical study of words the student should be supplied with a good dictionary, a book of synonyms, and blank note-books. A small vest-pocket note-book is desirable for jotting down words at a moment's notice.

The following exercises should be carefully practised, and can be indefinitely extended:

1. Write down in a column in your note-book the list of words hereunder. Then from memory write after each word its meaning and as many synonyms as you can. Compare the result with your dictionary.

copious	peculation	permeate
splenetic	impervious	obsequious
promiscuous	obsolete	deleterious
predatory	opprobrium	effloresce
miscreant	extenuate	indigent
propinquity	emolument	redundant
insidious	travesty	vicarious
circumscribe	vagary	initiative
tautology	sapient	lugubrious

2. Write down twenty-five words just as they occur to your mind, aiming to select the word next nearest in meaning, thus:

Abstemious, temperate, simple, genuine, reliable, stanch, enduring, firm, resolute, persevering, constant, invariable, immutable, stable, undeviating, steady, anchored, fixt, permanent, established, habitual, customary, usual, frequent, common.

3. Write down from memory a list of twenty-five words in contrast, thus:

Cold, hot, cool, excited, calm, storm, quiet, noisy, silent, talkative, reticent, frank, secretive, enlighten, conceal, disclose, mask, indicate, equivocate, straightforward, deception, fidelity, perversion, scrupulous, exaggeration.

4. Select an original subject and write down all the words you can call to mind bearing upon it. Then augment your list from your dictionary and book of synonyms. Write out your composition and compare your effort with the following:

Subject: "Our Honored Dead."

List of words:

Honors, fortitude, patriotic, patience, death, redeemed, garnered, memory, precious, martyred, heroes, love, pride, inspiration, invisible, gladness, tears, country, mourners, liberty, justice, cherish, fresh, inscribed, remembrance.

How bright are the honors which await those who, with sacred fortitude and patriotic patience, have endured all things that they might save their nation from division and from the power of corruption! The honored dead! They that die for a good cause are redeemed from death; their names are gathered and garnered; their memory is precious; each place grows proud for them who were born there. There is in every village, and in every neighborhood, a glowing pride in its martyred heroes; tablets preserve their names; pious love shall renew the inscriptions as time and the unfeeling elements efface them. And the national festivals shall give multitudes of precious names to the orator's lips. Children shall grow up under more sacred inspirations, whose elder brothers, dying nobly for their country, left a name that honored and inspired all who bore it.

Oh, tell me not that they are dead, that generous host, that army of invisible heroes! Are they dead that yet speak louder than we can speak, and a more universal language? Are they dead that yet act? Are they dead that yet move upon society and inspire the people with nobler motives and more heroic patriotism? Ye that mourn, let gladness mingle with your tears; he was your son, but now he is the nation's; he made your household bright, now his example inspires a thousand households; dear to his brothers and sisters, he is now brother to every generous youth in the land; before, he was narrowed, appropriated, shut up to you; now he is augmented, set free, and given to all; before, he was yours, now he is ours; he has died to the family that he might live to the nation. Not one name shall be forgotten or neglected, and it shall by and by be confest of our modern heroes, as it is of an ancient hero, that he did more for his country by his death than by his whole life.

O mother of lost children! sit not in darkness, nor sorrow when a nation honors. O mourners of the early dead! they shall live again, and live forever; your sorrows are our gladness; the nation lives because you gave it men that loved it better than their lives. And when the nation shall sit in unsullied garments of liberty with justice upon her forehead, love in her eyes, and truth on her lips, she shall not forget those whose blood gave vital currents to her heart, and whose life given to her shall live with her life till time shall be no more. Every mountain and hill shall have its treasured name, every river shall keep some solemn title, every valley and every lake shall cherish its honored register, and, till the mountains are worn out and the rivers forget to flow, till the clouds are weary of replenishing springs and the springs forget to gush and the rills to sing, shall their names be kept fresh with reverent honors which are inscribed upon the book of national remembrance.

"Our Honored Dead." HENRY WARD BEECHER.

5. Write a speech on the subject, "The Murderer's Secret," employing the following list of words:

Aged, man, sleep, assassin, window, noiseless, lonely, moon, room, sleeper, murderer, fatal, blow, death, secret, God, guilty, detection, conscience, torment, evil, entangle, violence, confession, suicide.

Then compare your speech with this:

An aged man without an enemy in the world, in his own house, and in his own bed, is made the victim of butcherly murder for mere pay. A healthful old man to whom sleep was sweet, the first sound slumbers of the night held him in their soft but strong embrace. The assassin enters, through the window already prepared, into an unoccupied apartment. With noiseless foot he paces the lonely hall half-lighted by the moon, he winds up the ascent of the stairs, and reaches the door of the chamber. Of this he moves the lock by soft continued pressure till it turns on its hinges, and he enters and beholds his victim before him. The room is uncommonly open to the admission of light. The face of the innocent sleeper is turned from the murderer, and the beams of the moon, resting on the gray locks of his aged temple, show him where to strike. The fatal blow is given, and the victim passes, without a struggle or a motion, from the repose of sleep to the repose of death. It is accomplished. The deed is done. He retreats, retraces his steps to the window, passes out through it as he came in, and escapes. He has done the murder. No eye has seen him. No ear has heard him. The secret is his own, and it is safe!

Ah! gentlemen, that was a dreadful mistake. Such a secret can be safe nowhere. The whole creation of God has neither nook nor corner where the guilty can bestow it and say it is safe. Not to speak of that Eye which glances through all disguises and beholds everything as in the splendor of noon, such secrets of guilt are never safe from detection even by men. True it is, generally speaking, that "murder will out." True it is that Providence hath so ordained and doth so govern things, that those who break the great law of Heaven by shedding man's blood seldom succeed in avoiding discovery. Especially in a case exciting so much attention as this, discovery must come, and will come, sooner or later. A thousand eyes turn at once to explore every man, every thing, every circumstance, connected with the time and place; a thousand ears catch every whisper; a thousand excited minds intensely dwell on the scene, shedding all their light, and ready to kindle the slightest circumstance into a blaze of discovery.

Meantime, the guilty soul can not keep its own secret. It is false to itself, or, rather, it feels an irresistible impulse of conscience to be true to itself. It labors under its guilty possession, and knows not what to do with it. The human heart was not made for the residence of such an inhabitant. It finds itself preyed on by a torment which it dares not acknowledge to God nor man. A vulture is devouring it, and it can ask no sympathy or assistance either from heaven or earth. The secret which the murderer possesses soon comes to possess him, and, like the evil spirits of which we read, it overcomes him, and leads him whithersoever it will. He feels it beating at his heart, rising to his throat, and demanding disclosure. He thinks the whole world sees it in his face, reads it in his eyes, and almost hears its workings in the very silence of his thoughts. It has become his master. It betrays his discretion, it breaks down his courage, it conquers his prudence. When suspicions from without begin to embarrass him, and the net of circumstances to entangle him, the fatal secret struggles with still greater violence to burst forth. It must be confest, it will be confest; there is no refuge from confession but suicide, and suicide is confession.

"The Murderer's Secret." DANIEL WEBSTER.

6. Write an essay on the subject "Family Government," using the following list of words:

Command, decision, consistency, firmness, law, enforce, penalties, inevitable, consequences, uniformity, respect, administration, justice, severity, leniency, contemptible, transgression, impunity, coercive, despotism, discipline, governed, slavery, free, self-control.

Compare your composition with this:

Whenever you *do* command, command with decision and consistency. If the case is one which really can not be otherwise dealt with, then issue your fiat, and, having issued it, never afterward swerve from it. Consider well beforehand what you are going to do, weigh all the consequences, think whether your firmness of purpose will be sufficient; and then, if you finally make the law, enforce it uniformly at whatever cost. Let your penalties be like the penalties inflicted by inanimate nature—inevitable. The hot cinder burns a child the first time he seizes it; it burns him the second time; it burns him the third time; it burns him every time; and he very soon learns not to touch the hot cinder. If you are equally consistent, if the consequences which you tell your child will follow certain acts follow with like uniformity, he will soon come to respect your laws as he does those of nature.

And this respect, once established, will prevent endless domestic evils. Of errors in education one of the worst is that of inconsistency. As in a community crimes multiply when there is no certain administration of justice, so in a family an immense increase of transgressions results from a hesitating or irregular infliction of penalties. A weak mother who perpetually threatens and rarely performs, who makes rules in haste and repents of them at leisure, who treats the same offense now with severity and now with leniency, according as the passing humor dictates, is laying up miseries both for herself and her children. She is making herself contemptible in their eyes; she is setting them an example of uncontrolled feelings; she is encouraging them to transgress by the prospect of probable immunity; she is entailing endless squabbles and accompanying damage to her own temper and the tempers of her little ones; she is reducing their minds to a moral chaos, which after-years of bitter experience will with difficulty bring into order.

Better even a barbarous form of domestic government carried out consistently than a humane one inconsistently carried out. Again we say, avoid coercive measures whenever it is possible to do so; but, when you find despotism really necessary, be despotic in good earnest. Bear constantly in mind the truth that the aim of your discipline should be to produce a self-governing being, not to produce a being to be governed by others. Were your children fated to pass their lives as slaves, you could not too much accustom them to slavery during their childhood; but, as they are by and by to be free men, with no one to control their daily conduct, you can not too much accustom them to self-control while they are still under your eye.

"Education." HERBERT SPENCER.

7. Carefully note the following phrases. Make similar lists of your own, gathered from your reading and observation.

kingly virtues
dazzling contrasts
barren phraseology
consummate prudence
legendary valor
teeming millions
triumphant victory
timid mediocrity
bloated epicure
unutterable forces
extreme rarity
unmasked pretension
youthful buoyancy
luminous insight
unfailing tact
matured skill
capacious understanding
lawless violence
searching sunlight
copious fountain
sun-baked hills
implacable fervor
enlightened judgment
touching fidelity
abundant recognition

laborious indolence
violet valley
panic terror
impregnable stronghold
unreasoning felicity
noble zeal
riotous vegetation
tacit assumption
unwearied enthusiasm
throbbing personality
utterly relentless
predestinated criminals
pitiless persecution
sublime achievement
fundamental principle
immeasurable power
unbending strength
twilight glimmerings
kindled imagination
softening influences
glorious iconoclasts
momentous crisis
trembling solicitude
inviolable justice
innocent stratagem

8. Note three special words each day in your reading or in the conversation of others, and employ them in your speech that day. Keep a record of such words for frequent review. If this practise is faithfully carried out your vocabulary will be surprizingly increased in a short time.

9. Write in your note-book, daily, at least seven words from the following lists, in the order given. Then after each word write a sentence illustrating its idiomatic use. Afterward compare with your dictionary.

WORD LIST—I. ABSTRACT RELATIONS

Essence, subjectiveness, pith, principle, quintessence, incarnation, soul.

Circumstance, phase, attitude, occasion, situation, juncture, place.

Contrary, opposed, antithetical, contrasted, conflicting, hostile, antipodean.

Agreement, accordance, unison, harmony, conformity, consonance, concord.

Equality, parity, balance, poise, evenness, symmetry, level.

Greatness, magnitude, immensity, enormity, infinity, largeness, might.

Vast, towering, stupendous, prodigious, astonishing, incredible, marvelous.

Supreme, paramount, preeminent, crowning, inimitable, superlative, incomparable.

Increase, exalt, strengthen, intensify, raise, augment, enlarge.

Disperse, scatter, dispel, apportion, sow, disseminate, spread.

Infinite, exhaustless, incomprehensible, perpetual, measureless, incalculable, boundless.

Continual, endless, interminable, unceasing, eternal, incessant, uninterrupted.

Previous, prior, preceding, antecedent, former, aforesaid, foregoing.

Venerable, superannuated, decrepit, antiquated, declining, patriarchal, waning.

Capricious, desultory, fitful, uncertain, whimsical, unsteady, spasmodic.
Variation, modification, change, alteration, permutation, qualification, deviation.
Fluctuate, waver, vacillate, oscillate, vary, flutter, scruple.
Power, strength, energy, force, virility, vitality, vigor.
Powerful, robust, potent, hardy, puissant, mighty, sturdy.
Calm, cool, tranquillize, assuage, appease, compose, palliate.

II. SPACE

Extent, expanse, scope, range, latitude, compass, field.
Diminish, compress, dwarf, circumscribe, contract, condense, lessen.
Proximity, nearness, propinquity, vicinity, adjacency, contiguity, neighborhood.
Abridge, curtail, shorten, reduce, abbreviate, prune, epitomize.
Height, eminence, elevation, altitude, loftiness, pitch, sublimity.
Encompass, surround, enclose, circumvent, gird, beset, encircle.
Rotund, round, cylindrical, spherical, bulbous, circular, complete.
Smooth, polished, slippery, velvety, lubricous, glabrous, glossy.
Velocity, swiftness, speed, expedition, celerity, rapidity, acceleration.
Gentle, easy, leisurely, imperceptible, gradual, deliberate, slow.
Discursive, devious, vagrant, circuitous, rambling, erratic, desultory.
Entrance, introgression, intrusion, incursive, invasion, admission, insinuation.
Expansion, enlargement, increase, augmentation, amplification, swell, inflation.
Emaciated, lean, gaunt, lanky, skinny, starved, meager.
Symmetry, shapeliness, finish, beauty, proportion, uniformity, regularity.
Involved, intricate, complicated, labyrinthine, winding, convoluted, twisted.
Protuberance, swelling, projection, protrusion, bulge, convexity, prominence.
Pointed, conical, tapering, pyramidal, sharp, keen, acute.

Propel, throw, pitch, project, fling, cast, toss.
Tremulous, shambling, convulsive, restless, agitated, shaking, unquiet.

III. MATTER

Subtile, weightless, ethereal, sublimated, volatile, buoyant, floating.
Congeal, coagulate, crystallize, petrify, solidify, consolidate, fix.
Flexible, supple, pliant, limber, plastic, tractable, malleable.
Powdery, granular, mealy, impalpable, efflorescent, sabulous, flocculent.
Ferment, effervesce, bubble, gurgle, foam, froth, boil.
Oily, unctuous, sebaceous, greasy, saponaceous, fatty, slippery.
Agreeable, refreshing, comforting, cordial, genial, palatable, sensuous.
Heat, caloric, fervor, warmth, incandescence, glow, hectic.
Pungent, strong, sharp, stinging, biting, acrimonious, peppery.
Fragrant, aromatic, spicy, balmy, scented, redolent, perfumed.
Inaudible, stifled, low, dull, muffled, hoarse, husky.
Scream, screech, shriek, yell, roar, shout, halloo.
Melodious, musical, tuneful, sweet, dulcet, mellifluous, euphonious.
Luminous, vivid, lucid, lambent, lustrous, scintillant, bright.
Turbid, muddy, obfuscated, cloudy, thick, fuliginous, muggy.
Behold, discern, perceive, descry, distinguish, recognize, see.
Visible, palpable, perceptible, discernible, apparent, obvious, plain.
Variegated, kaleidoscope, iridescent, opalescent, prismatic, diversified, tesselated.
Black, swarthy, sable, somber, dark, jetty, ebon.
Silence, stillness, peace, hush, lull, muteness, soundless.

IV. INTELLECT

Conception, thought, apprehension, perception, impression, idea, notion.
Alertness, vigilance, attention, prudence, forethought, precaution, watchfulness.

Discrimination, distinction, nicety, differentiation, distinguishing, estimation, discernment.

Reasonable, credible, probable, plausible, presumable, ostensible, likely.

Absolute, positive, definite, unequivocal, unmistakable, decisive, clear.

Sophistry, perversion, casuistry, equivocation, evasion, chicanery, speciousness.

Refute, disprove, invalidate, demolish, rebut, parry, expose.

Belief, credence, assurance, faith, confidence, dependence, credit.

Incredulous, supsicious, scrupulous, distrustful, skeptical, inconvincible, unbelieving.

Dissent, demur, differ, protest, repudiate, contradict, disagree.

Exact, definite, precise, literal, unerring, rigid, scrupulous.

Twaddle, jargon, moonshine, vagary, fustian, stuff, tomfoolery.

Acumen, subtlety, perspicacity, sagacity, acuteness, comprehension, intelligence.

Foolish, unwise, ridiculous, stupid, asinine, irrational, injudicious.

Madness, delirium, frenzy, lunacy, aberration, delusion, hallucination.

Portend, signify, augur, typify, presage, herald, foreshadow.

Conjecture, surmise, suspect, suppose, presume, divine, speculate.

Fabulous, legendary, chimerical, fantastical, imaginary, mythological, visionary.

Unreasonable, inconsistent, untenable, fallacious. groundless, illogical, invalid.

Ambiguous, equivocal, vague, indefinite, questionable, doubtful, dubious.

V. VOLITION

Persevering, unfaltering, industrious, persisting, unflinching, strenuous, unwavering.

Tergiversation, recantation, retraction, withdrawal, disavowal, renunciation, defection.

Attraction, allurement, enticement, cajolery, inducement, temptation, fascination.

Adequacy, abundance, copiousness, amplitude, profusion, luxuriance, plentitude.

Redundant, exuberant, inordinate, excessive, profuse, replete, extravagant.

Contemptible, meager, beggarly, miserable, shabby, wretched, paltry.

Inexpedient, objectionable, disadvantageous, inopportune, undesirable, inappropriate, ineligible.

Perfect, faultless, immaculate, spotless, impeccable, unblemished, complete.

Morbid, unsound, vitiated, contaminated, infirm, drooping, diseased.

Salubrious, wholesome, sanitary, invigorating, nutritious, hygienic, healthful.

Dulness, languor, sluggishness, drowsiness, lethargy, heaviness, torpidity.

Skill, adroitness, proficiency, facility, expertness, dexterity, mastery.

Ingenuous, unaffected, guileless, unsophisticated, artless, simple, docile.

Manageable, tractable, submissive, yielding, ductile, pliant, towardly.

Variance, disagreement, dissension, misunderstanding, division, disunion, breach.

Pacify, compose, reconcile, placate, conciliate, propitiate, harmonize.

Succumb, submit, yield, resign, bend, capitulate, surrender.

Accomplish, achieve, compass, consummate, perfect, complete, elaborate.

Defeat, conquer, silence, vanquish, discomfit, overcome, checkmate.

Prosperous, thriving, buoyant, fortunate, lucky, successful, affluent.

VI. AFFECTIONS

Insensible, apathetic, frigid, dull, phlegmatic, obtuse, cold.

Excitement, impetuosity, paroxysm, perturbation, vehemence, agitation, ferment.

Felicitous, delightful, charming, exquisite, lovely, winning, captivating.

Vivacity, animation, liveliness, jocundity, joviality, alacrity, life.
Lugubrious, funereal, somber, melancholy, gloomy, spiritless, mournful.
Lachrymose, melancholic, hypochondriacal, saturnine, splenetic, pensive, sad.
Facetiousness, waggery, smartness, whimsicality, banter, jocularity, humor.
Beautiful, handsome, lovely, elegant, comely, refined, dainty.
Pure, chaste, cultivated, refined, classical, esthetic, artistic.
Ridiculous, ludicrous, funny, laughable, grotesque, farcical, whimsical.
Confident, sanguine, buoyant, elated, enthusiastic, utopian, exultant.
Fear, diffidence, apprehension, misgiving, timidity, perturbation, trepidation.
Courage, bravery, valor, confidence, intrepidity, gallantry, daring.
Repugnance, disgust, loathing, antipathy, abhorrence, animosity, detestation.
Surprize, astonish, astound, amaze, bewilder, stagger, startle.
Illustrious, glorious, imperishable, brilliant, eminent, peerless, immortal.
Insolent, arrogant, imperious, haughty, dictatorial, arbitrary, supercilious.
Affectionate, sympathetic, loving, tender, ardent, rapturous, devoted.
Benevolence, unselfishness, philanthropy, benignity, kindness, charity, generosity.
Respect, courtesy, reverense, deference, veneration, esteem, regard.

CHAPTER V

POWER IN ENGLISH STYLE

An element of great power and effectiveness in public speaking is a good English style. Among the many definitions of this phrase are these: Newman: "Style is a thinking out into language." Wordsworth: "Style is the incarnation of thought." Buffon: "Style is the man." Dean Swift: "Style is proper words in proper places." Pater: "Truth! there can be no merit, no craft at all, without that." Phelps: "Style is the general term by which we designate the qualities of thought as exprest in language." W. J. Dawson: "Greatness of style springs from the great mind and the noble temper."

Style, then, is the result of a certain moral and mental discipline, in which a man at last expresses *himself*. As a result of this training words will fit naturally and readily into their proper places, while their arrangement will suggest clearness, rhythm, beauty, force, felicity, and other qualities. Carlyle says: "Care not for the reward of your speaking, but simply and with undivided mind for the *truth* of your speaking." Jean Paul Richter's counsel to the writer is equally applicable to the speaker: "Never write upon a subject without having first *read* yourself full of it, and never read without having first *thought* yourself hungry."

According to leading rhetoricians, the principal qualities to be developed are purity, precision, perspicuity, individuality, energy, elegance, and naturalness. To this end the writer and speaker will endeavor to make these a part of his general mental habits. As a man accustoms himself to think, so is he likely to speak, or "As a man thinketh, so is he." He should closely study such masters of prose style as Macaulay, Newman, Ruskin, Matthew Arnold, and others, reading them aloud, and committing them to writing.

A favorite model for students of English style is John Henry Newman, of whom Alexander Whyte says:

"The strength, the richness, the pliability, the acuteness, the subtlety, the spiritualness, the beauty, the manifold resources of the English language, are all brought out under Newman's hand, as under the hand of no other English author. 'Athanasius is a great writer,' says Newman, 'simple in his diction, clear, unstudied, direct, vigorous, elastic, and, above all, characteristic.' All of which I will repeat of Newman himself, and especially this—he is, above all, characteristic. If the English language has an angel residing in it and presiding over it, surely Newman is that angel. Or, at the least, the angel who has the guardianship of the English language committed to him must surely have handed his own pen to Newman as often as that master has sat down to write English. No other writer in the English language has ever written it quite like Newman. Every preface of his, every title-page of his, every dedication and advertisement of his, every footnote, every parenthesis of his, has a stamp upon it that at once makes you say—that is Newman! He is simply inimitable. He is simply alone as a writer, and has no fellow."

Contrast with this high tribute the eloquent words of Newman himself: "While the many use language as they find it, the man of genius uses it indeed, but subjects it withal to his own purposes, and molds it according to his own peculiarities. The throng and succession of ideas, thoughts, feelings, imaginations, aspirations, which pass within him, the abstractions, the juxtapositions, the comparisons, the discriminations, the conceptions, which are so original in him, his views of external things, his judgments upon life, manners, and history, the exercises of his wit, of his humor, of his depth, of his sagacity, all these innumerable and incessant creations, the very pulsation and throbbing of his intellect, does he image forth, to all does he give utterance, in a corresponding language, which is as multiform as this inward mental action itself and analogous to it, the faithful expression of his intense personality, attending on his own inward world of thought as its very shadow: so that we might as well say one man's shadow is another's as that the style of a really gifted mind can belong to any but himself. It follows him about *as* a shadow. His thought and feeling are personal, and so his language is personal."

According to Newman's definition, thought and speech are inseparable, so that a man who aspires to write well or to speak well should see to it that he first *thinks* well. Since the time of Cicero and Quintilian the advice given in this matter of English style has been to write, write, write. This applies to original writing as well as to copying the thoughts and language of others. This work should be done every day, and as much of it as possible. Macaulay wrote six pages every morning, reducing his first rough draft to two pages, and considered his day ill-spent when he neglected to do this. He was emphatic in his dislike for "fine writing," and said: "The feelings should, indeed, have their ornamental garb, but, like an elegant woman, they should be neither muffled nor exposed. The drapery should be so arranged as at once to answer the purposes of modest concealment and judicious display."

As a model of purity of style the Bible offers an incomparable text. In combining simplicity of expression and sublimity of thought what outside of its holy pages can equal this: "Let there be light: and there was light!" And yet according to the style of some speakers, this would be rendered, as William Matthews says: "Let there be light, and there was a solar illumination!" In all the noted lists of "One hundred best books" the Bible is given first place. Archbishop Fénelon says: "The Scripture surpasses the most ancient Greek authors vastly in native simplicity, loveliness, and grandeur. Homer himself never reached the sublimity of Moses' songs. Never did any ode, either Greek or Latin, come up to the loftiness of the Psalms. Neither Homer nor any other great poet equalled Isaiah, describing the majesty of God. What is there in antiquity that can be compared to the lamentations of Jeremiah, when he tenderly deplores the misery of his country, or the prophecy of Nahum, when he foresees in the spirit the proud Nineveh fall under the rage of an invisible army? Everything is painted in such a lively manner as strikes the imagination: the prophet far outdoes Homer. Read likewise Daniel denouncing to Belshazzar the divine vengeance ready to overwhelm him, and try if you can find anything in the most sublime original of antiquity that can be compared to those passages of Sacred Writ. As for the rest of Scripture, every portion of it is uniform and constant, every part bears the peculiar character that becomes it. In short, there is as much difference between the heathen poet and the prophets as there is between a false enthusiasm and the true."

Sympathy, simplicity, enthusiasm, vitality, power, loftiness of spirit, love of truth, and other such qualities in the public speaker should first characterize his thinking habits, that they may naturally reflect themselves in the personality of his English style. Daily practise in writing stimulates the mental faculties, promotes accuracy and precision, and tends to make one systematic and logical. The prudent writer or speaker will avoid all attempts at "flowers of rhetoric," "fine writing," and "perfumed fancy" as having a tendency to impoverish his natural expression.

The public speaker should write for the ear as well as for the eye. He will summon his audience before him, gather the people around him in imagination, and mentally voice his thoughts to them as he writes. He should frequently stop writing and read aloud what he has written to determine whether it fits the mouth and "speaks well." Otherwise he may be composing a very good essay but a very poor speech. The ear is the most exacting critic in this matter. It is quick to detect a word out of place, an inharmonious combination of sounds, or other infelicity of speech.

The public speaker will have a scholarly care about his habits of conversation. He will not only avoid loose and incorrect speech, but will constantly aim to express himself at his best, without resorting to pedantry or stiltedness.

"We must write as carefully, and as much as we can," says Quintilian; "for as the ground, by being dug to a great depth, becomes more fitted for fructifying and nourishing seeds, so improvement of the mind, acquired from more than mere superficial cultivation, pours forth the fruits of study in richer abundance, and retains them with greater fidelity. For without this precaution, the very faculty of speaking extempore will but furnish us with empty loquacity, and words born on the lips. In writing are the roots, in writing are the foundations of eloquence; by writing resources are stored up, as it were, in a sacred repository, whence they may be drawn forth for sudden emergencies, or as circumstances require."[1]

The constant aim of the writer and speaker should be toward simplicity. He should prefer the short Saxon word, whenever possible, instead of the usually ponderous importation from some other language. Simplicity begets clearness, and clearness of thought and expression are the fundamental qualities for deeply impressing an audience. Particularly should the student guard against a style like the following:

"All external objects are in their truest sense visible embodiments or incarnations of divine ideas which are roughly sculptured in the hard granite that underlies the living and breathing surface of the world above; penciled in delicate tracery upon each bark-flake that encompasses the tree-trunk, each leaf that trembles in the breeze, each petal that fills the air with fragrant effluence; assuming a living and breathing existence in the rhythmic throbbings of the heart-pulse that urges the life-stream through the body of every animated being; and attaining their greatest perfection in man, who is thereby bound by the very fact of his existence to outspeak and outact the divine ideas which are the true instincts of humanity, before they are crusht or paralyzed by outward circumstances."

The student is not recommended to devote himself too exclusively to any one writer. It is better to give some time

[1] Quintilian's *Institutes of Oratory, or, Education of an Orator*, Vol. 2; translated by Rev. John Selby Watson. George Bell & Sons.

to each of the recognized stylists. For simplicity he will study the Bible, Bunyan, Addison, and Lincoln; for elegance and resourcefulness, John Henry Newman, Washington Irving, and James Martineau; for rhetorical style, Macaulay; for narrative and character delineation, Dickens; for harmony, Ruskin and Hawthorne; for epigrammatic style, Emerson and Stephen Crane; for condensation, Bacon; for energy, Wendell Phillips, Edmund Burke, and Daniel Webster; for oratorical style, Edward Everett, William Ewart Gladstone, and other great political and pulpit speakers.

The following exercises will be found helpful:

1. Read daily two or more pages of a master of style, some of whose names have already been suggested. Do this systematically. Carefully note the selection and arrangement of words, the structure of sentences and paragraphs, the felicitous turns of expression, and other characteristics of the writer.

2. Copy in your own handwriting daily at least one page of some master stylist, carefully observing, as in your reading in the last-named exercise, special qualities in thought, word, and arrangement. Learn to "brood" over this exercise.

3. Read aloud daily two or more pages of some great oration. Take in as many words or phrases as you can with a quick glance of the eye, and speak the words to an imaginary audience. This will help you to cultivate a speaking rather than a reading style.

4. Read a page or a paragraph from some stylist, then close the book and write out the thought in your own words. Compare with the original, and note your faults.

5. As often as convenient, copy in your own handwri-

ting some portion of a great poem by Milton, Tennyson, Byron, Wordsworth, Cowper, Bryant, or other poet.

6. Write original compositions, both in essay and oratorical form, comparing them with the work of other writers and speakers, and subjecting them to the severest criticism. Earnestly endeavor to strengthen the weak points in your style. Remember that results worth while come only from long and laborious practise.

Many excellent specimens for study, both in prose and poetry, will be found at the back of this volume. Begin your work with the following short extracts:

1. The perfect loveliness of a woman's countenance can only consist in that majestic peace which is founded in the memory of happy and useful years, full of sweet records; and from the joining of this with that yet more majestic childishness, which is still full of change and promise—opening always—modest at once, and bright, with the hope of better things to be won, and to be bestowed. There is no old age where there is still that promise.

Thus, then, you have first to mold her physical frame, and then as the strength she gains will permit you, to fill and temper her mind with all knowledge and thoughts which tend to confirm its natural instincts of justice and refine its natural tact of love.

All such knowledge should be given her as may enable her to understand, and even to aid, the work of men; and yet it should be given, not as knowledge—not as if it were, or could be, for her an object to know, but only to feel, and to judge. It is of no moment, as a matter of pride or perfectness in herself, whether she knows many languages or one; but it is of the utmost that she should be able to show kindness to a stranger, and to understand the sweetness of a stranger's tongue. It is of no moment to her own worth or dignity that she should be acquainted with this science or that; but it is of the highest that she should be trained in habits of accurate thought; that she should understand the meaning, the inevitableness, and the loveliness of natural laws; and follow at least some one path of scientific attainment as far as to the threshold of that bitter valley of humiliation, into which only the wisest and bravest of men can descend, owning themselves forever children, gathering pebbles on a boundless shore. It is of little consequence how many positions of cities she knows, or how many dates of events, or names of celebrated persons—it is not the object of education to turn the woman into a dictionary; but it is deeply necessary that she should be taught to enter with her whole personality into the history she reads; to picture the passages of it vitally in her own bright imagination; to apprehend, with her fine instincts, the pathetic circumstances and dramatic relations which the historian too often only eclipses by his reasoning and disconnects by his arrangement: it is for her to trace the hidden equities of divine reward, and catch sight, through the darkness, of the fateful threads of woven fire that connect error with retribution. But chiefly of all, she is to be taught to extend the limits of her sympathy with respect to that history which is being forever determined as the moments pass in which she draws her peaceful breath, and to the contemporary calamity which, were it but rightly mourned by her, would recur no more hereafter. She is to exercise herself in imagining what would be the effects upon her mind and conduct, if she were daily brought into the presence of suffering which is not the less real because shut from her sight. She is to be taught somewhat to understand the nothingness of the proportion which that little world in which she lives and loves, bears to the world in which God lives and loves; and solemnly she is to be taught to strive that her thoughts of piety may not be feeble in proportion to the number they embrace, nor her prayer more languid than it is for the momentary relief from pain of her husband or her child, when it is uttered for the multitudes of those who have none to love them, and is "for all who are desolate and opprest."

"Sesame and Lilies." JOHN RUSKIN.

2. Ethereal Minstrel! Pilgrim of the sky!
Dost thou despise the earth where cares abound?
Or, while the wings aspire, are heart and eye
Both with thy nest upon the dewy ground?
Thy nest which thou canst drop into at will,
Those quivering wings composed, that music still!

To the last point of vision, and beyond,
Mount, daring warbler! that love prompted strain
('Twixt thee and thine a never-failing bond)
Thrills not the less the bosom of the plain.
Yet might'st thou seem, proud privilege! to sing
All independent of the leafy spring.

Leave to the Nightingale her shady wood:
A privacy of glorious light is thine;
Whence thou dost pour upon the world a flood
Of harmony, with instinct more divine;
Type of the wise, who soar, but never roam;
True to the kindred points of Heaven and Home!

"To a Skylark." WILLIAM WORDSWORTH.

3. There are two classes of permanent products raised and transmitted by human activity. One of them is *cooperative* and has a parallel in the life of other creatures. As the coral-reef is deposited in increments contributed by a constant animal succession, so the city, the harbor, the aqueduct, the road enlist and attest the labors of many generations, and owe their solidity and grandeur to prolonged experience and multitudinous skill. Such monuments record the power of the *social* spirit, and measure for us the greatness of *nations*.

The other class is purely *individual* and *personal,* and has no place except in human kind. An *Iliad,* an *Agamemnon,* a *Divina Commedia,* a *Hamlet,* a *Faust,* a *Madonna di San Sisto,* or a *Sinfonia Eroica* is a unique birth in which no sound mind can bear a part; and, go where it may, speak to what myriads it will, it is still an appeal of one soul to another, eliciting response as sharp and single as the echo to a solitary voice. Flowing forth from a single creative nature, it acts by its touch as an experiment in spiritual friendship, and gathers an ever-increasing group, held fast in fellowship of enthusiasm, and owing a common obligation to the genius which has discovered for them their true soul.

What and where, then, are the two members of this relation? Is the first of them nothing and nowhere? and is the homage it wrings from me paid to a blank? or to a dead book only—to blotted paper or colored canvas or an orchestral score? Heart-worship, like God, is "not of the dead, but of the living"; and that, in the thought-glance with which we look up to a Homer, a Dante, a Shakespeare, there should be no reciprocity possible—that in reverencing the prophets we do but decorate their tombs—that the touch which wakes such fires within us should be that of a *quenched* torch, would expel their chief meaning from the noblest relations subsisting among human minds.

A great, creative personality may be lonely and neglected in his day; and only when the reflection which he leaves of himself travels down the ages, does he select and gather together his natural associates and lovers: and shall he never hear the chorus of that great company, or know of that life which began for him when life had ended? Can a word that is immortal come from a speaker that is ephemeral?

"A Study of Religion." JAMES MARTINEAU.

4. Whence the sound
Of instruments, that made melodious chime,
Was heard, of harp and organ; and who moved
Their stops and chords, was seen; his volant touch
Instinct through all proportions, low and high,
Fled and pursued transverse the resonant fugue.

"Paradise Lost," Book XI.

Passion of sudden death! that once in youth I read and interpreted by the shadows of thy averted signs!—rapture of panic taking the shape (which among tombs in churches I have seen) of woman bursting her sepulchral bonds—of woman's

Ionic form bending forward from the ruins of the grave with arching foot, with eyes upraised, with clasped, adoring hands—waiting, watching, trembling, praying for the trumpet's call to rise from dust forever! Ah, vision too fearful of shuddering humanity on the brink of mighty abysses!—vision that didst start back, that didst reel away, like a shrivering scroll before the wrath of fire racing on the wings of the wind! Epilepsy so brief of horror, wherefore is it that thou canst die? Passing so suddenly into darkness, wherefore is it that thou sheddest thy sad funeral blights upon the gorgeous mosaic of dreams? Fragments of music too passionate, heard once and heard no more, what aileth thee, that thy deep rolling chords come up at intervals through all the worlds of sleep, and after forty years, have lost no element of horror?

I

Lo, it is summer—almighty summer! The everlasting gates of life and summer are thrown open wide; and on the ocean tranquil and verdant as a savannah, the unknown lady from the dreadful vision and I myself are floating—she upon a fairy pinnace, and I upon an English three-decker. Both of us are wooing gales of festive happiness within the domain of our common country, within that ancient watery park, within that pathless chase of ocean, where England takes her pleasure as a huntress through winter and summer, from the rising to the setting sun. Ah, what a wilderness of floral beauty was hidden, or was suddenly revealed, upon the tropic islands through which the pinnace moved! And upon her deck what a bevy of human flowers—young women how lovely, young men how noble, that were dancing together, and slowly drifting toward *us* amid music and incense, amidst blossoms from forests and gorgeous corymbi from vintages, amidst natural carolling, and the echoes of sweet girlish laughter. Slowly the pinnace nears us, gaily she hails us, and silently she disappears beneath the shadow of our mighty bows. But then, as at some signal from heaven, the music, and the carols, and the sweet echoing of girlish laughter—all are hushed. What evil has smitten the pinnace, meeting or overtaking her? Did ruin to our friends couch within our own dreadful shadow? Was our shadow the shadow of death? I looked over the bow for an answer, and, behold! the pinnace was dismantled; the revels and the revelers were found no more; the glory of the vintage was dust; and the forests with their beauty were left without a witness upon the seas. "But where," and I turned to our crew—"where are the lovely women that danced beneath the awning of flowers and clustering corymbi? Whither have fled the noble young men that danced with *them*?" Answer there was none. But suddenly the man at the masthead, whose countenance darkened with alarm, cried out, "Sail on the weather beam! Down she comes upon us; in seventy seconds she also will founder."

II

I looked to the weather side, and the summer had departed. The sea was rocking and shaking with gathering wrath. Upon its surface sat mighty mists, which grouped themselves into arches and long cathedral aisles. Down one of these, with the fiery pace of a quarrel from a crossbow, ran a frigate right athwart our course. "Are they mad?" some voice exclaimed from our deck. "Do they woo their ruin?" But in a moment, as she was close upon us, some impulse of a heady current or local vortex gave a wheeling bias to her course, and off she forged without a shock. As she ran past us, high aloft amongst the shrouds stood the lady of the pinnace. The deeps in malice opened ahead to receive her, the billows were fierce to catch her. But far away she was borne upon the desert spaces of the sea; while still by sight I followed her, she ran before the howling gale, chased by angry seabirds and by maddening billows; still I saw her, as at the moment when she ran past us, standing amongst the shrouds, with her white draperies streaming before the wind. There she stood, with hair disheveled, one hand clutched amongst the tackling—rising, sinking, fluttering trembling, praying—there for leagues I saw her as she stood, raising at intervals one hand to heaven, amidst the fiery crests of the pursuing waves and the raving of the storm; until at last, upon a sound from afar of malicious laughter and mockery, all was hidden forever in driving showers; and afterward, but when I know not, nor how.

"Dream-Fugue." THOMAS DE QUINCEY.

5. The Present Age. In these brief words what a world of thought is comprehended; what infinite movements; what joys and sorrows; what hope and despair; what faith and doubt; what silent grief and loud lament; what fierce conflicts and subtle schemes of policy! what private and public revolutions! In the period through which many of us have passed, what thrones have been shaken; what hearts have bled; what millions have been butchered by their fellow-creatures; what hopes of philanthropy have been blighted! And at the same time what magnificent enterprises have been achieved; what new provinces won to science and art; what rights and liberties secured to nations! It is a privilege to have lived in an age so stirring, so pregnant, so eventful. It is an age never to be forgotten. Its voice of warning and encouragement is never to die. Its impression on history is indelible. Amidst its events, the American Revolution, the first distinct, solemn assertion of the rights of men; and the French Revolution, that volcanic force which shook the earth to its center, are never to pass from men's minds. Over this age the night will, indeed, gather more and more as time rolls away; but in that night two forms will appear, Washington and Napoleon, the one a lurid meteor, the other a benign, serene, and undecaying star. Another American name will live in history, your Franklin; and the kite which brought lightning from heaven will be seen sailing in the clouds by remote posterity, when the city where he dwelt may be known only by its ruins. There is, however, something greater in the age than its greatest men; it is the appearance of a new power in the world, the appearance of the multitude of men on the stage where as yet the few have acted their parts alone. This influence is to endure to the end of time. What more of the present is to survive? Perhaps much

of which we now take no note. The glory of an age is often hidden from itself. Perhaps some word has been spoken in our day which we have not deigned to hear, but which is to grow clearer and louder through all ages. Perhaps there sleeps in his cradle some reformer who is to move the Church and the world, who is to open a new era in history, who is to fire the human soul with new hope and new daring. What else is to survive the age? That which the age has little thought of, but which is living in us all; I mean the soul, the immortal spirit. Of this all ages are the unfoldings, and it is greater than all. We must not feel, in the contemplation of the vast movements in our own and former times, as if we ourselves were nothing. I repeat it, we are greater than all. We are to survive our age, to comprehend it, and to pronounce its sentence.

"The Present Age." W. E. CHANNING.

6. Or stay at home, and take up one of those daily prints, which are so true a picture of the world; look down the columns of advertisements, and you will see the catalog of pursuits, projects, aims, anxieties, amusements, indulgences, which occupy the mind of man. He plays many parts: here he has goods to sell, there he wants employment; there again he seeks to borrow money, here he offers you houses, great seats or small tenements; he has food for the million, and luxuries for the wealthy, and sovereign medicines for the credulous, and books, new and cheap, for the inquisitive. Pass on to the news of the day, and you will learn what great men are doing at home and abroad: you will read of wars and rumors of wars; of debates in the legislature; of rising men, and old statesmen going off the scene; of political contests in this city or that county; of the collision of rival interests. You will read of the money market, and the provision market, and the market for metals; of the state of trade, the call for manufactures, news of ships arrived in port, of accidents at sea, of exports and imports, of gains and losses, of frauds and their detection. Go forward, and you arrive at discoveries in art and science, discoveries (so-called) in religion, the court and royalty, the entertainments of the great, places of

amusement, strange trials, offenses, accidents, escapes, exploits, experiments, contests, ventures. Oh, this curious, restless, clamorous, panting being which we call life! And is there to be no end to all this? Is there no object in it? It never has an end, it is forsooth its own object!

"God's Will the End of Life." JOHN HENRY NEWMAN.

CHAPTER VI

HOW TO DEVELOP THE IMAGINATION

A public speaker should cultivate the habit of making vivid mental pictures of what he sees and reads. This is one of the best remedies for self-consciousness. It also develops the power of concentration, gives freshness and reality to a speaker's utterance, and greatly increases the interest of his audience. The attentive hearer keenly follows the operation of a speaker's mind, is inclined to see what he sees, and is quick to detect mental wandering away from the thought. The more vividly and accurately the speaker mentally pictures what he is saying, the more clearly and satisfactorily will his audience be imprest by his message.

Imagination, like any other faculty, can be cultivated by judicious practise. There is so much material on every hand that the public speaker will do well to choose subjects for practise such as he is likely to use. He should have special regard for mental pictures that embody harmony, beauty, and symmetry. He should endeavor to work out such pictures into the smallest detail, making them as complete as possible. This work of the imagination should become more and more selective, and less a thing of chance. Sir Benjamin Brodie says: "Physical investigation, more than anything besides, helps to teach us the actual value and right use of the imagination—of that wondrous faculty which, when left to ramble uncontrolled, leads us astray into a wilderness of perplexities and errors, a land of mists and shadows; but which, properly controlled by experience and reflection, becomes the noblest attribute of man, the source of poetic genius, the instrument of discovery in science, without the aid of which Newton would never have invented fluxions, nor Davy have decomposed the earths and alkalis, nor would Columbus have found another continent."

Imagination may be defined as a mental image of something not present to the senses. When properly developed it enables a public speaker to summon before his mental vision experiences and observations of the past, and to live them over again. This imparts spontaneity and intensity to his words, and wins both the attention and the confidence of his audience. A well-developed imagination broadens the view of the speaker, quickens his sensibilities, and gives him a larger sympathy for mankind. If, as Carlyle says, "Man carries under his hat a private theater, wherein a greater drama is acted than is ever performed on the mimic stage, beginning and ending in eternity," how careful every one should be, and especially the public speaker, in choosing the scenes, characters, and plays to be presented there!

Begin your practise with a simple picture like the following:

1. The past rises before me like a dream. Again we are in the great struggle for national life. We hear the sounds of preparation—the music of boisterous drums—the silver voices of heroic bugles. We see thousands of assemblages, and hear the appeals of orators. We see the pale cheeks of women, and the flushed faces of men; and in those assemblages we see all the dead whose dust we have covered with flowers. We lose sight of them no more. We are with them when they enlist in the great army of freedom. We see them part with those they

love. Some are walking for the last time in quiet, woody places, with the maidens they adore. We hear the whisperings and the sweet vows of eternal love as they lingeringly part forever. Others are bending over cradles, kissing babes that are asleep. Some are receiving the blessings of old men. Some are parting with mothers who hold them and press them to their hearts again and again, and say nothing. Kisses and tears, tears and kisses; divine mingling of agony and love! And some are talking with wives, and endeavoring with brave words, spoken in the old tones, to drive from their hearts the awful fear. We see them part. We see the wife standing in the door with the babe in her arms—standing in the sunlight sobbing. At the turn of the road a hand waves—she answers by holding high in her loving arms the child. He is gone, and forever.

R. G. INGERSOLL.

"A Vision of War and a Vision of the Future."

Now close your eyes and recall the mental picture of what you saw and the order in which you saw it. Tell it aloud in your own words. What sounds did you hear? Describe the concourse of people you saw, the mother, the wife. Did you see the husband departing? Did you experience any feeling in reading this scene? Describe it.

Reread the extract and endeavor to get a more detailed mental impression of the picture. Again close your eyes and describe as minutely as you can just what you saw.

Repeat the exercise with the following pictures:

2. Science and revelation concur in teaching that this ball of earth, which man inhabits, is not the only world; that millions of globes like ours roll in the immensity of space. The sun, the moon, "those seven nightly wandering fires," those twinkling stars, are worlds. There, doubtless, dwell other moral and intellectual natures, passing what man calls time, in one untired pursuit of truth and duty; still seeking, still exploring, never satisfying, never satiating, the ethereal, moral, intellectual thirst;

whose delightful task it is, as it should be ours, to learn the will of the Eternal Father—to seek the good, which to that end, for them and to us who seek, hides; and finding, to admire, adore, and praise, "Him first! Him last, Him midst and without end."

Imagine one of these celestial spirits, bent on this great purpose, descending upon our globe, and led by chance to a European plain, at the point of some great battle; on which, to human eye, reckless and blind to overruling heaven, the fate of states and empires is suspended.

On a sudden, the field of combat opens on his astonished vision. It is a field which men call "glorious." A hundred thousand warriors stand in opposed ranks. Light gleams on their burnished steel. Their plumes and banners wave. Hill echoes to hill the noise of moving rank and squadron—the neigh and tramp of steeds—the trumpet, drum, and bugle call. There is a momentary pause—a silence like that which precedes the fall of a thunderbolt—like that awful stillness, which is precursor to the desolating rage of the whirlwind. In an instant, flash succeeding flash, pours columns of smoke along the plain. The iron tempest sweeps, heaping man, horse, and car in undistinguished ruin. In shouts of rushing hosts—in shock of breasting steeds—in peals of musketry—in artillery's roar—in sabers' clash—in thick and gathering clouds of smoke and dust, all human eye and ear and sense are lost. Man sees naught but the sign of onset. Man hears naught but the cry of "onward."

Not so the celestial stranger. His spiritual eye, unobscured by artificial night, his spiritual ear, unaffected by mechanic noise, witness the real scene, naked in all its cruel horrors.

He sees lopped and bleeding limbs scattered; gashed, dismembered trunks, outspread, gore-clothed, lifeless; brains bursting from crushed skulls, blood gushing from sabered necks, severed heads, whose mouths mutter rage amidst the palsying of the last agony.

He hears the mingled cry of anguish and despair issuing from a thousand bosoms in which a thousand bayonets turn; the convulsive scream of anguish from heaps of mangled, half-expiring victims, over whom the heavy artillery wheels lumber and crush into one mass, bone and muscle and sinew, while the fetlock of the warhorse drips with blood starting from the last palpitation of the burst heart on which the hoof pivots.

"This is not earth"—would not such a celestial stranger exclaim?—"this is not earth, this is hell! This is not man, but demon, tormenting demon."

Thus exclaiming, would he not speed away to the skies—his immortal nature unable to endure the folly, the crime, and the madness of man?

"The Field of Battle." ROBERT HALL.

3. And I saw a new heaven and a new earth: for the first heaven and the first earth are passed away; and the sea is no more. And I saw the holy city, new Jerusalem, coming down out of heaven from God, made ready as a bride adorned for her husband. And I heard a great voice out of the throne saying, Behold, the tabernacle of God is with men, and He shall dwell with them, and they shall be His peoples, and God Himself shall be with them, and be their God: and He shall wipe away every tear from their eyes; and death shall be no more; neither shall there be mourning, nor crying, nor pain, any more: the first things are passed away. And He that sitteth on the throne said, Behold, I make all things new. And He saith, Write: for these words are faithful and true. And He said unto me, They are come to pass. I am the Alpha and the Omega, the beginning and the end. I will give unto him that is athirst of the fountain of the water of life freely. He that overcometh shall inherit these things; and I will be his God, and he shall be My son. But for the fearful, and unbelieving, and abominable, and murderers, and fornicators, and sorcerers, and idolaters, and all liars, their part shall be in the lake that burneth with fire and brimstone; which is the second death.

And there came one of the seven angels who had the seven bowls, who were laden with the seven last plagues; and he spake with me, saying, Come hither, I will show thee the bride, the wife of the Lamb. And he carried me away in the spirit to a mountain great and high, and showed me the holy city Jerusalem, coming down out of heaven from God, having the glory of God; her light was like unto a stone most precious, as it were a jasper stone, clear as crystal: having a wall great and high; having twelve gates, and at the gates twelve angels; and names written thereon, which are the names of the twelve tribes of the children of Israel: on the east were three gates; and on the north three gates; and on the south three gates; and on the west three gates. And the wall of the city had twelve foundations, and on them twelve names of the twelve apostles of the Lamb. And he that spake with me had for a measure a golden reed to measure the city, and the gates thereof, and the wall thereof. And the city lieth foursquare, and the length thereof is as great as the breadth: and he measured the city with the reed, twelve thousand furlongs: the length and the breadth and the height thereof are equal. And he measured the wall thereof, a hundred and forty and four cubits, according to the measure of a man, that is, of an angel. And the building of the wall thereof was jasper: and the city was pure gold, like unto pure glass.

The foundations of the wall of the city were adorned with all manner of precious stones. The first foundation was jasper; the second, sapphire; the third, chalcedony; the fourth, emerald; the fifth, sardonyx; the sixth, sardius; the seventh, chrysolite; the eighth, beryl; the ninth, topaz; the tenth, chrysoprase; the eleventh, jacinth; the twelfth, amethyst. And the twelve gates were twelve pearls; each one of the several gates was of one pearl: and the street of the city was pure gold, as it were transparent glass. And I saw no temple therein; for the Lord God the Almighty and the Lamb are the temple thereof. And the city hath no need of the sun, neither of the moon, to shine upon it: for the glory of God did lighten it, and the lamp thereof is the Lamb. And the nations shall walk amidst the light thereof: and the kings of the earth bring their glory into it. And the gates thereof shall in nowise be shut by day (for there shall be no night there): and they shall bring the glory and the honor of the nations into it: and there shall in nowise enter into it anything unclean, or he that maketh an abomination and a lie: but only they that are written in the Lamb's book of life.

And he showed me a river of water of life, bright as crystal, proceeding out of the throne of God and of the Lamb, in the midst of the street thereof. And on this side of the river and on that was the tree of life, bearing twelve manner of fruits, yielding its fruit every month: and the leaves of the tree were for the healing of the nations. And there shall be no curse any more: and the throne of God and of the Lamb shall be therein: and His servants shall serve Him; and they shall see His face; and His name shall be on their foreheads. And there shall be night no more; and they need no light of lamp, neither light of sun; for the Lord God shall give them light: and they shall reign forever and ever.

Rev. xxi., xxii., 1-5. THE BIBLE [Am. Rev. Ver.]

4. At the fair grounds at San José, California, recently, about two thousand spectators were gathered about a balloon in which an ascension was to be made by Professor Hoff. While the balloon was being filled the professor called for several assistants, and a man by the name of Macado was one of those who stept forward. When all was ready the aeronaut called out, "Let go!" and the balloon quickly rose. As Macado endeavored to step away he became entangled in the ropes and was lifted from the ground. He realized the peril of his situation, and as the balloon arose he took a firm hold upon the rope. The excited crowd below could hear his cries to the man in the balloon, "Save me! Save me!" The aeronaut, finding he could not draw the man up to him, decided that a descent must be made. He let the gas out of the balloon and slowly it started to descend. The young man held on to the rope with dogged determination while he was carried half a mile before he reached the ground. Many people find themselves in the course of their lives in situations where they can do nothing to help themselves, and all they can do is to stand still and trust God. The grit to hold on is a great thing. This is what Paul meant when he wrote the Ephesians about putting on the whole armor of God and then adds the words, "Having done all, ... stand!"

"Pluck to Hold On." LOUIS ALBERT BANKS.

5. I visited the Garden of Gethsemane for the second time at sundown on Sunday evening. I left at a little distance my dragoman and two others, dwellers in Jerusalem, who chanced to be with us that day, that I might be alone with my thoughts, that I might read again the Scripture narrative of our Lord's agony in the garden, and that I might make the scene of His sufferings real and personal. Some have said that the present garden is not sufficiently lonely and secluded to harmonize with the descriptions given by the evangelists, and that possibly the agony of our Lord occurred in the larger garden, which existed, as it is supposed, in that day, and not in the portion of the garden now shown. But it seemed to me to be a place of peculiar loneliness and seclusion. The Mount of Olives overhangs it on the one side and the embattled walls of Jerusalem on the other. It is a fitting spot for one desiring to be alone with God at evening's holy hour, or under the shadows cast by the olive-trees under the light of the Passover moon. An American woman has furnished a sufficient amount of money to maintain a tank of water in the garden. This provision enables the guardians to keep the flowers constantly in bloom and the grass perpetually fresh and green. It was an admirable gift; it symbolizes the place which the garden and its sacred scenes must ever have in the minds of Christians throughout the whole world. Thoughts of wonderful tenderness came into my mind on that Sunday evening, amid the fading light of day and the gathering shadows of evening. Perhaps near the spot where I stood did Christ endure the bloody sweat of agony untold; perhaps it was here that the angel came and ministered unto Him when He was exhausted with "strong crying and tears."

> Under the olive boughs,
> Falling like ruby beads,
> The blood drops from His brows;
> He bleeds! My Savior bleeds!

Josephus tells us that the suburbs of Jerusalem abound with gardens and pleasure-grounds. The word "garden," it ought to be borne in mind, was then used with a somewhat different meaning from that which we now give to the name. The Garden of Gethsemane is now more truly a garden, in our use of the word, than it was in Christ's day. Then the word garden meant substantially what we mean by the word orchard. This garden, however, will ever be associated with but a single event, the agony of the Son of God on the evening preceding His death on the cross. Here was fulfilled the prophecy of Isaiah regarding the Christ: "I have trodden the wine-press alone." The word Gethsemane means an olive-press. The garden is but a few paces to the south from the so-called tomb of the Virgin. The entrance is from the Mount of Olives toward the southeast. The olive-oil yielded by the trees in the garden is still sold for a high price, and many rosaries are still made from the olive stones.

This garden was to me holy ground; here, if ever, I felt like taking my shoes from off my feet. Yonder, on Calvary, Christ's body was crucified; but here in Gethsemane was the crucifixion of His soul. Yonder He gave up his life; here He yielded His soul in sweet obedience to the Father's will. There the letter of the law was satisfied; here the weight of the law, in its spiritual import, fell on the soul of Christ. In this garden His "own familiar friend betrayed Him." Here the Captain of our salvation experienced the truth that the soul of His sufferings was the suffering of His soul. And here in the quiet of my own heart, at evening's holy hour, I strove to dedicate myself afresh in unswerving loyalty to my crucified Lord, and in unceasing love for the souls of men for whom He died.

ROBERT STUART MACARTHUR.

"Sunday Night Lectures on The Land and the Book."

CHAPTER VII

DRAMATIC POWER IN SPEAKING

The dramatic element in speaking is by no means the exclusive property of the stage. It has its appropriate and legitimate place in platform and pulpit delivery. The extent to which it should be employed depends upon the subject and the occasion. When properly used it is a source of great power and effectiveness.

This is not a recommendation, however, of paroxysms of feeling, wild gesticulation, tearing and combing of the hair with the fingers, violent pacing up and down the platform, and other manifestations of old-style oratory, happily now obsolete, but rather to suggest a power which, when properly used, will give life, variety, intensity, and color to the spoken message.

In reciting dramatic scenes the voice should be varied so as to faithfully impersonate each character distinctly and naturally. This affords the best kind of practise for the speaking voice.

The study of dramatic literature gives life and vividness to a speaker's style, develops his imagination, and broadens his conception of humanity. It teaches him to speak from the heart to the heart. It educates his emotions for instant use.

The effect of strong dramatic utterance is illustrated in the story of Whitefield addressing his audience, of whom some were sailors, when he said:

"Well, my boys, we have a clear sky, and are making fine headway over a smooth sea before a light breeze, and we shall soon lose sight of land. But what means this sudden lowering of the heavens, and that dark cloud arising from beneath the western horizon? Hark! Don't you hear distant thunder? Don't you see those flashes of lightning? This is a storm gathering! Every man to his duty! How the waves rise and dash against the ship! The air is dark! —the tempest rages!—our masts are gone—the ship is on her beam-ends! What next?" This appeal instantly brought the sailors to their feet, with a shout: "The long-boat!—take to the long-boat."

This study will also give vigor and action to the speaker. The orator is not a statue, but "an animal galvanic battery on two legs," as Nathan Sheppard has it. The body, the hand, the face, the eye, the mouth, all should respond to the speaker's inner thought and feeling. It should be said of him as of Wendell Phillips:

> Pure and eloquent blood
> Spoke in his cheek, and so distinctly wrought
> That one might almost say his body thought.

The public speaker should be a man of great earnestness and of strong healthy passions. These qualities can best be cultivated by the daily practising aloud of dramatic scenes. Care must be taken not to exaggerate objective effects. Gesture, facial expression, and bodily action must be subordinated to the thought.

It is said of the elder Salvini that in studying the part of *Othello,* he instructed his attendants to tie him securely to a chair, in order that he might develop his subjective expression as much as possible. When at last he appeared on the stage the critics marveled at his impersonation of a part that had almost invariably been overdone in style and action.

"All true action in the pulpit," says Doctor Kennard, "must first proceed from the soul. In other words, it has a psychic base and spring. If the man's soul is in a healthy and vigorous state, inspired by his theme, his thought will swim to the surface and reflect itself in his physical features and organs. By a subtle psychological law the whole nervous and muscular system responds to the sympathetic impulses of the emotions and will; feeling and purpose mysteriously and spontaneously press at every gate of the eyes, the lips, the cheeks, the hands, the feet, for *expression*. The preacher's heart, swelling with inspired energetic conviction and emotion, lifts itself up like a great tidal wave, overflows its banks and pours itself forth in expressions of the features, glances of the eyes, quivering of the mouth, tones of the voice and movements of the limbs, so that the physical structure becomes simply the complex and delicate organ of expression for the brain, and heart, and will."[1]

The emotions of the speaker must first be awakened, then judiciously trained to respond instantly to his demands. They must first be intelligently controlled that they may be safely and unconsciously liberated at the moment of use in public speaking. Shakespearian numbers are particularly recommended because of their scope and fidelity.

The following scenes will give material for practise of this kind. Further selections will be found in the latter part of the book.

---

[1] *Psychic Power in Preaching*, J. Spencer Kennard, D.D

KING HENRY VIII

Act III, Scene 2—Wolsey After His Fall

Scene: *An antechamber in Henry VIII.'s palace.*

Wol. So, farewell to the little good you bear me.
Farewell! a long farewell, to all my greatness!
This is the state of man; to-day he puts forth
The tender leaves of hope; to-morrow blossoms,
And bears his blushing honors thick upon him;
The third day comes a frost, a killing frost,
And, when he thinks, good easy man, full surely
His greatness is a-ripening, nips his root,
And then he falls, as I do. I have ventur'd,
Like little wanton boys that swim on bladders,
This many summers in a sea of glory,
But far beyond my depth; my high-blown pride
At length broke under me, and now has left me
Weary and old with service, to the mercy
Of a rude stream, that must forever hide me.
Vain pomp and glory of this world, I hate ye;
I feel my heart new-opened. Oh, how wretched
Is that poor man that hangs on princes' favors!
There is, betwixt that smile we would aspire to,
That sweet aspect of princes, and their ruin,
More pangs and fears than wars or women have;
And when he falls, he falls like Lucifer,
Never to hope again.

Enter Cromwell

Why, how now, Cromwell?
Crom. I have no power to speak, sir.
Wol. What! amazed
At my misfortunes? can thy spirit wonder
A great man should decline? Nay, an you weep,
I am fall'n indeed.

Crom. How does your grace?
Wol. Why, well;
Never so truly happy, my good Cromwell.
I know myself now; and I feel within me
A peace above all earthly dignities,
A still and quiet conscience. The king has cur'd me,
I humbly thank his grace; and from these shoulders,
These ruin'd pillars, out of pity, taken
A load would sink a navy—too much honor;
Oh, 'tis a burden, Cromwell, 'tis a burden
Too heavy for a man that hopes for heaven!
Crom. I am glad your grace has made that right use of it.
Wol. I hope I have; I am able now, methinks,
(Out of a fortitude of soul I feel,)
To endure more miseries and greater far
Than my weak-hearted enemies dare offer.
What news abroad?
Crom. The heaviest and the worst
Is your displeasure with the king.
Wol. God bless him!
Crom. The next is, that Sir Thomas More is chosen
Lord Chancellor in your place.
Wol. That's somewhat sudden;
But he's a learned man. May he continue
Long in his highness' favor, and do justice
For truth's sake and his conscience; that his bones,
When he has run his course and sleeps in blessings,
May have a tomb of orphans' tears wept on 'em!
What more?
Crom. That Cranmer is return'd with welcome,
Install'd Lord Archbishop of Canterbury.
Wol. That's news indeed.
Crom. Last, that the Lady Anne,
Whom the king hath in secrecy long married,
This day was view'd in open as his queen,
Going to chapel; and the voice is now
Only about her coronation.

Wol. There was the weight that pull'd me down.
O Cromwell!
The king has gone beyond me; all my glories
In that one woman I have lost forever.
No sun shall ever usher forth mine honors,
Or gild again the noble troops that waited
Upon my smiles. Go, get thee from me, Cromwell;
I am a poor fall'n man, unworthy now
To by thy lord and master. Seek the king;
That sun, I pray, may never set! I have told him
What and how true thou art; he will advance thee;
Some little memory of me will stir him—
I know his noble nature—not to let
Thy hopeful service perish too; good Cromwell,
Neglect him not; make use now, and provide
For thine own future safety.
Crom. O my lord,
Must I, then, leave you? must I needs forego
So good, so noble, and so true a master?
Bear witness, all that have not hearts of iron,
With what a sorrow Cromwell leaves his lord.
The king shall have my service; but my prayers
Forever and forever shall be yours.
Wol. Cromwell, I did not think to shed a tear
In all my miseries; but thou hast forc'd me,
Out of thy honest truth, to play the woman.
Let's dry our eyes; and thus far hear me, Cromwell;
And, when I am forgotten, as I shall be,
And sleep in dull cold marble, where no mention
Of me more must be heard of, say, I taught thee,
Say, Wolsey, that once trod the ways of glory,
And sounded all the depths and shoals of honor,
Found thee a way, out of his wreck, to rise in;
A sure and safe one, tho thy master miss'd it.
Mark but my fall, and that which ruin'd me.
Cromwell, I charge thee, fling away ambition!
By that sin fell the angels; how can man, then,
The image of his Maker, hope to win by it?

Love thyself last; cherish those hearts that hate thee;
Corruption wins not more than honesty.
Still in thy right hand carry gentle peace,
To silence envious tongues. Be just, and fear not;
Let all the ends thou aim'st at be thy country's,
Thy God's and truth's; then, if thou fall'st, O Cromwell,
Thou fall'st a blessed martyr! Serve the king;
And,—prithee lead me in;
There take an inventory of all I have,
To the last penny; 'tis the king's; my robe,
And my integrity to Heaven, are all
I dare not call mine own. O Cromwell, Cromwell!
Had I but serv'd my God with half the zeal
I served my king, He would not in mine age
Have left me naked to mine enemies!

Crom. Good sir, have patience.

Wol. So I have. Farewell.
The hopes of court! my hopes in heaven do dwell. [*Exeunt.*

HENRY V

Part of Act IV

Enter Chorus

Chorus. Now entertain conjecture of a time,
When creeping murmur, and the poring dark,
Fills the wide vessel of the universe.
From camp to camp, through the foul womb of night,
The hum of either army stilly sounds,
That the fix'd sentinels almost receive
The secret whispers of each other's watch:
Fire answers fire; and through their paly flames
Each battle sees the other's umber'd face:
Steed threatens steed, in high and boastful neighs
Piercing the night's dull ear; and from the tents,
The armorers, accomplishing the knights,

With busy hammers closing rivets up,
Give dreadful note of preparation.
The country cocks do crow, the clocks do toll,
And the third hour of drowsy morning name.
Proud of their numbers, and secure in soul,
The confident and overlusty French
Do the low-rated English play at dice:
And chide the cripple tardy-gaited night,
Who, like a foul and ugly witch, doth limp
So tediously away. The poor condemned English,
Like sacrifices, by their watchful fires
Sit patiently, and inly ruminate
The morning's danger; and their gesture sad,
Investing lank-lean cheeks, and war-worn coats,
Presenteth them unto the gazing moon
So many horrid ghosts. Oh, now, who will behold
The royal captain of this ruin'd band,
Walking from watch to watch, from tent to tent,
Let him cry—Praise and glory on his head!
For forth he goes, and visits all his host;
Bids them good-morrow with a modest smile;
And calls them brothers, friends, and countrymen.
Upon his royal face there is no note,
How dread an army hath enrounded him;
Nor doth he dedicate one jot of color
Unto the weary and all-watched night:
But freshly looks, and overbears attaint
With cheerful semblance, and sweet majesty;
That every wretch, pining and pale before,
Beholding him, plucks comfort from his looks;
A largess universal, like the sun,
His liberal eye doth give to every one,
Thawing cold fear that, mean and gentle all,
Behold, as may unworthiness define,
A little touch of Harry in the night.
And so our scene must to the battle fly;
Where, (O for pity!) we shall much disgrace—
With four or five most vile and ragged foils,

Right ill-disposed in brawl ridiculous—
The name of Agincourt: Yet, sit and see;
Minding true things by what their mockeries be.

[*Exit.*

SCENE: *The English camp. Characters: The Dukes of* GLOSTER *and* BEDFORD, *the King's brothers, the Earls of* WESTMORELAND, SALISBURY, EXETER, *and others.*

West. Of fighting men they have full threescore thousand.
Exe. There's five to one; besides, they all are fresh.
Sal. God's arm strike with us! 'tis a fearful odds.
God be wi' you, princes all; I'll to my charge:
If we no more meet, till we meet in heaven,
Then, joyfully—my noble lord of Bedford—
My dear lord Gloster,—and my good lord Exeter,—
And my kind kinsman,—warriors all, adieu!
Bed. Farewell, good Salisbury; and good luck go with thee.
[*Exit* SALISBURY.

Enter KING HENRY

West. O that we now had here
But one ten thousand of those men in England,
That do no work to-day!
K. Hen. What's he that wishes so?
My cousin Westmoreland?—No, my fair cousin:
If we are mark'd to die, we are enough
To do our country loss; and if to live,
The fewer men, the greater share of honor.
God's will! I pray thee, wish not one man more.
By Jove, I am not covetous for gold;
Nor care I who doth feed upon my cost;
It yearns me not if men my garments wear;
Such outward things dwell not in my desires:
But if it be a sin to covet honor,
I am the most offending soul alive.

No, 'faith, my coz, wish not a man from England:
God's peace! I would not lose so great an honor,
As one man more, methinks, would share from me,
For the best hope I have. O, do not wish one more:
Rather proclaim it, Westmoreland, through my host,
That he which hath no stomach to his fight,
Let him depart, his passport shall be made,
And crowns for convoy put into his purse:
We would not die in that man's company,
That fears his fellowship to die with us.
This day is call'd the feast of Crispian:
He that outlives this day, and comes safe home,
Will stand a tiptoe when this day is nam'd,
And rouse him at the name of Crispian.
He that shall live this day, and see old age,
Will yearly on the vigil feast his neighbors,
And say to-morrow is Saint Crispian:
Then will he strip his sleeve, and show his scars,
And say, these wounds I had on Crispian's day.
Old men forget; yet all shall be forgot,
But he'll remember, with advantages,
What feats he did that day! Then shall our names,
Familiar in his mouth as household words—
Harry the king, Bedford and Exeter,
Warwick and Talbot, Salisbury and Gloster,—
Be in their flowing cups freshly remember'd:
This story shall the good man teach his son;
And Crispin Crispian shall ne'er go by,
From this day to the ending of the world,
But we in it shall be remembered;
We few, we happy few, we band of brothers:
For he, to-day, that sheds his blood with me,
Shall be my brother; be he ne'er so vile,
This day shall gentle his condition:
And gentlemen in England, now a-bed,
Shall think themselves accurst, they were not here;
And hold their manhoods cheap, whiles any speaks,
That fought with us upon Saint Crispian's day.

Enter SALISBURY

Sal. My sovereign lord, bestow yourself with speed,
The French are bravely in their battles set,
And will with all expedience charge on us.
K. Hen. All things are ready, if our minds be so.
West. Perish the man whose mind is backward now!
K. Hen. Thou dost not wish more help from England, cousin?
West. God's will, my liege, would you and I alone,
Without more help, could fight this royal battle!
K. Hen. Why, now thou hast unwish'd five thousand men;
Which likes me better, than to wish us one.—
You know your places: God be with you all!

Tucket. Enter MONTJOY

Mont. Once more I come to know of thee, King Harry,
If for thy ransom thou wilt now compound,
Before thy most assured overthrow?
For, certainly, thou art so near the gulf,
Thou needs must be englutted. Besides, in mercy,
The Constable desires thee thou wilt mind
Thy followers of repentance; that their souls
May make a peaceful and a sweet retire
From off these fields, where (wretches) their poor bodies
Must lie and fester.
K. Hen. Who hath sent thee now?
Mont. The Constable of France.
K. Hen. I pray thee, bear my former answer back;
Bid them achieve me, and then sell my bones.
Good God! why should they mock poor fellows thus?
The man that once did sell the lion's skin
While the beast lived, was kill'd with hunting him.
A many of our bodies shall, no doubt,
Find natives' graves: upon the which, I trust,
Shall witness live in brass of this day's work;
And those that leave their valiant bones in France,
Dying like men, tho buried in your dunghills,
They shall be famed; for there the sun shall greet them,

And draw their honors reeking up to heaven;
Let me speak proudly,—Tell the Constable,
We are but warriors for the working day:
Our gayness and our gilt are all besmirch'd
With rainy marching in the painful field;
There's not a piece of feather in our host,
(Good argument, I hope, we will not fly,)
And time hath worn us into slovenry:
But, by the mass, our hearts are in the trim:
And my poor soldiers tell me, yet ere night
They'll be in fresher robes: or they will pluck
The gay new coats o'er the French soldiers' heads,
And turn them out of service. If they do this,
(As, if God please, they shall,) my ransom then
Will soon be levied. Herald, save thou thy labor,
Come thou no more for ransom, gentle herald;
They shall have none, I swear, but these my joints:
Which if they have as I will leave 'em them,
Shall yield them little, tell the Constable.
Mont. I shall, King Harry. And so fare thee well:
Thou never shalt hear herald any more. [*Exit.*
K. Hen. I fear, thou'lt once more come again for ransom.

Enter the DUKE OF YORK

York. My Lord, most humbly on my knees I beg
The leading of the vaward.
K. Hen. Take it, brave York.—Now, soldiers, march away;—
And how thou pleasest, God, dispose the day!
[*Exeunt.*

SCENE: *The field of battle. Characters: Captain* GOWER, *an English captain, and Captain* FLUELLEN, *a Welsh captain.*

Flu. Kill the poys and the luggage! 'tis expressly against the law of arms: 'tis as arrant a piece of knavery, mark you now, as can be offert in the 'orld: In your conscience now, is it not?

Gow. 'Tis certain there's not a boy left alive; and the

cowardly rascals that ran from the battle have done this slaughter: besides, they have burned and carried away all that was in the king's tent; wherefore the king, most worthily, hath caused every soldier to cut his prisoner's throat. O, 'tis a gallant king!

Flu. Ay, he was porn at Monmouth, Captain Gower: What call you the town's name, where Alexander the pig was porn?

Flu. Alexander the Great?

Flu. Why, I pray you, is not pig great? The pig, or the great, or the mighty, or the huge, or the magnanimous, are all one reckonings, save the phrase is a little variations.

Gow. I think Alexander the Great was born in Macedon; his father was called Philip of Macedon, as I take it.

Flu. I think it is in Macedon where Alexander is porn. I tell you, captain,—if you look in the maps of the 'orld, I warrant, you shall find in the comparisons between Macedon and Monmouth, that the situations, look you, is both alike. There is a river in Macedon; and there is also moreover a river at Monmouth; it is called Wye, at Monmouth; but it is out of my prains, what is the name of the other river; but 'tis all one, 'tis alike as my fingers is to my fingers, and there is salmons in both. If you mark Alexander's life well, Harry of Monmouth's life is come after it indifferent well; for there is figures in all things. Alexander, (God knows, and you know,) in his rages, and his furies, and his wraths, and his cholers, and his moods, and his displeasures, and his indignations, and also being a little intoxicates in his prains, did, in his ales and his angers, look you, kill his pest friend, Clytus.

Gow. Our king is not like him in that; he never killed any of his friends.

Flu. It is not well done, mark you now, to take the tales out of my mouth, ere it is made an end and finished. I speak but in the figures and comparisons of it: As Alexander is kill his friend Clytus, being in his ales and his cups; so also Harry Monmouth, being in his right wits and his goot judgments; is turn away the fat knight with the great pelly-doublet: he was full of jests, and gipes, and knaveries, and mocks; I am forget his name.

Gow. Sir John Falstaff.

Flu. That is he: I can tell you, there is goot men porn at Monmouth.

Gow. Here comes his majesty.

ALARUM. *Enter* KING HENRY *with a part of the English forces;* WARWICK, GLOSTER, EXETER, *and others.*

K. Hen. I was not angry since I came to France,
Until this instant.—Take a trumpet, herald;
Ride thou unto the horsemen on yon hill;
If they'll do neither, we will come to them;
Or void the field; they do offend our sight:
If they'll do neither, we will come to them;
And make them skirr away as swift as stones
Enforced from the old Assyrian slings:
Besides, we'll cut the throats of those we have;
And not a man of them, that we shall take,
Shall taste our mercy:—Go, and tell them so.

Enter MONTJOY

Exe. Here comes the herald of the French, my liege.

Glo. His eyes are humbler than they used to be.

K. Hen. How now? what means this, herald? know'st thou not,
That I have fined these bones of mine for ransom?
Com'st thou again for ransom?

Mont. No, great king:
I come to thee for charitable license,
That we may wander o'er this bloody field,
To book our dead, and then to bury them:
To sort our nobles from our common men;
For many of our princes (wo the while!)
Lie drown'd and soak'd in mercenary blood;
(So do our vulgar drench their peasant limbs
In blood of princes; and their wounded steeds
Fret, fetlock deep in gore, and, with wild rage,

Yerk out their armed heels at their dead masters,
Killing them twice.) O give us leave, great king,
To view the field in safety, and dispose
Of their dead bodies.
K. Hen. I tell thee truly, herald,
I know not, if the day be ours, or no;
For yet a many of your horsemen peer,
And gallop o'er the field.
Mont. The day is yours.
K. Hen. Praised be God, and not our strength for it!—
What is this castle call'd, that stands hard by?
Mont. They call it Agincourt.
K. Hen. Then we call this the field of Agincourt,
Fought on the day of Crispin Crispians.

SCENES FROM "THE RIVALS"

By Richard B. Sheridan

Act II, Scene I

Capt A. Now for a parental lecture. I hope he has heard nothing of the business that has brought me here. I wish the gout had held him fast in Devonshire, with all my soul!

Enter Sir Anthony

Capt. A. Sir, I am delighted to see you here, and looking so well!—your sudden arrival at Bath made me apprehensive for your health.

Sir A. Very apprehensive, I dare say, Jack.—What, you are recruiting here, hey?

Capt. A. Yes, sir, I am on duty.

Sir A. Well, Jack, I am glad to see you, tho I did not expect it; for I was going to write to you on a little matter of business.—Jack, I have been considering that I grow old and infirm, and shall probably not trouble you long.

Capt. A. Pardon me, sir, I never saw you look more strong and hearty, and I pray fervently that you may continue so.

Sir A. I hope your prayers may be heard, with all my heart. Well, then, Jack, I have been considering that as I am so strong and hearty, I may continue to plague you for a long time.—Now, Jack, I am sensible that the income of your commission, and what I have hitherto allowed you, is but a small pittance for a lad of your spirit.

Capt. A. Sir, you are very good.

Sir A. And it is my wish, while yet I live, to have my boy make some figure in the world.—I have resolved, therefore, to fix you at once in a noble independence.

Capt. A. Sir, your kindness overpowers me.—Yet, sir, I presume you would not wish me to quit the army?

Sir A. Oh! that shall be as your wife chooses.

Capt. A. My wife, sir!

Sir A. Ay, ay, settle that between you,—settle that between you.

Capt. A. A wife, sir, did you say?

Sir A. Ay, a wife: why, did not I mention her before?

Capt. A. Not a word of her, sir.

Sir A. Oddso! I mustn't forget her, tho.—Yes, Jack, the independence I was talking of is by a marriage,—the fortune is saddled with a wife,—but, I suppose, that makes no difference?

Capt. A. Sir! sir! you amaze me!

Sir A. Why, what's the matter with the fool? Just now you were all gratitude and duty.

Capt A. I was sir,—you talked to me of independence and a fortune, but not a word of a wife.

Sir A. Why, what difference does that make? Odds life, sir! if you have the estate, you must take it with the live stock on it, as it stands.

Capt. A. Pray, sir, who is the lady?

Sir A. What's that to you sir?—Come, give me your promise to love, and to marry her directly.

Capt. A. Sure, sir, this is not very reasonable, to summon my affections for a lady I know nothing of!

Sir A. I am sure, sir, 'tis more unreasonable in you to object to a lady you know nothing of.

Capt. A. You must excuse me, sir, if I tell you, once for all, that in this point I can not obey you.

Sir A. Harkye, Jack!—I have heard you for some time with patience—I have been cool—quite cool; but take care—you know I am compliance itself—when I am not thwarted; no one more easily led—when I have my own way;—but don't you put me in a frenzy.

Capt. A. Sir, I must repeat it—in this, I can not obey you.

Sir A. Now, hang me, if ever I call you Jack again while I live!

Capt. A. Nay, sir, but hear me.

Sir A. Sir, I won't hear a word—not a word! not one word! so give me your promise by a nod—and I'll tell you what, Jack—I mean, you dog—if you don't, by—

Capt. A. What, sir, promise to link myself to some mass of ugliness!

Sir A. Zounds! sirrah! the lady shall be as ugly as I choose: she shall have a hump on each shoulder; she shall be as crooked as the crescent; her one eye shall roll like the bull's in Cox's Museum; she shall have a skin like a mummy,—she shall be all this, sirrah!—yet I'll make you ogle her all day, and sit up all night, to write sonnets on her beauty.

Capt. A. This is reason and moderation indeed!

Sir A. None of your sneering, puppy! no grinning, jackanapes!

Capt. A. Indeed, sir, I never was in a worse humor for mirth in my life.

Sir A. 'Tis false, sir; I know you are laughing in your sleeve; I know you'll grin when I am gone, sirrah!

Capt. A. Sir, I hope I know my duty better.

Sir A. None of your passion, sir! none of your violence, if you please. It won't do with me, I promise you.

Capt. A. Indeed, sir, I never was cooler in my life.

Sir A. 'Tis a lie!—I know you are in a passion in your heart; I know you are, you hypocritical young dog; but it won't do.

Capt. A. Nay, sir, upon my word—

Sir A. So you will fly out! Can't you be cool, like me!—

What good can passion do?—passion is of no service, you impudent, insolent, overbearing reprobate!—There, you sneer again!—don't provoke me!—but you rely upon the mildness of my temper—you do, you dog! You play upon the meekness of my disposition! Yet take care—the patience of a saint may be overcome at last!—but mark!—I give you six hours and a half to consider of this: if you then agree, without any condition, to do everything on earth that I choose, why—confound you, I may in time forgive you. If not, zounds! don't enter the same hemisphere with me! don't dare to breathe the same air, or use the same light with me; but get an atmosphere and a sun of your own! I'll strip you of your commission; I'll lodge a five-and-three-pence in the hands of trustees, and you shall live on the interest. I'll disown you; I'll disinherit you, and, hang me! if ever I call you Jack again! [*Exit.*

Capt. A. Mild, gentle, considerate father! I kiss your hands.

II

Act III, Scene I

Capt. A. 'Tis just as Fag told me, indeed!—Whimsical enough, 'faith! My father wants to force me to marry the very girl I am planning to run away with! He must not know of my connection with her yet awhile. He has too summary a method of proceeding in these matters; however, I'll read my recantation instantly. My conversion is something sudden, indeed; but I can assure him it is very sincere.

Enter SIR ANTHONY

Sir A. No—I'll die sooner than forgive him! Die, did I say? I'll live these fifty years to plague him. At our last meeting his impudence had almost put me out of temper—an obstinate, passionate, self-willed boy! Who can he take after? This is my return for putting him, at twelve years old, into a marching regiment, and allowing him fifty pounds a year, besides his pay, ever since! But I have done with him—he's anybody's son for me—I never will see him more—never—never—never—never.

Capt. A. Now for a penitential face!

Sir A. Fellow, get out of my way!

Capt. A. Sir, you see a penitent before you.

Sir A. I see an impudent scoundrel before me.

Capt. A. A sincere penitent. I am come, sir, to acknowledge my error and to submit entirely to your will.

Sir A. What's that?

Capt. A. I have been revolving, and reflecting, and considering on your past goodness, and kindness, and condescension to me.

Sir A. Well, sir!

Capt. A. I have been likewise weighing and balancing what you were pleased to mention concerning duty, and obedience, and authority.

Sir A. Why, now, you talk sense, absolute sense; I never heard anything more sensible in my life. Confound you, you shall be Jack again!

Capt. A. I am happy in the appellation.

Sir A. Why, then, Jack, my dear Jack, I will now inform you who the lady really is. Nothing but your passion and violence, you silly fellow, prevented me telling you at first. Prepare, Jack, for wonder and rapture—prepare! What think you of Miss Lydia Languish?

Capt. A. Languish! What, the Languishes of Worcestershire?

Sir A. Worcestershire! No! Did you never meet Mrs. Malaprop and her niece, Miss Languish, who came into our country just before you were last ordered to your regiment?

Capt. A. Malaprop! Languish! I don't remember ever to have heard the name before. Yet stay: I think I do recollect something. Languish—Languish! She squints, don't she? A little red-haired girl?

Sir A. Squints! A red-haired girl! Zounds, no!

Capt A. Then I must have forgot: it can't be the same person.

Sir A. Jack, Jack! what think you of blooming, love-breathing seventeen?

Capt. A. As to that, sir, I am quite indifferent; if I can please you in the matter, 'tis all I desire.

Sir A. Nay, but Jack, such eyes! such eyes! so innocently wild! so bashfully irresolute! Not a glance but speaks and kindles some thought of love! Then, Jack, her cheeks! her cheeks, Jack! so deeply blushing at the insinuations of her tell-tale eyes! Then, Jack, her lips! Oh, Jack, lips, smiling at their own discretion! and, if not smiling, more sweetly pouting—more lovely in sullenness! Then, Jack, her neck! Oh, Jack! Jack!

Capt. A. And which is to be mine, sir, the niece or the aunt?

Sir A. Why, you unfeeling, insensible puppy, I despise you! When I was of your age, such a description would have made me fly like a rocket! The aunt, indeed! Odds life! when I ran away with your mother, I would not have touched anything old or ugly to gain an empire!

Capt. A. Not to please your father, sir?

Sir A. To please my father—zounds! not to please—Oh! my father? Oddso! yes, yes! if my father, indeed, had desired—that's quite another matter. Tho he wasn't the indulgent father that I am, Jack.

Capt. A. I dare say not, sir.

Sir A. But, Jack, you are not sorry to find your mistress is so beautiful?

Capt. A. Sir, I repeat it, if I please you in this affair, 'tis all I desire. Not that I think a woman the worse for being handsome; but, sir, if you please to recollect, you before hinted something about a hump or two, one eye, and a few more graces of that kind. Now, without being very nice, I own I should rather choose a wife of mine to have the usual number of limbs, and a limited quantity of back; and tho one eye may be very agreeable, yet, as the prejudice has always run in favor of two, I would not wish to affect a singularity in that article.

Sir A. What a phlegmatic sot it is! Why, sirrah, you are an anchorite! a vile, insensible stock! You a soldier! you're a walking block, fit only to dust the company's regimentals on! Odds life, I've a great mind to marry the girl myself!

Capt. A. I am entirely at your disposal, sir, if you should think of addressing Miss Languish yourself, I suppose you would have me marry the aunt; or if you should change your mind, and take the old lady, 'tis the same to me—I'll marry the niece.

Sir A. Upon my word, Jack, thou art either a very great hypocrite, or—but, come, I know your indifference on such a subject must be all a lie—I'm sure it must. Come, now, hang your demure face; come, confess, Jack, you have been lying, haven't you? You have been playing the hypocrite, hey? I'll never forgive you, if you haven't been lying and playing the hypocrite.

Capt. A. I am sorry, sir, that the respect and duty which I bear to you should be so mistaken.

Sir A. Respect and duty! But come along with me. I'll write a note to Mrs. Malaprop, and you shall visit the lady directly. Her eyes shall be the Promethean torch to you—come along, I'll never forgive you if you don't come back stark mad with rapture and impatience—if you don't, 'egad, I'll marry the girl myself. [*Exeunt.*

CHAPTER VIII

HOW TO TRAIN THE MEMORY

The extemporaneous style of delivery should be the ultimate aim of every public speaker. To this end the memory should be cultivated to the highest possible degree. Many persons despair because of their poor and unreliable memories, but they are unwilling to give the time and practise necessary to develop them. There is no royal road to this as to any other branch of study. The memory can be cultivated, however, by any one having the necessary perseverance and application.

Memory is largely a matter of association of ideas. If we cultivate the habit of being *interested,* we are at the same time strengthening the memory. Memory depends upon securing vivid first impressions. These come through concentration, and we concentrate when we are sufficiently interested.

There are numerous so-called "memory systems," but the objection usually offered to them is that the end does not justify the means. If the average student had sufficient time and patience to carry the exercises to completion, he would doubtless be greatly benefited, but in most cases he soon becomes disheartened and gives up his study before any substantial results are possible.

What constitutes a good memory? One might answer, the ability to recall accurately and instantly the greatest number of things at the moment of need. A well-trained memory, then, may be likened unto a series of pigeon-holes, in which knowledge may be found so systematized as to make it easily available.

If the memory be poor it will be helpful at first to inquire into the reason for this condition. Such questions may be asked as: Is it lack of proper practise? Is it due to ill health? Is it lack of observation or of interest? Is there a systematic plan of gathering and recording knowledge? Are the daily habits of thinking and reading well-ordered? Is there lack of thoroughness, accuracy, and deliberateness? These and similar questions should be answered frankly, and a determined effort made to correct such faults as are noted.

To strengthen the memory it is advisable to form the habit of making comparisons and contrasts. In reading a book one should take notes and at the first opportunity try to repeat from memory, to some other person, the general ideas of what has been read. It is helpful also to interrogate one's self as to what has been seen or read. A good exercise is to read a passage from some writer and endeavor to repeat the same ideas in different words and in as many ways as possible. Vivid picturing of the thought helps to impress it upon the mind, and frequent repetition of a passage or speech will gradually fix it in the memory.

Committing to heart each day a verse or prose extract will train the memory with surprizing rapidity. An exercise that has been used with good results is to enter a room, take a quick glance around, walk out, and write down what you remember of the things that you have seen. The same exercise can be applied to passing a shop-window.

The following selections are suggested for memorizing,

the student taking a passage for each day. He may indefinitely extend the list at his own taste and discretion.

1. Let every dawn of morning be to you as the beginning of life, and every setting sun be to you as its close. Then let every one of these short lives leave its sure record of some kindly thing done for others; some goodly strength or knowledge gained for yourself.

JOHN RUSKIN.

2. The day returns and brings us the petty round of irritating concerns and duties. Help us to play the man, help us to perform them with laughter and kind faces; let cheerfulness abound with industry. Give us to go blithely on our business all this day, bring us to our resting beds weary and content and undishonored, and grant us in the end the gift of sleep.

"Morning Prayer." ROBERT LOUIS STEVENSON.

3. Let no soft slumber close my eyes,
Ere I have recollected thrice
The train of actions through the day.
Where have my feet marked out their way?
What have I learnt where'er I've been,
From all I've heard, from all I've seen?
What know I more that's worth the knowing?
What have I done that's worth the doing?
What have I sought that I should shun?
What duties have I left undone,
Or into what new follies run?
These self-inquiries are the road
That leads to virtue and to God.

"Self-Inquiry." *From the Greek of* PYTHAGORAS.

4. A little thing, a sunny smile,
A loving word, at morn,
And all day long the sun shone bright,
The cares of life were made more light,
And sweetest hopes were born.

A little thing, a hasty word,
  A cruel frown, at morn,
And aching hearts went on their way
And toiled throughout a dreary day,
  Disheartened, sad and lorn.

"In the Morning." COL. ROBERT G. INGERSOLL.

5. Do not keep the alabaster boxes of your love and tenderness sealed up until your friends are dead. Fill their lives with sweetness. Speak approving, cheering words while their ears can hear them and while their hearts can be thrilled and made happier; the kind things you mean to say when they are gone, say before they go. The flowers you mean to send for their coffin, send to brighten and sweeten their homes before they leave them. If my friends have alabaster boxes laid away, full of fragrant perfumes of sympathy and affection, which they intend to break over my body, I would much rather that they would bring them out in my weary and troubled hours, and open them, that I may be refreshed and cheered while I need them. I would rather have a plain coffin, without a flower, a funeral without a eulogy, than a life without the sweetness of love and sympathy. Let us learn to anoint our friends beforehand for their burial. Post-mortem kindness does not cheer the burdened spirit. Flowers on the coffin cast no fragrance backward over the weary way.

COL. ROBERT G. INGERSOLL.

6. Now Love is the remedy, the great sweetener of the mind and body. It produces harmony, and harmony is equilibrium—health.

This must first be established in the mind through belief and trust in the Infinite Love, and Omnipresent Good, then the practise of love and self-forgetfulness toward others.

If we would attract love to ourselves, we must feel it for others, and make ourselves lovable; and that should be our whole concern, to love more and more, and think less and less of self; then we will grow sweet and wholesome, and fragrant as a flower. The blood will be pure and rich, and filled with vitality, and, in short, all things will become new, for the former things will have passed away.

"Spiritual Realizations." FLORENCE WILLARD DAY.

7. So live that when thy summons comes to join
The innumerable caravan that moves
To that mysterious realm, where each shall take
His chamber in the silent halls of death,
Thou go not, like the quarry slave at night,
Scourged to his dungeon, but, sustained and soothed
By an unfaltering trust, approach thy grave
Like one who wraps the drapery of his couch
About him, and lies down to pleasant dreams.

"Thanatopsis." WILLIAM CULLEN BRYANT.

8. Some men employ their health, an ugly trick,
In making known how oft they have been sick.
And give us in recitals of disease,
A doctor's trouble, but without the fees;
Relate how many weeks they kept their bed,
How an emetic or cathartic sped:
Nothing is slightly touched, much less forgot.
Nose, ears, and eyes seem present on the spot.
Now the distemper, spite of draft or pill,
Victorious seemed, and now the doctor's skill;
And now,—alas, for unforeseen mishaps!
They put on a damp nightcap and relapse:
They thought they must have died, they were so bad;
Their peevish hearers almost wish they had.

"Descanting on Illness." WILLIAM COWPER.

CHAPTER IX

POWER OF ILLUSTRATION

A story well-told, or an illustration that illustrates, gives an added power to public speaking. Illustrations not only stimulate the imagination of the hearer, but also move the heart and arouse special interest. Appropriateness, clearness, and fluency are essential to successful story-telling. Hesitation, lack of memory, and irrelevancy invariably invite disaster. It is not always necessary nor desirable that a story be memorized and repeated in exact words, but the thought and the order of the thought, as well as the particular points to be made, should be clearly fixed in the mind. It is good practise to rehearse a story several times, endeavoring to vary the phraseology.

Some one has likened illustrations unto windows that let the light in. Because of their concrete character they make a strong and direct appeal to the hearer, touching, as they usually do, his personal experience. For this reason illustrations should be chosen, whenever possible, upon subjects that are familiar to the audience. There must, however, be something to illustrate. Stories introduced merely for their own sake, or to fill up gaps, or to disguise poverty of thought, are undesirable and ineffective. Phillips Brooks goes further and says: "We confine too much the office of illustration if we give it only the duty of making truth clear to the understanding and do not also allow it the privilege of making truth glorious to the imagination."

Abstract philosophy and close argument, if long continued in speech, become wearisome to an audience. They demand some relief. A good illustration, skilfully introduced, rests the mind of the listener, lends variety and vivacity to the speaker's style, and drives home his message with increased effectiveness.

Henry Ward Beecher owed much of his power and success to his resourcefulness in this respect. He says:

"The effect of illustrations upon ideality is very great. They bring into play the imaginative faculty, which is only another name for ideality. Now all great truth is beautiful. It carries in it elements of taste and fitness. The 'beauty of holiness' we find spoken of in the Word of God, and this is a beauty that does not belong to anything material. God is transcendently a lover of beauty, and all the issues of the divine soul are, if we could see them as He sees them, beautiful, just as self-denial and love are beautiful, and as purity and truth and all good things are beautiful.

"It is not, therefore, in the interest of truth that a man should sift it down to the merest bare nuggets of statement that it is susceptible of; and this is not best for an audience. It is best that a truth should have argument to substantiate it, and analysis and close reasoning; yet when you come to give it to an audience you should clothe it with flesh, so that it shall be fit for their understandings. In no other way can you so stir up that side of the mind to grasp your statements and arguments easily, and prepare it to remember them. You can not help your audience in any other way so well as by keeping alive in them the sense of the imagination and making the truth palpable to them, because it is appealing to the taste, to the sense of the beautiful in imagery as well as to the sense of truth."[1]

[1] *Yale Lectures on Preaching*, Henry Ward Beecher.

A speaker's illustrations should be as new and as varied as possible. Objection is sometimes raised to compilations of stories for illustration, on the ground that they soon become hackneyed. But this need not be the case if the speaker recasts the story in his own words and gives it a new application. The sources for material of this character are numerous. In addition to the regular collections of stories, the daily newspapers, magazines and other periodicals offer an almost inexhaustible supply of suggestions. The Bible itself is a storehouse of illustration and parable. Personal observation, however, will give the public speaker his best and most valuable material for illustration. Such material will not only have the quality of originality, but will palpitate with life and freshness, coming directly out of every-day human experience. The speaker should cultivate the habit of closely observing and noting things he sees around him. He should accustom himself to the exercise of mentally describing such things to himself, and at the first opportunity he should tell them to another. In this way the habit will gradually become an unconscious one, and the speaker will seldom feel at a loss for illustrative material.

It is well to keep two special books, one in which to write every story to be preserved for future use, the other in which to paste printed clippings.

The following extracts are intended to be suggestive. Those that the speaker wishes to use should be committed to memory, and repeated aloud in varied language as already mentioned.

1. You remember that in Prussia there was a law which exempted the only son of a widow from going to war; but it is said that so closely were they driven at one time for recruits, that the

law was for a time rescinded, and the widow's only son was taken. Suppose such a thing happened here, and there should be a widow whose only son was demanded of her. See her come forward, saying, "Ay, take him; my country is dearer to me even than he is." She puts him forward, and says, "Go forth, my son, to die if it be necessary; I give thee up, I give thee willingly." You see the red, red eye of the widow; she hath wiped it dry, but she hath wept in secret; and if we steal behind the door when her son is gone, and see her pouring out whole floods of sorrow, we can tell how great must have been her love for her country which made her give up him—her all. Beloved, we never should know Christ's love in all its heights and depths if He had not died; nor could we tell the Father's deep affection if He had not given His Son to die.

LOUIS ALBERT BANKS.

"Spurgeon's Illustrative Anecdotes."

2. During a heavy storm off the coast of Spain, a dismasted merchantman was observed by a British frigate drifting before the gale. Every eye and glass were on her, and a canvas shelter on a deck almost level with the sea suggested the idea that there yet might be life on board. With all his faults, no man is more alive to humanity than the rough and hardy mariner; and so the order instantly sounds to put the ship about, and presently a boat puts off with instructions to bear down upon the wreck. Away after that drifting hulk go these gallant men through the swell of a roaring sea; they reach it; they shout; and now a strange object rolls out of that canvas screen against the lee shroud of a broken mast. Hauled into the boat, it proves to be the trunk of a man, bent head and knees together, so dried and shriveled as to be hardly felt within the ample clothes, and so light that a mere boy lifted it on board. It is laid on the deck; in horror and pity the crew gather round it; it shows signs of life; they draw nearer; it moves, and then mutters—mutters in a deep, sepulchral voice—*"There is another man."* Saved himself, the first use the saved one made of speech was to seek to save another. Oh! learn that blest lesson. Be daily practising it. And so long as in our homes, among our friends, in this

wreck of a world which is drifting down to ruin, there lives an unconverted one, there is *"another man,"* let us go to that man, and plead for Christ; go to Christ and plead for that man; the cry, "Lord save me, I perish, changed into one as welcome to a Savior's ear, 'Lord save them, they perish.' "

"The Messenger." THOMAS GUTHRIE.

3. I will show you three fools. One is yonder soldier, who has been wounded on the field of battle, grievously wounded, well nigh unto death; the surgeon is by his side, and the soldier asks him a question. Listen, and judge of his folly. What question does he ask? Does he raise his eyes with eager anxiety and inquire if the wound be mortal, if the practitioner's skill can suggest means of healing, or if the remedies are within reach and the medicine at hand? No, nothing of the sort; strange to tell, he asks, "Can you inform me with what sword I was wounded and by what Russian I have been thus grievously mauled? I want," he adds, "to learn every minute particular respecting the origin of my wound." The man is delirious or his head is affected. Surely such questions at such a time are proof enough that he is bereft of his senses.

There is another fool. The storm is raging, the ship is flying impetuous before the gale, the dark scud moves swiftly over head, the masts are creaking, the sails are rent to rags, and still the gathering tempest grows more fierce. Where is the captain? Is he busily engaged on the deck, is he manfully facing the danger, and skilfully suggesting means to avert it? No, sir, he has retired to his cabin, and there with studious thoughts and crazy fancies he is speculating on the place where this storm took its rise. "It is mysterious, this wind; no one ever yet," he says, "has been able to discover it." And so he, reckless of the vessel, the lives of the passengers, and his own life, is careful only to solve his curious questions. The man is mad, sir; take the rudder from his hand; he is clean gone mad! If he should ever run on shore, shut him up as a hopeless lunatic.

The third fool I shall doubtless find among yourselves. You are sick and wounded with sin, you are in the storm and hurricane of Almighty vengeance, and yet the question which you would ask of me this morning would be, "Sir, what is the origin of evil?" You are mad, sir, spiritually mad.

"Spurgeon's Illustrative Anecdotes." LOUIS ALBERT BANKS.

4. I remember once riding from Buffalo to the Niagara Falls. I said to a gentleman, "What river is that, sir?"

"That," he said, "is Niagara River."

"Well, it is a beautiful stream," said I; "bright and fair and glassy. How far off are the rapids?"

"Only a mile or two," was the reply.

"Is it possible that only a mile from us we shall find the water in the turbulence which it must show near the falls?"

"You will find it so, sir." And so I did find it; and the first sight of Niagara I shall never forget.

Now launch your bark on that Niagara River; it is bright, smooth, beautiful and glassy. There is a ripple at the bow; the silver wake you leave behind adds to your enjoyment. Down the stream you glide, oars, sails and helm in proper trim, and you set out on your pleasure excursion.

Suddenly some one cries out from the bank:

"Young men, ahoy!"

"What is it?"

"The rapids are below you."

"Ha! ha! we have heard of the rapids; but we are not such fools as to get there. If we go too fast, then we shall up with the helm and steer to the shore; we will set the mast in the socket, and hoist the sail, and speed to the land. Then on, boys; don't be alarmed, there is no danger."

"YOUNG MEN, AHOY THERE!"

"What is it?"

"THE RAPIDS ARE BELOW YOU."

"Ha! ha! we will laugh and quaff; all things delight us. What care we for the future! No man ever saw it. Sufficient for the day is the evil thereof. We will enjoy life while we may; we will catch pleasure as it flies. This is enjoyment; time enough to steer out of danger when we are sailing swiftly with the current."

"YOUNG MEN, AHOY!"

"What is it?"

"BEWARE! BEWARE! THE RAPIDS ARE BELOW YOU!"

Now you see the water foaming all around. See how fast you pass that point! Up with the helm! Now turn! Pull hard! *Quick!* QUICK! QUICK! *Pull hard for your lives!* Pull till the blood starts from your nostrils and the veins start like whipcords upon your brow! Set the mast in the socket! hoist the sail! ah! ah! it is too late! *"Shrieking,* HOWLING, BLASPHEMING, *over they go!"*

Thousands go over the rapids of intemperance every year through *the power of habit,* crying all the while: "When I find out that it is injuring me, I will give it up!"

"The Power of Habit."[1] JOHN B. GOUGH.

5. I read a story the other day of some Russians crossing wide plains studded over here and there with forests. The villages were ten or a dozen miles from each other, the wolves were out, the horses were rushing forward madly, the travelers could hear the baying of the wolves behind them; and, tho the horses tore along with all speed, yet the wolves were fast behind, and they only escaped, as we say, "by the skin of their teeth," managing just to get inside some hut that stood in the road, and to shut to the door. Then they could hear the wolves leap on the roof; they could hear them dash against the sides of the hut; they could hear them gnawing at the door, and howling, and making all sorts of dismal noises; but the travelers were safe, because they had entered in by the door, and the door was shut. Now, when a man is in Christ, he can hear, as it were, the devils howling like wolves, all fierce and hungry for him; and his own sins, like wolves, are seeking to drag him down to destruction. But he has got in to Christ, and that is such a shelter that all the devils in the world, if they were to come at once, could not start a single beam of that eternal refuge; it must stand fast, tho the earth and heaven should

---

[1] "Platform Echoes," copyrighted 1877 by A. D. Worthington & Co., Hartford, Conn.

pass away. Now, to every man and woman Christ says that if they have entered in by the door, they shall be saved.
Selected. SPURGEON.

6. The dissipations of social life are blasting and destroying a vast multitude. With many life is a masquerade ball, and as at such entertainments gentlemen and ladies put on the garb of kings and queens, or mountebanks or clowns, and at the close put off the disguise, so a great many pass their whole life in a mask, taking off the mask at death. While the masquerade ball of life goes on, they trip merrily over the floor, gemmed hand is stretched to gemmed hand, gleaming brow bends to gleaming brow. On with the dance! Flush and rustle and laughter of immeasurable merrymaking. But after a while the languor of death comes on the limbs and blurs the eyesight. Lights lower. Floor hollow with sepulchral echo. Music saddened into a wail. Lights lower. Now the maskers are only seen in the dim light. Now the fragrance of the flowers is like the sickening odor that comes from garlands that have lain long in the vaults of cemeteries. Lights lower. Mists gather in the room. Glasses shake as tho quaked by sullen thunder. Sight caught in the curtain. Scarf drops from the shoulder of beauty a shroud. Lights lower. Over the slippery boards in dance of death glide jealousies, envies, revenges, lust, despair and death. Stench of lamp-wicks almost extinguished. Torn garlands will not half cover the ulcerated feet. Choking damps. Chilliness. Feet still. Hands closed. Voices hushed. Eyes shut. Lights out.
"Lights Out."[1] T. DEWITT TALMAGE.

7. One of our railroad engineers, some years since, was running an express train of ten filled cars. It was in the night, and a very dark night too. His train was behind time, and he was putting the engine to the utmost speed of which it was capable, in order to reach a certain point at the proper hour. He was running on a straight and level track, and at this unusual velocity, when a conviction struck him that he must stop.

"A something seemed to tell me," he said, "that to go ahead was dangerous, and that I must stop if I would save life. I looked back at my train and it was all right. I strained my eyes and peered into the darkness, and could see no signal of danger, nor anything betokening danger, and there, in the daytime, I could have seen five miles. I listened to the working of my engine, tried the water, looked at the gage, and all was right. I tried to laugh myself out of what I considered a childish fear; but, like Banquo's ghost, it would not down at my bidding, but grew stronger in its hold upon me. I thought of the ridicule I would have heaped upon me if I did stop; but it was all of no avail. The conviction—for by this time it had ripened into a conviction—that I must stop, grew stronger, and I resolved to do so. I shut off, and blew the whistle for brakes accordingly. I came to a dead halt, got off, and went ahead a little way without saying anything to anybody what was the matter. I had a lamp in my hand, and had gone but about sixty feet when I saw what convinced me that premonitions are sometimes possible. I dropt the lantern from my nerveless grasp and sat down on the track utterly unable to stand."

He goes on to tell that there some one had drawn a spike which had long fastened a switch rail, and opened a switch which always had been kept locked, which led on to a track—only about one hundred and fifty feet long—which terminated in a stone quarry!

"Here it was, wide open, and had I not obeyed my premonitory warning—call it what you will—I should have run into it, and at the end of the track, only about ten rods long, my heavy engine and train, moving at the rate of forty-five miles an hour, would have come into collision with a solid wall of rock eighteen feet high! The consequences, had I done so, can neither be imagined nor described, but they could by no possibility have been otherwise than fatally horrible."

"A Premonition." ANONYMOUS.

8. "Do you see this lock of hair?" said an old man to me.

"Yes; but what is it? It is, I suppose, a curl from the head of a dear child long since dead."

"It is not. It is a lock of my own hair; and it is now nearly seventy years since it was cut from this head."

"But why do you prize a lock of your own hair so much?"

"It has a story belonging to it, a strange one. I keep it thus with care because it speaks to me more of God, and of His special care, than anything else I possess. I was a little child of four years old, with long curly locks, which in the sun, or rain, or wind, hung down my cheeks uncovered. One day my father went into the woods to cut up a log, and I went with him. I was standing a little way behind him, or rather at his side, watching with interest the strokes of the heavy ax as it went up and came down upon the wood, sending off splinters with every stroke, in all directions. Some of the splinters fell at my feet, and I eagerly stooped to pick them up. In doing so I stumbled forward, and in a moment my curly head lay upon the log. I had fallen just at the moment when the ax was coming down with all its force. It was too late to stop the blow. Down came the ax. I screamed, and my father fell to the ground in terror. He could not stay the stroke, and in the blindness which the sudden horror caused, he thought he had killed his boy. We soon recovered—I from my fright, and he from terror. He caught me in his arms, and looked at me from head to foot to find the deadly wound which he was sure he had inflicted. Not a drop of blood nor a scar was to be seen. He knelt upon the grass and gave thanks to a gracious God. Having done so, he took up his ax, and found a few hairs upon its edge. He turned to the log he had been splitting, and there was a single curl of his boy's hair, sharply cut through and laid upon the wood. How great the escape! It was as if an angel had turned aside the edge at the moment it was descending upon my head.

"That lock he kept all his days as a memorial of God's care and love. That lock he left me on his death-bed. I keep it with care. It tells me of my father's God and mine. It rebukes unbelief and alarm. It bids me trust Him forever. I have had many tokens of fatherly love in my threescore years and ten, but somehow this speaks most to my heart. It is the oldest and perhaps the most striking. It used to speak to my father's heart; it now speaks to mine."

"The Lock of Hair." ANONYMOUS.

9. Last summer I saw Moscow, in some respects the most splendid city under the sun. The emperor afterward asked me if I had seen it, for Moscow is the pride of Russia. I told him yes, and that I had seen Moscow burn. I will tell you what I meant. After examining nine hundred brass cannons which were picked out of the snow after Napoleon retreated from Moscow, each cannon deep cut with the letter "N," I ascended a tower of some two hundred and fifty feet, just before sunset, and on each platform there were bells, large and small, and I climbed up among the bells, and then, as I reached the top, all the bells underneath me began to ring, and they were joined by the bells of fourteen hundred towers and domes and turrets. Some of the bells sent out a faint tinkle of sound, a sweet tintinnabulation that seemed a bubbling of the air, and others thundered forth boom after boom, boom after boom, until it seemed to shake the earth and fill the heavens—sounds so weird, so sweet, so awful, so grand, so charming, so tremendous, so soft, so rippling, so reverberating—and they seemed to wreathe and whirl and rise and sink and burst and roll and mount and die. When Napoleon saw Moscow burn, it could not have been more brilliant than when I saw the fourteen hundred turrets aflame with the sunset; and there were roofs of gold, and walls of malachite, and pillars of porphyry, and balustrades of mosaic, and architecture of all colors mingling the brown of autumnal forests and the blue of summer heavens, and the conflagration of morning skies, and the emerald of rich grass, and the foam of tossing seas. The mingling of so many sounds was an entrancement almost too much for human nerves and human eyes and human ears. I expect to see nothing to equal it until you and I see heaven. But that will surpass it and make the memory of what I saw that July evening in Moscow almost tame and insipid. All heaven aglow and all heaven

a-ring, not in the sunset, but in the sunrise. Voices of our own kindred mingling with the doxologies of empires. Organs of eternal worship responding to the trumpets that have wakened the dead. Nations in white. Centuries in coronation. Anthems like the voice of many waters. Circle of martyrs. Circle of apostles. Circle of prophets. Thrones of cherubim. Thrones of seraphim. Throne of archangel. Throne of Christ. Throne of God. Thrones! Thrones! Thrones! The finger of God points that way. Stop not until you reach that place. Through the atoning Christ, all I speak of and more may be yours and mine. Do you not now hear the chime of the bells of that metropolis of the universe! Do you not see the shimmering of the towers? Good-morning.

"The Bells of Moscow."[1] T. DE WITT TALMAGE.

Velpean, the eminent French surgeon, successfully performed a perilous operation on a five-year-old child. The mother, overjoyed, called upon him and said:

"Monsieur, I do not know how to express my gratitude. May I present you, however, with this pocketbook, embroidered with my own hands?"

"Madam," said Velpean, "my art is not merely a matter of feeling. My life has its necessities, like yours. Allow me to decline your charming gift and request a more substantial remuneration."

"But, monsieur, what do you wish? Fix the fee yourself."

"Five thousand francs, madam."

She quietly opened the pocketbook, which contained ten one-thousand-franc notes, counted out five, and politely handing them to Velpean, retired.

ANONYMOUS.

[1] Copyright 1900, by Louis Klopsch.

CHAPTER X

POWER IN CONVERSATION

Conversation offers one of the best and most practical helps to the study of public speaking. Here common faults of speech can be readily noted, and habits of fluent and natural expression established. The facility and self-confidence gained here will be valuable in speaking before an audience.

Probably nothing betrays a man so unmistakably as his style of conversation. The quality of his voice, his use of words, his ability to put his ideas into forceful and effective speech, all disclose his breeding and education. The value of conversation as an educational force is emphasized by President Eliot, of Harvard, who says: "I recognize but one mental acquisition as an essential part of the education of a lady or gentleman, namely, an accurate and refined use of the mother-tongue." Dr. Nicholas Murray Butler, of Columbia, says: "First among the evidences of an education I name correctness and precision in the use of the mother-tongue."

The best public speaking and preaching of to-day is mainly colloquial or conversational in style. Hence conversation offers the best models for study and practise. The ability to speak to the point, to describe vividly a recent journey, or to tell an interesting story, is a practical and direct preparation for the larger work of public address. The practise of communicating to others what one has seen or heard, will gradually awaken a desire to speak before a larger audience.

The conversation of children often serves as the best model of easy unaffected speech. Their vivacity and genuineness might well be copied by those who wish to move and influence men.

The student of public speaking should be careful not to indulge at any time in loose and incorrect speech. In his daily conversation he should exercise the utmost care in pronouncing every word clearly and correctly, in pure-toned voice, and usually in a low key. He should avoid everything that is slipshod in speech, high pitch, rapid rate, half-closed mouth, and the disposition to be vociferous.

Dr. Richard Storrs, the gifted and eloquent preacher, has recommended conversation as one of the best means of refreshing the mind and replenishing it with active force. He says: "Conversation, if practised as it ought to be, as a commerce of thought between responsive and interchanging minds, is an invaluable aid toward gaining the art of easy and self-possest public speech. I do not think we have as much of it as we ought, or that it holds the place which it should in our plans of life, as a real educational force. It is much the same exercise, if you analyze it, as public speaking. Of course it is not the same altogether. In public speech your utterance of thought is more prolonged; it is monolog not dialog. You miss the help which comes from interjected remarks or replies; and you are not so immediately conscious of the sympathy or the collision of the adjacent minds. Still, conversation is much the same form of mental activity, and it always helps the public speaker. It trains the mind to think rapidly, and to formulate thought with facility and success; and each sense of such success, which is gained in conversation, will give one more confidence when he stands before an audience.

The following extracts in conversational style will serve as introductory practise along these lines. They should be read aloud, with natural and spontaneous expression, and with due regard to clear and correct enunciation.

1. "I am willing to amuse you if I can, sir; quite willing; but I can not introduce a topic, because how do I know what will interest you? Ask me questions, and I will do my best to answer them."

"Then, in the first place, do you agree with me that I have a right to be a little masterful, abrupt, perhaps exciting sometimes, on the grounds I stated—namely, that I am old enough to be your father, and that I have battled through a varied experience with many men of many nations, and roamed over half the globe, while you have lived quietly with one set of people in one house?"

"Do as you please, sir."

"That is no answer; or rather, it is a very irritating, because a very evasive one; reply clearly."

"I don't think, sir, you have a right to command me, merely because you are older than I, or because you have seen more of the world than I have; your claim to superiority depends on the use you have made of your time and experience."

"Humph! Promptly spoken. But I won't allow that, seeing that it would never suit my case, as I have made an indifferent, not to say a bad use of both advantages. Leaving superiority out of the question then, you must still agree to receive my orders now and then, without being piqued or hurt by the tone of command—will you?"

I smiled: I thought to myself Mr. Rochester *is* peculiar—he seems to forget that he pays me 30 pounds per annum for receiving his orders.

"The smile is very well," said he, catching instantly the passing expression; "but speak, too."

"I was thinking, sir, that very few masters would trouble themselves to inquire whether or not their paid subordinates were piqued and hurt by their orders."

"Paid subordinates! What, you are my paid subordinate, are you? Oh, yes, I had forgotten the salary! Well, then, on that mercenary ground, will you agree to let me hector a little?"

"No, sir, not on that ground, but on the ground that you did forget it, and that you care whether or not a dependent is comfortable in his dependency, I agree heartily."

"And will you consent to dispense with a great many conventional forms and phrases, without thinking that the omission arises from insolence?"

"I am sure, sir, I should never mistake informality for insolence: one I rather like, the other nothing free-born would submit to even for a salary."

"Humbug! Most things free-born will submit to anything for a salary; therefore keep to yourself, and don't venture on generalities of which you are intensely ignorant. However, I mentally shake hands with you for your answer, despite its inaccuracy, and as much for the manner in which it was said as for the substance of the speech. The manner was frank and sincere; one does not often see such a manner; no, on the contrary, affectation, or coldness, or stupid, coarse-minded misapprehension of one's meaning are the usual rewards of candor. Not three in three thousand raw school-girl governesses would have answered me as you have just done. But I don't mean to flatter you; if you are cast in a different mold to the majority, it is no merit of yours: Nature did it. And then, after all, I go too fast in my conclusions; for what I yet know, you may be no better than the rest; you have intolerable defects to counterbalance your few good points."

"And so may you," I thought. My eye met his as the idea crossed my mind. He seemed to read the glance, answering as if its import had been spoken as well as imagined—

"Yes, yes, you are right," said he; "I have plenty of faults of my own: I know it, and I don't wish to palliate them, I assure you. God wot, I need not be too severe about others; I have a past existence, a series of deeds, a color of life to contemplate within my own breast which might well call my sneers and censures from my neighbors to myself. I started, or rather (for, like other defaulters, I like to lay half the blame on ill fortune and adverse circumstances), was thrust on to a wrong tack at the age of one-and-twenty, and have never recovered the right course since: but I might have been very different; I might have been as good as you—wiser—almost as stainless. I envy you your peace of mind, your clean conscience, your unpolluted memory. Little girl, a memory without blot or contamination must be an exquisite treasure—an inexhaustible source of pure refreshment: is it not?"

"How was your memory when you were eighteen, sir?"

"All right then; limpid, salubrious: no gush of bilge-water had turned to fetid puddle. I was your equal at eighteen—quite your equal. Nature meant me to be on the whole a good man, Miss Eyre: one of the better kind; and you see I am not so. You would say you don't see it: at least I flatter myself I read as much in your eye (beware, by the by, what you express with that organ, I am quick at interpreting its language). Then, take my word for it, I am not a villian; you are not to suppose that—not to attribute to me any such bad eminence; but owing, I verily believe, rather to circumstances than to my natural bent, I am a trite, commonplace sinner, hackneyed in all the poor petty dissipations with which the rich and worthless try to put on life. Do you wonder that I avow this to you? Know that in the course of your future life you will often find yourself elected the involuntary confidante of your acquaintances' secrets: people will instinctively find out, as I have done, that it is not your forte to tell of yourself, but to listen while others talk of themselves; they will feel, too, that you listen with no malevolent scorn of their indiscretion, but with a kind of innate sympathy, not the less comforting and encouraging because it is very unobtrusive in its manifestations."

"How do you know?—how can you guess all this, sir?"

"I know it well; therefore I proceed almost as freely as if I were writing my thoughts in a diary. You would say, I should have been superior to circumstances: so I should—so I should; but you see I was not. When fate wronged me, I had not the wisdom to remain cool: I turned desperate; then I degenerated. Now, when any vicious simpleton excites my disgust by his paltry ribaldry, I can not flatter myself that I am better than he: I am forced to confess that he and I are on a level. I wish I had stood firm—God knows I do! Dread remorse when you are tempted to err, Miss Eyre: remorse is the poison of life."

"Repentance is said to be its cure, sir."

"It is not its cure. Reformation may be its cure; and I could reform—I have strength yet for that—if—but where is the use of thinking of it, hampered, burdened, curst as I am? Besides, since happiness is irrevocably denied me, I have a right to get pleasure out of life; and I *will* get it, cost what it may."

"Then you will degenerate still more, sir."

"Possibly: yet why should I, if I can get sweet, fresh pleasure? And I may get it as sweet and fresh as the wild honey the bee gathers on the moor."

"It will sting—it will taste bitter, sir."

"How do you know?—you never tried it. How very serious—how very solemn you look; and you are as ignorant of the matter as this cameo head" (taking one from the mantelpiece). "You have no right to preach to me, you neophyte, that have not passed the porch of life, and are absolutely unacquainted with its mysteries."

"I only remind you of your own words, sir: you said error brought remorse, and you pronounced remorse the poison of existence."

"And who talks of error now? I scarcely think the notion that flitted across my brain was an error. I believe it was an inspiration rather than a temptation: it was very genial, very soothing—I know that. Here it comes again! It is no devil, I assure you; or if it be, it has put on the robes of an angel of light. I think I must admit so fair a guest when it asks entrance to my heart."

From "Jane Eyre." CHARLOTTE BRONTE.

2. Altho he had arrived at his journey's end for the day at noon, he had since insensibly walked about the town so far and so long that the lamplighters were now at their work in the streets and the shops were sparkling up brilliantly. Thus reminded to turn toward his quarters, he was in the act of doing so, when a very little hand crept into his and a very little voice said:

"Oh, if you please, I am lost!"

He looked down, and saw a very little fair-haired girl.

"Yes," she said, confirming her words with a serious nod. "I am, indeed. I am lost."

"What is your name?"

"Polly."

"What is your other name?"

The reply was prompt but unintelligible.

Imitating the sound, as he caught it, he hazarded the guess, "Trivits?"

"Oh, no!" said the child, shaking her head. "Nothing like that."

"Say it again, little one."

An unpromising business. For this time it had quite a different sound.

He made the venture: "Paddens?"

"Oh no!" said the child. "Nothing like that."

"Once more. Let us try it again, dear."

A most hopeless business. This time it swelled into four syllables. "It can't be Tappitarver?" said Barbox Brothers, rubbing his head with his hat in discomfiture.

"No! It ain't," the child quietly assented.

On her trying this unfortunate name once more, with extraordinary efforts at distinctness, it swelled into eight syllables at least.

"Ah! I think," said Barbox Brothers, with a desperate air of resignation, "that we had better give it up."

"But I am lost," said the child nestling her little hand more closely in his, "and you'll take care of me, won't you?"

If ever a man were disconcerted by division between compassion on the one hand, and the very imbecility of irresolution on the other, here the man was. "Lost!" he repeated, looking down at the child. "I am sure I am. What is to be done!"

"Where do *you* live?" asked the child, looking up at him wistfully.

"Over there," he answered, pointing vaguely in the direction of the hotel.

"Hadn't we better go there?" said the child.

"Really," he replied, "I don't know but what we had."

So they set off, hand in hand—he, through comparison of himself against his little companion, with a clumsy feeling on him as if he had just developed into a foolish giant; she, clearly elevated in her own tiny opinion by having got him so neatly out of his embarrassment.

"We are going to have dinner when we get there, I suppose?" said Polly.

"Well," he rejoined, "I—yes, I suppose we are."

"Do you like your dinner?" asked the child.

"Why, on the whole," said Barbox Brothers, "yes, I think I do."

"I do mine," said Polly. "Have you any brothers and sisters?"

"No, have you?"

"Mine are dead."

"Oh!" said Barbox Brothers. With that absurd sense of unwieldiness of mind and body weighing him down, he would not have known how to pursue the conversation beyond this curt rejoinder, but that the child was always ready for him.

"What," she asked, turning her soft hand coaxingly in his, "are you going to do to amuse me after dinner?"

"Upon my soul, Polly," exclaimed Barbox Brothers, very much at a loss, "I have not the slightest idea!"

"Then I tell you what," said Polly. "Have you got any cards at the house?"

"Plenty," said Barbox Brothers, in a boastful vein.

"Very well. Then I'll build houses, and you shall look at me. You mustn't blow, you know."

"Oh no!" said Barbox Brothers. "No, no, no! No blowing! Blowing's not fair."

He flattered himself that he had said this pretty well for an idiotic monster; but the child, instantly perceiving the awkwardness of his attempt to adapt himself to her level, utterly destroyed his hopeful opinion of himself by saying, compassionately: "What a funny man you are!"

Feeling, after this melancholy failure, as if he every minute grew bigger and heavier in person and weaker in mind, Barbox gave himself up for a bad job. No giant ever submitted more meekly to be led in triumph by all-conquering Jack, than he to be bound in slavery to Polly.

"Do you know any stories?" she asked him.

He was reduced to the humiliating confession: "No."

"What a dunce you must be, mustn't you?" said Polly.

He was reduced to the humiliating confession: "Yes."

"Would you like me to teach you a story? But you must remember it, you know, and be able to tell it right to somebody else afterward?"

He professed that it would afford him the highest mental gratification to be taught a story, and that he would humbly endeavor to retain it in his mind. Whereupon Polly, giving her hand a new little turn in his, expressive of settling down for enjoyment, commenced a long romance, of which every relishing clause began with the words: "So this," or "And so this." As, "So this boy"; or, "So this fairy"; or, "And so this pie was four yards round and two yards and a quarter deep." The interest of the romance was derived from the intervention of this fairy to punish this boy for having a greedy appetite. To achieve which purpose, this fairy made this pie, and this boy ate and ate and ate and his cheeks swelled and swelled and swelled. There were many tributary circumstances, but the forcible interest culminated in the total consumption of the pie and the bursting of this boy. Truly he was a fine sight, Barbox Brothers, with serious attentive face, an ear bent down, much jostled on the pavements of the busy town, but afraid of losing a single incident of the epic, lest he should be examined in it by and by and found deficient.

"Barbox Brothers & Co." CHARLES DICKENS.

3. We took possession of the private box assigned to us: and Mrs. Fletcher seated herself in the place of honor—each of the young ladies taking it by turns to occupy the other corner. Miss Minny and Master Jones occupied the middle places; and it was pleasant to watch the young gentleman throughout the performance of the comedy—during which he was never quiet for two minutes—now shifting his chair, now swinging to and fro upon it, now digging his elbows into the capacious sides of Mrs. Captain Flather, now beating with his boots against the front of the box or trampling upon the skirts of Mrs. Flather's satin garment.

He occupied himself unceasingly, too, in working up and down Mrs. F's double-barreled French opera-glass—not a little to the detriment of that instrument and the wrath of the owner; indeed, I have no doubt that had not Mrs. Flather reflected that Mrs. Colonel Jones gave some of the most elegant parties in London, to which she was very anxious to be invited, she would have boxed Master Augustine's ears in the presence of the whole audience of Covent Garden.

One of the young ladies was, of course, obliged to remain in the back row with Mr. Spec. We could not see much of the play over Mrs. F's turban; but I trust we were not unhappy in our retired position. O Miss Emily! O Miss Louisa! there is one who would be happy to sit for a week close by either of you, tho it were on one of those abominable little private-box chairs. I know, for my part, that every time the box-keeperess popped in her head, and asked if we would take any refreshment, I thought the interruption odious.

Our young ladies, and their stout chaperon and aunt, had come provided with neat little bouquets of flowers, in which they evidently took a considerable pride, and which were laid, on their first entrance, on the ledge in front of our box.

But presently, on the opposite side of the house, Mrs. Cutbush, of Pocklington Gardens, appeared with her daughters, and bowed in a patronizing manner to the ladies of our party, with whom the Cutbush family had a slight acquaintance.

Before ten minutes, the bouquets of our party were whisked away from the ledge of the box. Mrs. Flather dropt hers to the ground, where Master Jones's feet speedily finished it; Miss Louisa Twigg let hers fall into her lap, and covered it with her pocket-handkerchief. Uneasy signals passed between her and her sister. I could not, at first, understand what event had occurred to make these ladies so unhappy.

At last the secret came out. The Misses Cutbush had bouquets like little haystacks before them. Our small nosegays, which had quite satisfied the girls until now, had become odious in their little jealous eyes; and the Cutbushes triumphed over them.

I have joked the ladies subsequently on this adventure; but not one of them will acknowledge the charge against them. It was mere accident that made them drop the flowers—pure accident. They jealous of the Cutbushes—not they, indeed; and, of course, each person on this head is welcome to his own opinion.

How different, meanwhile, was the behavior of my young friend Master Jones, who is not as yet sophisticated by the world. He not only nodded to his father's servant, who had taken a place in the pit, and was to escort his young master home, but he discovered a school-fellow in the pit likewise. "By Jove, there's Smith!" he cried out, as if the sight of Smith was the most extraordinary event in the world. He pointed out Smith to all of us. He never ceased nodding, winking, grinning, telegraphing, until he had succeeded in attracting the attention not only of Master Smith, but of the greater part of the house; and whenever anything in the play struck him as worthy of applause, he instantly made signals to Smith below, and shook his fist at him, as much as to say, "By Jove, old fellow, ain't it good? I say, Smith, isn't it *prime*, old boy?" He actually made remarks on his fingers to Master Smith during the performance.

I confess he was one of the best night's entertainment to me. How Jones and Smith will talk about that play when they meet after holidays! And not only then will they remember it, but all their lives long. Why do you remember that play you saw thirty years ago, and forget the one over which you yawned last week? "Ah, my brave little boy," I thought in my heart, "Twenty years hence you will recollect this, and have forgotten many a better thing. You will have been in love twice or thrice by that time, and have forgotten it; you will have buried your wife and forgotten her; you will have had ever so many friendships and forgotten them. You and Smith won't care for each other, very probably; but you'll remember all the actors and the plot of this piece we are seeing."

I protest I have forgotten it myself. In our back row we could not see or hear much of the performance (and no great loss)—fitful bursts of elocution only occasionally reaching us, in which we could recognize the well-known nasal twang of the excellent Mr. Stupor, who performed the part of the young hero; or the ringing laughter of Mrs. Belmore, who had to giggle through the whole piece.

It was one of Mr. Boyster's comedies of English life. Frank Nightrake (Stupor) and his friend Bob Fitzoffley appeared in the first scene, having a conversation with that impossible valet of English comedy, whom any gentleman would turn out-of-doors before he could get through half a length of the dialog assigned. I caught only a glimpse of this act. Bob, like a fashionable young dog of the aristocracy (the character was played by Bulwer, a meritorious man, but very stout, and nearly fifty years of age), was drest in a rhubarb-colored body-coat with brass buttons, a couple of under-waistcoats, a blue satin stock with a paste brooch in it, and an eighteen-penny cane, which he never let out of his hand, and with which he poked fun at everybody. Frank Nightrake, on the contrary, being at home, was attired in a very close-fitting chintz dressing-gown, lined with glazed red calico, and was seated before a large pewter teapot, at breakfast. And, as your true English comedy is the representation of nature, I could not but think how like these figures on the stage, and the dialog which they used, were to the appearance and talk of English gentlemen of the present day.

The dialog went on somewhat in the following fashion:

Bob Fitzoffley (enters whistling).—"The top of the morning to thee, Frank! What! at breakfast already? At chocolate and the *Morning Post*, like a dowager of sixty? Slang *(he pokes the servant with his cane)*, what has come to thy master, thou

Prince of Valets! thou pattern of Slaveys! thou swiftest of Mercuries! Has the Honorable Francis Nightrake lost his heart, or his head, or his health?"

Frank (laying down the paper).—"Bob, Bob, I have lost all three! I have lost my health, Bob, with thee and thy like, over the Burgundy at the club; I have lost my head, Bob, with thinking how I shall pay my debts; and I have lost my heart, Bob, oh, to such a creature!"

Bob.—"A Venus, of course?"

Slang.—"With the presence of Juno."

Bob.—"And the modesty of Minerva."

Frank.—"And the coldness of Diana."

Bob.—"Pish! What a sigh is that about a woman! Thou shalt be Endymion, the nightrake of old, and conquer this shy goddess. Hey, Slang?"

Herewith Slang takes the lead of the conversation, and propounds a plot for running away with the heiress; and I could not help remarking how like the comedy was to life—how the gentlemen always say "thou" and "prythee" and "go to," and talk about heathen goddesses to each other; how their servants are always their particular intimates; how when there is serious love-making between a gentleman and lady, a comic attachment invariably springs up between the valet and the waiting-maid of each; how Lady Grace Gadabout, when she calls upon Rose Ringdove to pay a morning visit, appears in a low satin dress, with jewels in her hair; how Saucebox, her attendant, wears diamond brooches, and rings on all her fingers: while Mrs. Tallyho, on the other hand, transacts all the business of life in a riding-habit, and always points her jokes by a cut of the whip.

This playfulness produced a roar all over the house, whenever it was repeated, and always made our little friends clap their hands and shout in a chorus.

Like that *bon-vivant* who envied the beggars staring into the cookshop windows, and wished he could be hungry, I envied the boys, and wished I could laugh, very much. In the last act, I remember—for it is now very nearly a week ago—everybody took refuge either in a secret door, or behind a screen, or curtain, or under a table, or up a chimney: and the house roared as each person came out from his place of concealment. And the old fellow in top-boots, joining the hands of the young couple (Fitzoffley, of course, pairing off with the widow), gave them his blessing, and thirty thousand pounds.

And ah, ye gods! if I wished before that comedies were like life, how I wished that life was like comedies! Whereon the drop fell; and Augustus, clapping to the opera-glass, jumped up, crying—"Hurray! now for the pantomime."

WILLIAM MAKEPEACE THACKERAY.

"An Evening at the Theater," from *"Sketches and Travels in London."*

4. *Dogb.* First, who think you the most desartless man to be constable?

1 Watch. Hugh Oatcake, sir, or George Seacoal; for they can write and read.

Dogb. Come hither, neighbor Seacoal: God hath blest you with a good name: to be a well-favored man is the gift of fortune; but to write and read comes by nature.

2 Watch. Both which, master constable—

Dogb. You have; I knew it would be your answer. Well, for your favor, sir, why, give God thanks, and make no boast of it; and for your writing and reading, let that appear when there is no need of such vanity. You are thought here to be the most senseless and fit man for the constable of the watch; therefore bear you the lantern. This is your charge: you shall comprehend all vagrom men; you are to bid any man stand, in the prince's name.

"Much Ado About Nothing." SHAKESPEARE.

CHAPTER XI

POWER IN EXTEMPORANEOUS SPEAKING

The question of the use of manuscript in speaking before an audience has been widely discust. If it were left to the public, the decision would be unanimously in favor of the extemporaneous style. An audience has a distinct prejudice against a speech or sermon read from a paper. If a speaker refers even to notes, it is considered a point against him. The public expect to see the speaker unencumbered by written notes of any kind. If he has to use them, they conclude he is not master of himself nor of the occasion.

If an address is read from a paper, the listener feels he could as well read it himself at his own home. In the speech or sermon that is read he misses the action of the speaker, the eye to eye communication, the free and spontaneous expression of the voice and body, the direct appeal, the varied pausing, and the infinite shades of modulation attached to extemporaneous delivery. A read speech is likely to be too right-onward in its movement, savoring of the essay, and losing much of the personal element so necessary to effective speaking.

In the early training of a public speaker it is perhaps advisable in most cases to adhere to the manuscript. But as confidence is gained the aim should be to speak entirely without notes of any kind. In these first efforts there should be the most rigid preparation, and in some instances careful memorization. As the speaker gains experience he will find himself more and more able to speak with less detailed preparation, and finally he may be able to do well from merely a clearly defined brief.

Oliver Wendell Holmes said: "The orator—I do not mean the poor slave of a manuscript, who takes his thought chilled and stiffened from its mold, or the impassioned speaker who pours it forth corruscating from the furnace —the orator only becomes our master at the moment when he is himself captured, taken possession of by a sudden rush of fresh inspiration. How well we know the flash of the eye, the thrill of the voice, which are the signature and symbol of nascent thought—thought just entering into consciousness, in which condition, as in the case of the chemist's elements, it has a combining force at other times wholly unknown."

This certainly is a plea for the extemporaneous style. This form of address has the advantage of being more conversational and direct than the reading style. It enables the speaker to take constant note of the effect he is producing upon his audience, and to change his method and arrangement to meet unexpected conditions. There is a freshness and a spontaneity about this style that pleases and fascinates an audience, which can not usually be said of the cold made-to-order phraseology of the manuscript speaker. The extemporaneous style gives the speaker unlimited scope for timely observation, the introduction of new illustrations and arguments, for repetition of ideas when required by special circumstances, and numerous other advantages. If the *whole man* should speak, how can this be done if his eyes are glued to a written page?

There is also the question of the vast amount of time that would be saved by the speaker and minister if he could so train himself as not to be obliged to memorize his addresses. Beecher's words regarding the preacher apply also to the average public speaker, who spends days and nights in toil and anxiety over his forthcoming address. Beecher says: "We do not desire to have preaching made less thorough or less instructive, but it is desirable that it should be less burdensome. Many and many a minister is a prisoner all the week to his two sermons. In them he has poured his whole life, and when they are done there is little of him left for pastoral labors and social life. Few men there are who are upborne and carried forward by their sermons. Few men ascend, as the prophet did, in a chariot of fire. The majority of preachers are consciously harnessed, and draw heavily and long at the sermon, which tugs behind them. In every way, then, it is desirable that preaching should be made more easy, that men should learn to take advantage of their own temperament, and that they should learn the best plans and methods."

Henry Ward Beecher was himself the ideal type of extemporaneous speaker. Dr. Wilkinson pays this high tribute to him: "Mr. Beecher's genius had its own elements and its own accompaniments. What are these? One accompaniment was a well-tempered, wonderfully elastic, wonderfully responsive body. This he cared for scrupulously, to maintain it at the highest point of effectiveness. His voice was a living instrument, in native power unsurpassed, and never impaired through ill-health in the owner. Every muscle of his flesh, every bone and nerve and sinew of his frame, the very blood in throat and cheek and brow, was absolutely obedient to the demand of the orator; and the demand of the orator was immense, for Mr. Beecher's instinct of mimicry was boundless. From long habit on Mr. Beecher's part, of absolute command over audiences, his face grew leonine in expression, and the leonine expression itself was constantly more and more a means of such command. Audiences love to be mastered—by a master; and they easily recognize a master by his looks."[1]

It is true that there are some men who can never hope to become successful extemporaneous speakers. These, of course, must continue to use their manuscript, and forego the advantages of the other style. Doctor Storrs tells of his struggle and determination to acquire the ability to speak without notes. He joined a debating society and during his seminary course did everything he could to advance himself in this way, but with little success. He speaks of his first public efforts to preach without notes as like swimming up the rapids. Then he experimented by having some notes before him, or a "skeleton" of his discourse, but he felt himself worse off than ever. For him, at least, this method proved a failure, obstructing the freedom, freshness, and vigor of his thought. The manuscript in any form, however slight, checked his spontaneity, made him jerky and self-conscious, so that at last he gave himself up wholly to a determined effort to speak entirely without notes of any kind. He refers to the first sermon he preached in Brooklyn thus: "I was called upon unexpectedly for the service, as I was passing through the city, and when I had with me no manuscript sermons. But I had a subject in mind on which I had written not long before, in which I had been at the time much interested, and

[1] William Cleaver Wilkinson, *Masters of Pulpit Discourse*.

of which I had made a thorough analysis. The course of thought pursued in the sermon was fresh in my mind, tho the notes were not with me. I preached in a lecture-room, which was wholly filled with attentive hearers. I had no sort of fear of the congregation, which was entirely made up of strangers to me; and I found as I went on, in the treatment of the subject with which I had made myself previously familiar, that the mind worked with a facility, a force, a sense of exhilaration, which I never had had in reading from a manuscript. I enjoyed the service, and had a certain sense of Christian success in it. The people were interested, and their interest had an instant reflex influence upon my own mind, so that the success became duplicated. It seemed to me, at the end, that it must be always easy and pleasant, under similar conditions, to repeat that experiment."[1]

Notwithstanding this promising experience, however, the first sermon he preached there, after his installation, was, to use his own words, "nearly a dead failure." Perhaps he had overprepared himself, like the overtrained athlete. There was too much dependence upon verbal memory, and too little upon spontaneous expression. But for sixteen years he persevered and at last was rewarded with the satisfaction of having achieved his long-cherished purpose. These experiences he sets forth most interestingly in the lectures embodied in his book.

In recommending the extemporaneous style of speaking or preaching, too much emphasis can not be placed upon the necessity of the most thorough preparation of the subject matter. There should be the same amount of care and industry and faithfulness as is given to an address in-

[1] Richard S. Storrs, *Preaching Without Notes.*

tended to be read. The speaker should, indeed, write out his speeches in detail, even tho he does not intend to speak from his notes.

Phillips Brooks does not believe in an arbitrary rule in this matter. He thinks some men are made for manuscripts, and some for the open platform. "To exclude either class from the ministry," he says, "or to compel either class to use the methods of the other, would rob the pulpit by silencing some of its best men." But according to Cardinal Newman, the manuscript, when used, needs an apology. He says: "While, then, a preacher will find it becoming and advisable to put into writing any important discourse beforehand, he will find it equally a point of propriety and expedience not to read it in the pulpit. I am not of course denying his right to use a manuscript, if he wishes; but he will do well to conceal it, as far as he can, unless, which is the most effectual concealment, whatever be its counterbalancing disadvantages, he prefers, mainly not verbally, to get it by heart. To conceal it, indeed, in one way or other, will be his natural impulse; and this very circumstance seems to show us that to read a sermon needs an apology. For, why should he commit it to memory, or conceal his use of it, unless he felt that it was more natural, more decorous, to do without it? And so again, if he employs a manuscript, the more he appears to dispense with it, the more he looks off from it, and directly addresses his audience, the more will he be considered to preach; and, on the other hand, the more will he be judged to come short of preaching the more sedulous he is in following his manuscript line after line, and by the tone of his voice makes it clear that he has got it safely before him. What is this but a popular testimony to the fact that preaching is not reading, and reading is not preaching?"[1]

It must be admitted, then, that the speaker who depends upon a manuscript limits himself in independence and power. The fact that, as Bautain says, "There are men organized to speak well, as there are birds organized to sing well, bees to make honey, and beavers to build," is not a valid plea for the easier and more comfortable method of reading instead of speaking one's message. Properly done the extemporaneous style at first means increased labor, and greater risk and responsibility, but in the end it will yield the highest possible results in convincing and persuasive speech.

M. de Cormenin gives this stirring advice to French preachers in regard to their congregations: "Take strong hold of their attention. Stir up their pity or indignation, their sympathies, or their pride. Appear to be animated by their breath, all the while you are communicating yours to them. When you have in some degree detached their souls from their bodies and they come and group themselves of their own accord at the foot of the pulpit, riveted beneath the influence of your glance; then do not dally with them, for they are yours, your soul having, as it may be truly said, passed into theirs. Look, now, how they follow its ebb and flow! how they will as you will! how they act as you act! But persist, give them no rest; press your discourse home—and you will soon see all bosoms panting because yours pants; all eyes kindling because yours emit flame, or filling with tears because you grow tender. You will see all the hearers hanging on your lips through the attraction of persuasion; or, rather, you

[1] John Henry Newman, *Idea of a University.*

will see nothing, for you yourself will be under the spell of your own emotion; you will bend, you will succumb under your own genius, and you will be more eloquent the less effort you make to appear so."[1]

How can any man thus press his advantage home if his eyes be fixt upon a written manuscript, and having, perhaps, the constant fear that he will "lose his place." How incongruous and aimless does it seem in the speaker to gesticulate and twist the body while he is bent over the printed page. The popular ideal of speaking and preaching demands, as has already been said, the eye to eye communication of the speaker, the magnetism of direct appeal, the fire and freedom of the *whole man* unencumbered by manuscript or reading-desk. This was the method generally used by the great Greek and Roman orators and by most of the distinguished speakers of modern times. It is the style of delivery that should be assiduously cultivated by every man aspiring to become a thoroughly proficient public speaker.

[1] Quoted by J. Spencer Kennard, D.D., in *Psychic Power in Preaching*.

CHAPTER XII

POWER IN HOLDING AN AUDIENCE

It may seem superfluous to say that a public speaker should be heard in order to successfully hold an audience, but it is nevertheless true that many speakers are not heard with ease and satisfaction. This is often due to the habit of speaking through half-closed teeth and mouth. A public speaker should train himself to naturally open his mouth wide enough to give the greatest freedom to his voice and articulation. The long sound of *a* in father and in similar words is frequently obscured. This long open position of the mouth is illustrated in the following sentence: Thou art thy father's child.

If the reader will pronounce these words before a looking-glass he will observe the long opening of the mouth necessary to their correct pronunciation. If the correct mouth position in these or any other sounds is modified in the least degree, the pronunciation will be correspondingly incorrect.

In practising distinct enunciation avoid the two extremes of slovenliness and pedantry. Pronunciation and articulation should never attract the attention of the listener. They should be simply and unobtrusively correct. Some one said of a certain preacher: "He speaks so distinctly I do not understand anything he says." The listener's attention was so completely attracted to the manner of speaking that he lost sight of the subject.

For most occasions the speaker will require his chest tones for his public speaking work. This gives fulness, resonance, and depth to utterance; it is less taxing upon the speaker, if combined, as it should be, with abdominal breathing; and it is more agreeable to the listening ear. Head tones are responsible for much of the nasal twang heard on every side, and are largely the cause of weak and sore throats and "Monday-morning prostrations."

A public speaker should cultivate a conversational style of address. The day of stilted and bombastic oratory is passed. Audiences like and demand the most direct kind of speaking possible, and in words at once simple and idiomatic. Flowery speech, overwrought perorations, and oratorical flights are not now tolerated. This does not imply that intensity, progress, climax, and even a peroration have not their proper place and use, but it does mean that modern taste demands a colloquial style of utterance, adapted to the practical needs of men. Public speaking is merely heightened conversation, and the closer a man keeps to lines of naturalness and simplicity the greater will be his chances of success.

The preacher should be particularly careful not to fall into a certain uniform "tone," or as some one has called it, "a sanctimonious whine," but as a man talking to other men he should always employ a man's voice, use it in a manly style, and project it with manly force and vigor. Intoning, drawling, chanting, monotony and other unnatural tricks of delivery should be studiously avoided. This applies equally to "ministerial tone," singsong, wailing, clipping of consonants, undue prolongation of vowels, and other vocal eccentricities.

A speaker of real power must learn to emphasize his important thoughts, not by mere loudness of voice, nodding of the head, or slapping the hands loudly together, but rather by inflection, change of pitch, judicious pausing, and by other intellectual means. Here, again, the public speaker might take a lesson from the actor who spends hours in careful and painstaking study of the emphasis of a single speech. Intelligent emphasis will do much toward guiding one away from meaningless declamation. It is the best evidence that the speaker knows "what he is talking about."

The beginning of an address or sermon calls for no particular action or gesture. The commencement should be a gradual unfoldment of the speaker's powers, vocal, physical and mental. As he enters more deeply into his thought, some slight gesture may be appropriately used, and changes made in his attitude and standing position. Gesture and action of the body should be used sparingly, however, it being better to use too little than too much. The extremes of standing stock-still or restlessly moving about are to be avoided. No better advice on this subject has ever been given than to "suit the action to the word, the word to the action."

When the speaker stands to address his audience, he should assume a modest and easy attitude, and look his hearers straight in the eyes. The weight of the body should be on the forward part of the foot—not on the heels—the entire foot touching the floor. The knees should be straight. In turning from side to side the movements should be made at the waist, not at the neck. The latter give a jerky effect, and impair the freedom of the throat. It is advisable at the outset to direct the voice to some one sitting at the back of the room.

When special effects are demanded by the thought, care should be taken not to employ too loud nor too high-keyed a voice, but rather to depend upon increased intensity, roundness, and depth of tone. The voice should be adapted to the size of the room in which one is speaking. When possible it is well to test the voice there beforehand. This is particularly desirable when one is to speak in an unusually large auditorium, or in one with which he is not familiar. If there is an echo, or should the audience be unusually scattered, there is special necessity for deliberate and distinct utterance.

In reading from a manuscript or book it should be so held, or placed upon a reading-stand, as to give an unobstructed view of the speaker's face. Anything that is to be read before an audience, be it sermon, speech, Bible, report, or announcement, should be thoroughly practised aloud in advance.

Once the speaker secures a hold upon his audience this advantage should not be relaxed until the end of his address. The voice may be softened and shaded, as the thought subsides and varies, but the nervous and concentrated energy of the speaker should continue to exercise its powerful control over the audience.

A public speaker will find it advantageous to cultivate a discriminating musical ear. There is the music of speech as there is of song. Symmetrical flow and rhythm and melody play an important part in fascinating the listener, and give added ease and fluency to the spoken word. Effects of onomatopœia—words that partly disclose their meaning in their sound—should be studied and intelligently used as elements of effective speech.

Varied thought calls for appropriate and natural variety in speech. A "wriggling" voice is not to be encouraged, nor should the same variety be too often repeated lest it, too, by its very repetition, become monotonous. A just sense of vocal values, of perspective, of modulation adapted to the thought, will best guide the speaker. He will also cultivate lightness of touch. Sounds that come down like a heavy foot soon become burdensome to the ear. The greatest skill and judgment are needed in varying the voice in force, color, key, and flexibility, to properly meet the demands of diversified thought.

The successful speaker should have force in his style. Not merely the force of loudness, but the force of earnestness and sincerity. It is the power behind the man that makes for effective oratory, the power "speaking on the tongue, beaming from the eye, informing every feature, and urging the whole man onward, right onward to his object," this is truly the kind of eloquence to which every worthy public speaker should aspire.

Shrieking emphasis, vehement declamation, startling explosives, stamping the foot, pounding the desk or pulpit, are not evidences of self-possession nor of eloquence, and fail to inspire confidence on the part of the hearer. The cart-tail orator may harangue and scold his audience, but it is out of place in dignified address.

A deliberate style of speaking is desirable for most occasions. This prevents the crowding of words and obscuring of the thought. Frequent and varied pausing gives dignity and self-possession to the speaker, while at the same time the hearer has the opportunity of securing clear-cut impressions of his thought. He can follow the speaker with less effort, consequently both his interest and pleasure are enhanced. Deliberateness does not mean a tedious drawing out of sounds or an exaggerated slowness of speech, but an orderly movement in which passes, both grammatical and rhetorical, find their natural and effective place.

The style of speaking insisted upon at our national political conventions offers many valuable suggestions. There the speaker must have something to say, and he must say it briefly. A tedious talker will not be tolerated. The speech must have tact, force, and substance, and it must bear the unmistakable marks of genuineness.

The final test of all public speaking is whether the listener is persuaded to act in accordance with the speaker's views. If, however, the listener's mental resolution to act upon the advice of the speaker evaporates as soon as he is beyond the speaker's voice and influence, the speaking has failed. The speaker must drive home the truth, reenforced by as many suggestions as he can possibly give to the hearer.

Then, again, as referred to in a preceding chapter, there is the personality of the speaker as a force in holding an audience. The greatest power in the world is personal, and as Doctor Bradford says: "Personal power culminates when wisdom and knowledge are married to goodness and love."

A powerful personality will be found then, where brain and heart have been trained in loyal service to others, where a man feels an eager enthusiasm in his work, and where his sympathies are so broad and so deep that they will lead him, if need be, to offer himself a living sacrifice in behalf of his cause.

To maintain his hold upon the people, and to touch them on all sides, the speaker must be all-round in his taste and development. Music, poetry, the drama, science and literature must all have their proper place in his life. How pathetic is this confession of Darwin:

"Up to the age of thirty or beyond it, poetry of many kinds gave me great pleasure; and even as a schoolboy I took intense delight in Shakespeare, especially in the historical plays. I have also said that pictures formerly gave me considerable and music very great delight. But now for many years I can not endure to read a line of poetry. I have tried lately to read Shakespeare, and found it so intolerably dull that it nauseated me. I have also almost lost my taste for pictures or music. . . . My mind seems to have become a kind of machine for grinding general laws out of large collections of facts; but why this should have caused the atrophy of that part of the brain alone, on which the higher tastes depend, I can not conceive. . . . If I had to live my life again, I would have made a rule to read some poetry and listen to some music at least once every week; for perhaps the parts of my brain now atrophied would thus have been kept alive through use. The loss of these tastes is a loss of happiness, and may possibly be injurious to the intellect, and more probably to the moral character, by enfeebling the emotional part of our nature."

A public speaker can not hope to be successful in holding an audience without a deep-seated and well-directed sympathetic nature. "The secret of lasting success," says a writer, "in social conversation, in platform speech, in pulpit sermon, is sympathy, *sympathy*, SYMPATHY. In the public speaker and the private speaker, there should ever be sympathy for class or for mass, for the family or for the individual."

The speaker should have a definite purpose in view. There can be little power or satisfactory result in haphazard effort. He should know whether he is merely to entertain, or to instruct, convince, and persuade. Much will depend upon the occasion. A pulpit address will differ materially from an after-dinner speech, and what would be appropriate in a court of law, or in a scientific disquisition, might be uninteresting and out of place before a popular audience.

It is said that in a certain tribe of savages a man is allowed to speak at their councils only so long as he can stand on one foot. When the other toe touches the ground his time is up. What a relief this would be at times to some of our own long-suffering audiences!

A public speaker should be careful not to exceed his time limit. Many an otherwise admirable address has been ruined by being too long drawn out. It is dangerous to be too discursive, to succumb to the temptation to add "one more story." The old-time "Finally," "Lastly," "In conclusion," "One word more and I have done" have proved a pitfall to many a public speaker. It is an art to know how to successfully end a speech, to finish well within the prescribed time, and to leave your audience before they leave you.

CHAPTER XIII

POWER IN PRAYER

There is an inexhaustible power and efficacy in prayer, known only to those who have faithfully practised it. The praying that is done in secret will materially affect the style of one's public prayer. But whatever the form may be, this is true: "Who rises from prayer a better man, his prayer is answered."

Spurgeon in one of his addresses to his students says that prayer should be marked by solemnity, humility, and reverence. He deprecates long prayers. Frequent repetition and hackneyed expressions are to be avoided. One should cultivate a heavenly attitude of mind in prayer. God is to be entreated, not commanded. The eyes should be closed, that the Lord alone may be the object of prayer. Sickening superabundance of endearing words, and rhetorical display, have no place in earnest and effective prayer.

Learning to pray is like learning to do anything else. It comes from diligent practise. The question is sometimes asked by divinity students to what extent public prayer should be prepared in advance. No general rule can be laid down for this, as so much depends upon circumstances. There should be, however, in every case, a preparation of the heart, in which actual words may not be committed to memory, but in which the general ideas of the prayer have been thought out and arranged in order in the mind.

Unseeming hesitation in public prayer, lack of appropriate words, and discursiveness, sometimes robs prayer of real effectiveness. Spontaneity, sincerity, tenderness, and God-wardness are some of the characteristics of devout and heartfelt prayer.

The great preachers of the world have recognized the supreme power of prayer. In speaking of Dr. Russell H. Conwell, the Baptist divine, of Philadelphia, a writer says: "He is a man of prayer and a man of work. Loving, great-hearted, unselfish, cheery, practical, hard-working, he yet draws his greatest inspiration from that silent inner communion with the Master he serves with such single-hearted, unfaltering devotion."

This is Dr. Conwell's own tribute to prayer: "There is planted in every human heart this knowledge, namely, that there is a power beyond our reach, a mysterious potency shaping the forces of life, which if we would win we must have in our favor. There come to us all events over which we have no control by physical or mental power. Is there any hope of guiding those mysterious forces? Yes, friends, there is a way of securing them in our favor or preventing them from going against us. How? It is by prayer. When a man has done all he can do, still there is a mighty, mysterious agency over which he needs influence to secure success. The only way he can reach that is by prayer."

Prayer must be earnest, a thing of the heart. It should not be a thing of the lip, of formality, of a wandering mind. It should be real, soaring, confident—prayer such as this is a great force in personal power.

Thomas Guthrie, in his touching sermon, "The Necessity and Power of Prayer," says: "Child of God! pray on. By prayer thy hand can touch the stars, thy arm stretch up to heaven. Nor let thy holy boldness be dashed by the thought that prayer has no power to bend these skies, and bring down thy God. When I pull on the rope which fastens my frail and little boat to a distant and mighty ship, if my strength can not draw its vast bulk to me, I can draw myself to it—to ride in safety under the protection of its guns; to enjoy in want the fulness of its stores. And it equally serves my purpose, and supplies my needs, that prayer, altho it were powerless to move God to me, moves me to God. If He does not descend to earth, I—as it were—ascend to heaven."

Where can we find better advice upon the subject of prayer than in the Bible itself? Here we read:

"Thou, when thou prayest, enter into thy closet, and when thou hast shut thy door, pray to thy Father which is in secret, and thy Father which seeth in secret shall reward thee openly. But when ye pray, use not vain repetitions, as the heathen do; for they think that they shall be heard for their much speaking. Be not ye therefore like unto them: for your Father knoweth what things ye have need of, before ye ask him. After this manner therefore pray ye: Our Father which art in heaven, Hallowed be thy name. Thy kingdom come. Thy will be done in earth, as *it is* in heaven. Give us this day our daily bread. And forgive us our debts, as we forgive our debtors. And lead us not into temptation, but deliver us from evil: for thine is the kingdom, and the power, and the glory, forever. Amen." (*Matt.* vi., 6-13.)

"The sacrifice of the wicked is an abomination to the Lord: but the prayer of the upright is his delight." (*Prov.* xv., 1.)

"And Jesus said unto them, Because of your unbelief:

for verily I say unto you, if ye have faith as a grain of mustard seed, ye shall say unto this mountain, Remove hence to yonder place; and it shall remove; and nothing shall be impossible unto you." (*Matt.* xvii., 20.)

"Pray for them which despitefully use you, and persecute you." (*Matt.* v., 44.)

"Watch and pray, that ye enter not into temptation." (*Matt.* xxvi., 41.)

"What things soever ye desire, when ye pray, believe that ye receive them, and ye shall have them." (*Mark* xi., 24.)

"Take ye heed, watch and pray: for ye know not when the time is." (*Mark* xiii., 33.)

"Men ought always to pray, and not to faint." (*Luke* xviii., 1.)

"We know not what we should pray for as we ought: but the Spirit itself maketh intercession for us with groanings which can not be uttered." (*Rom.* viii., 26.)

"I will pray with the spirit, and I will pray with the understanding also." (*I Cor.* xiv., 15.)

"Pray without ceasing." (*I Thess.* v., 17.)

"I will therefore that men pray everywhere, lifting up holy hands, without wrath and doubting." (*I Tim.* ii., 8.)

"Is any among you afflicted? let him pray." (*James* v., 13.)

"Praying always with all prayer and supplication in the Spirit." (*Eph.* vi., 18.)

"And being in an agony he prayed more earnestly." (*Luke* xxii., 44.)

"Elias was a man subject to like passions as we are, and he prayed earnestly that it might not rain: and it rained not on the earth by the space of three years and six months." (*James* v., 17.)

"But we will now give ourselves continually to prayer, and to the ministry of the word." (*Acts* vi., 4.)

"Be careful for nothing; but in every thing by prayer and supplication with thanksgiving let your requests be made known unto God." (*Phil.* iv., 6.)

"And the prayer of faith shall save the sick, and the Lord shall raise him up; and if he have committed sins, they shall be forgiven." (*James* v., 15.)

"Confess your faults one to another, and pray one for another, that ye may be healed. The effectual fervent prayer of a righteous man availeth much." (*James* v., 16.)

Prayer, then, should be founded upon faith and earnestness. We must avoid vain repetition or doubting, and with thanksgiving and confidence make our requests known unto God. We should pray often, not only for ourselves but for one another, fervently, believingly, both with the spirit and the understanding. Such prayers, especially from one that is righteous, will avail much, such prayers can not fail to be a source of real power.

The Rev. Louis Albert Banks, in his suggestive book, "Windows for Sermons," speaking of genuine prayer, says:

"One of the greatest secrets of effective prayer is that the attitude of the heart shall be right toward God. The heart that recognizes the divine wisdom and love and trusts to them will pray as simply as a child asking help from its mother. One of the most beautiful prayers I have ever read is that of Fénelon. 'O Lord! I know not what I should ask of Thee. Thou knowest only what I want; and Thou lovest me, if I am Thy friend, better than I can love myself. O Lord! give to me, Thy child, what is proper, whatsoever it may be. I dare not ask either crosses or comforts. I only present myself before Thee. I open my heart to Thee.

Behold my wants, which I myself am ignorant of; but do Thou behold, and do, according to Thy mercy, smite or heal, depress me or raise me up. I adore all Thy purposes without knowing them. I am silent; I offer myself in sacrifice. I abandon myself to Thee. I have no more desire but to accomplish Thy will. Lord, teach me how to pray. Dwell Thou Thyself in me by the Holy Spirit. *Amen.*' "

In public prayer the minister uses his supremest faculty, that of communion with God. He speaks on behalf of his people, and must voice their needs and sentiments. His language should be simple and fitting, and his sympathies large enough to include all. It will be seen, therefore, that prayer is too important a matter to be left to the chance of the moment. It demands the same care and thought and meditation as are given to the preparation of the sermon.

The style and manner of public prayer are suggested by Professor Schenck in these words: "Terms of familiarity and endearment should be avoided, since we are addressing the Infinite and Holy God. Simple and chaste language should be used, easily understood by the ignorant and distrest and also proper to use before the throne of the Most High. The tone of the voice should be easily heard by all, from the first word of the prayer to the last, and should be earnest but never loud nor boisterous, since God is near by and loves to hear His people pray. The posture should be reverent; usually the minister should stand with claspt hands, without gesture, and the people should listen with bowed heads."[1]

The criticism is often made that public prayer is too general and does not meet the specific needs of people.

---

[1] Ferdinand S. Schenck, D.D., *Modern Practical Theology*. Funk & Wagnalls Company.

Spurgeon speaks of this generalization in prayer as disastrous. He pleads for definite prayer, asking clearly and distinctly for certain mercies. "If a regiment of soldiers should all fire off their guns anyhow, possibly somebody might be killed, but the majority of the enemy would be missed." So, in prayer, the speaker should have a target at which he aims, a clearly defined purpose on behalf of his people. In this way public prayer may be made a source of infinite power to both minister and congregation.

CHAPTER XIV

POWER IN SILENCE AND REPOSE

Paradoxical tho it may seem, there is an eloquence and a power in silence which every speaker should seek to cultivate. A man who knows how and when to listen is not only open to increase his store of knowledge, but will often receive credit for wisdom he does not really possess. The habit of silence gives time for necessary meditation and for accumulating power for subsequent use. It makes one acquainted with the inner life. It is the most direct means of developing spiritual power.

A silent man is usually a thinking man. He takes time to think, to test his ideas before giving them expression, to formulate his thought into clear and logical sequence. He obeys the admonition to "Think before you speak," consequently his thoughts when exprest carry weight because of their clearness and maturity. There are far too few of these silent men who take time to think, and too many who talk first and think afterward.

Cardinal Newman doubtless had in mind this lack of genuine thinking when he said: "What is more common than the sight of grown men, talking on political or moral or religious subjects, in that offhand, idle way, which we signify by the word *unreal?* 'That they simply do not know what they are talking about,' is the spontaneous silent remark of any man of sense who hears them. Hence such persons have no difficulty in contradicting themselves in successive sentences without being conscious of it. Hence others, whose defect in intellectual training is more latent, have their most unfortunate crotchets, as they are called, or hobbies, which deprive them of the influence which their estimable qualities would otherwise secure. Hence others can never look straight before them, never see the point, and have no difficulties in the most difficult subjects. Others are hopelessly obstinate and prejudiced, and, after they have been driven from their opinions, return to them the next moment without even an attempt to explain why. Others are so intemperate and intractable that there is no greater calamity for a good cause than that they should get hold of it."

Too much introspection and meditation may make one morbid, but intelligent self-analysis, reasonably pursued, is necessary to the highest growth. Periods of silence and relaxation offer the best conditions for this work and study. When one thinks of the noise and nervousness of modern city life, of the "bottled-lightning quality of Americans," it is reasonable to assume that only by carefully planned times for silence and quiet meditation can one hope to develop the highest and best in one's spiritual nature.

The knowledge gathered in these moments of silence, if properly applied, brings one into more intimate touch with the truth. A man finds out what things weaken his power, as well as what things contribute to it, and he can, if he will, change from destructive to constructive effort. With this new knowledge comes increased responsibility, but there comes, too, increased pleasure in the work of readjustment and of self-mastery.

The practise of silence brings reserve power, and poise,

by which a man trains himself to be equal to emergencies as they arise. In this listening attitude he hears whisperings from secret spiritual sources that otherwise could not be discerned. It is from these moments that he draws his deepest and most enduring inspiration. Every man has his own individual mind-world to explore. No one else can possibly do it for him. Its infinite possibilities must remain unrealized and undeveloped unless he is in some way led to do this work for himself.

Through relaxation and repose a man rests his physical and mental machinery, generates unsuspected energy, and at the moment of need is conscious of new and vastly increased power. To learn to "let go," to thoroughly relax both mind and body, usually requires patient and persistent practise. In the end it will repay the student manyfold in increased health and self-control.

Many persons waste valuable energy in unnecessary muscular contraction. They frown in reading a newspaper, sit anxiously in a car as if to help it to its destination, or at night they endeavor to hold the bed up lest it fall to pieces. Many times each hour they expend their power in such useless habits as clenching the fist, drumming with the fingers or tapping with the foot, biting the lips, rocking the body, or indulging in needless anxiety, anger or other excitement. These habits are a constant drain upon even the strongest constitutions, and eventually lead to physical and mental impoverishment and sometimes to nervous prostration.

Relaxation and repose act as a soothing influence to the nerves. They take the tension off the mental machinery, rest the body, and restore a man to his normal condition. As a man gradually forms this habit of doing his work without tension, he finds he can accomplish more and better work than he ever did before. It is this freedom from nerve-destroying contraction and anxiety that Carlyle has in mind when he says:

"Give us, oh, give us the man who sings at his work! He will do more in the same time—he will do it better—he will persevere longer. One is scarcely sensible of fatigue whilst he marches to music. The very stars are said to make harmony as they revolve in their spheres. Wondrous is the strength of cheerfulness, altogether past calculation in its powers of endurance. Efforts, to be permanently useful, must be uniformly joyous, a spirit all sunshine, graceful from very gladness, beautiful because bright."

Ruskin says: "All one's life is a music if one touches the notes rightly and in time—but there must be no hurry." The story of the creation—six days labor and then *rest*—is a rebuke to the ceaseless heart-breaking pace of the average American. "You wear too much expression on your faces," said Dr. Clouston, a Scottish medical man, in speaking of Americans. "You are living like an army with all its reserves engaged in action. The duller countenances of the British population betoken a better scheme of life. They suggest stores of reserved nervous force to fall back upon, if any occasion should arise that requires it. This inexcitability, this presence at all times of power not used, I regard as the great safeguard of our British people. The other thing in you gives me a sense of insecurity, and you ought somehow to tone yourselves down. You really do carry too much expression, you take too intensely the trivial moments of life."

A mental attitude of calmness may be brought about by realizing the positive injury that is being done by contracted muscles. The mind should be emptied as far as possible of all disturbing thoughts, such as fear, worry, resentment, and anger. The reader may experiment at once by allowing the hand and arm to relax at the side or wherever it may fall. It should be made to feel as heavy as lead—not held down, but down because of its own weight. This "limp" attitude may be gradually extended to other parts of the body, until finally one may lie down and give oneself up completely to the comfortable feeling of repose and relaxation. A wonderful power and facility will come after a little practise.

RELAXATION EXERCISES

The following exercises may be practised for a few minutes daily:

1. Lie down. Make yourself limp and passive. Lightly toss one hand in the air, and allow it to drop of its own weight where it will. Repeat with the other hand. Then do the same with the legs, one at a time. Raise the head and let it drop. Roll the body over from side to side, allowing the arms, legs and head to fall where they like. In a few minutes the entire body should become thoroughly relaxed. It will greatly assist at first to cultivate a lazy or drowsy feeling in doing this exercise.

2. Now rest the mind along with your relaxed body, still lying down. Learn to "let go" all mental strain. Gently direct the mind in turn to the feet, arms, head, back, throat, stomach, knees, abdomen, heart, and tongue. Do this very slowly and patiently. Then combine with this exercise thoughts of health, and ease, and power. You

will be surprised at the feeling of rest and renewed energy that you will shortly experience.

3. Stand erect. Droop the head and shoulders. Shake the body thoroughly, while relaxed as much as possible, allowing the arms to go loosely where they may.

4. Support yourself on one foot by holding a chair. Vigorously shake the other leg. Reverse.

5. While standing, relax both arms and shake them vigorously. Repeat with the hands alone.

6. Sit in a chair. Relax the arms, head and waist. Gradually let go of the entire body. Make the feet to rest heavily on the floor. Assume a feeling of drowsiness.

7. Walk around the room, with body, head, and arms relaxed, in imitation of intoxication.

8. Drop gently forward to one knee, then to the other, then to one hand, and to the other, then let the whole body drop to the floor. These movements should be done slowly, without jarring of any kind.

9. Hold the arm at the side, bent at the elbow, and rapidly vibrate it up and down so as to shake the head and upper body. Then relax thoroughly. Repeat with the other arm.

10. With arm extended straight out at side, palm of the hand down, rapidly vibrate the arm up and down. Then relax and repeat with the other arm.

11. Sit as perfectly still as you can, relaxed, for two minutes.

12. Stand as still as possible for one minute.

13. Stand on tiptoe, reach as high as you can with your hands, tense the whole body until it trembles, then slowly relax into a sitting position on a chair. Repeat several times, each time relaxing a little longer.

14. While walking, inhale slowly and rhythmically, mentally counting ten to ten steps, then slowly and evenly exhale in the same way. Avoid jerking the breaths. They should be slow and even.

15. Inhale deeply, filling out the chest and abdomen to their fullest capacity, then gently and slowly relax as you completely exhale.

CHAPTER XV

WORLD'S GREAT SERMONS THAT DEVELOP POWER[1]

In the following list of sermons will be found many of the great masterpieces of the pulpit. The subjects treated are of vital importance to any man seeking to develop power of character. Their aim for the most part is to solve the perplexing problems of right living. The list is suggestive rather than exhaustive. The sermons are recommended to the reader for their unusual power and inspiration.

VOLUME I

PREFACE . . . . GRENVILLE KLEISER
INTRODUCTION . . . . LEWIS O. BRASTOW
The Creation of the World . . . . BASIL
Excessive Grief at the Death of Friends . . CHRYSOSTOM
The Recovery of Sight by the Blind . . . . AUGUSTINE
Christ's Real Body Not in the Eucharist . . . . WYCLIF
The Ascension of Christ . . . . SAVONAROLA
The Method and Fruits of Justification . . . . LUTHER
On Christian Love . . . . LATIMER
The Safety of the Virtuous . . . . MELANCHTHON
The First Temptation of Christ . . . . KNOX
Enduring Persecution for Christ . . . . CALVIN

---

[1] *The World's Great Sermons*, compiled by Grenville Kleiser, are published in ten pocket-size volumes by Funk & Wagnalls Company.

VOLUME II

The Activity of Faith, or Abraham's Imitators . . HOOKER
Christ's Advent to Judgment . . . . . . JEREMY TAYLOR
Making Light of Christ and Salvation . . . . . . BAXTER
Funeral Sermon on the Death of the Grande Condé . BOSSUET
The Heavenly Footman . . . . BUNYAN
The Reasonableness of a Resurrection . . . . TILLOTSON
The Redeemer's Tears Over Lost Souls . . . . . . HOWE
The Passion of Christ . . . . BOURDALOUE
The Saints Converse with God . . . . FENELON
The Image of God in Man . . . . SOUTH

VOLUME III

The Small Number of the Elect . . . . . . MASSILLON
Paul Before Felix and Drusilla . . . . SAURIN
Spiritual Light . . . . EDWARDS
God's Love to Fallen Man . . . . JOHN WESLEY
The Method of Grace . . . . WHITEFIELD
The Hour and the Event of All Time . . . . . . BLAIR
The Sovereignty of God . . . . TIMOTHY DWIGHT
Marks of Love to God . . . . ROBERT HALL
The Fall and Recovery of Man . . . . EVANS
Christ's Resurrection an Image of Our New Life
SCHLEIERMACHER
Messiah's Throne . . . . JOHN M. MASON

VOLUME IV

The Government of God Desirable . . . LYMAN BEECHER
The Character of Christ . . . . CHANNING
The Expulsive Power of a New Affection . . . CHALMERS
The Missionary Cause . . . . . . ALEXANDER CAMPBELL
Preparation for Consulting the Oracles of God EDWARD IRVING
Alive in God . . . . THOMAS ARNOLD
A Day in the Life of Jesus of Nazareth . . . . WAYLAND

VOLUME IV—CONTINUED

The Mysteries of Christianity . . . . VINET
The Heavenly Inheritance . . . . SUMMERFIELD
God's Will the End of Life . . . . J. H. NEWMAN
Unconscious Influence . . . . BUSHNELL

VOLUME V

The New Heart . . . . GUTHRIE
The Valley of Dry Bones . . . . MAURICE
Parting Words . . . . MARTINEAU
The Triumph of the Church . . . . MANNING
The Prominence of Atonement . . . . EDWARDS A. PARK
The Resurrection of Our Lord . . . . SIMPSON
The Transient and Permanent in Christianity THEODORE PARKER
The True Christian Ministry . . . . MACLEOD
The Reversal of Human Judgment . . . . MOZLEY

VOLUME VI

Immortality . . . . H. W. BEECHER
Nicodemus: The Seeker After Religion . . . . . CHAPIN
In Memoriam—Thomas Carlyle . . . . STANLEY
God Calling to Man . . . . VAUGHAN
Christian Victory . . . . NEWMAN HALL
The Loneliness of Christ . . . . ROBERTSON
Eternal Atonement . . . . HITCHCOCK
The Shaking of the Heavens and the Earth . . . KINGSLEY
Religion in Common Life . . . . CAIRD
The Permanent Motive in Missionary Work . . . . STORRS
Zeal in the Cause of Christ . . . . PUNSHON

VOLUME VII

The Colonization of the Desert . . . . HALE
The Miraculous Stilling of the Storm . . . . MAGEE
The Wonderful Testimonies . . . . SEISS
The Pattern of Service . . . . MACLAREN

VOLUME VII—CONTINUED

VOLUME VIII

VOLUME IX

VOLUME IX—CONTINUED

VOLUME X

CHAPTER XVI

BOOKS THAT HELP TO DEVELOP POWER

This list is prepared in response to numerous requests for names of books that develop personal power.

ALDEN, R. M. . . . . The Art of Debate
ALLEN, James . . . . As a Man Thinketh
ALLEN, James . . . . Entering the Kingdom
ARISTOTLE . . . . Rhetoric and Poetics
ARMITAGE, T. . . . . Preaching
AYRES, A . . . . The Essentials of Elocution

BAKER, G. P. . . . . . . The Principles of Argumentation
BANKS, L. A. . . . . Anecdotes and Morals
BANKS, L. A. . . . . . Spurgeon's Illustrative Anecdotes
BANKS, L. A. . . . . Windows for Sermons
BAUTIN, M. . . . . . . The Art of Extempore Speaking
BEECHER, H. W. . . . . . . Yale Lectures on Preaching
BELL, D. G. . . . . Bell's Standard Elocutionist
BELL, D. G. . . . . The Mechanism of Speech
BERTRAM, R. A.
A Homiletic Cyclopedia of Illustrations in Morals
BLACKIE, J. S. . . . . Self-Culture
BRASTOW, L. O. . . . . . Representative Modern Preachers
BROADUS, J. A. . . . . Preparation and Delivery of Sermons
BRYAN, W. J. . . . . The World's Famous Orations

CHRISTLIEB, T. . . . . Lectures on Preaching
CICERO . . . . On Oratory and Orators
CORSON, Hiram . . . . . The Voice and Spiritual Education

DALE, R. W. . . . . Yale Lectures on Preaching
DAY, H. N. . . . . The Art of Discourse
DELAUMOSNE, Abbe M. . . . . The Art of Oratory
DRESSER, H. W. . . . . The Power of Silence

ESENWEIN, J. B. . . . How to Attract and Hold an Audience

FARRAR, F. W. . . . . The Life of Christ
FENELON, Francis . . . Dialogues Concerning Eloquence
FERNALD, J. C. English Synonyms, Antonyms, and Prepositions
FERNALD, J. C. . . . . . . Connectives of English Speech
FERNALD, J. C. . . . . Scientific Side-Lights
FUNK, I. K. . . . . The Next Step in Evolution

GENUNG, J. F. . . . . . . Practical Elements in Rhetoric
GORDON, G. A. . . . . Through Man to God
GUTHRIE, Thomas . . . . Gems of Illustration

HEATH, L. M. . . . . Platform Pearls
HIGGINSON, T. W. . . . Hints on Writing and Speech-Making
HOLYOAKE, G. J. . . . . . . Public Speaking and Debate
HOOD, E. P. . . . . The Throne of Eloquence
HOPPIN, J. M. . . . . Homiletics
HOYT, A. S. . . . . The Work of Preaching
HOYT, J. K. . . . . The Cyclopedia of Practical Quotations

INGALESE, R. . . . . . . History and Power of the Mind

JAMES, W. . . . . Talks to Teachers on Psychology
JEBB, R. C. . . . . The Attic Orators
JEFFERSON, C. E. . . . . Quiet Hints for Growing Preachers

KELLY, Thomas . . . Pulpit Trees and Homiletic Undergrowth
KENNARD, J. S. . . . . . . Psychic Power in Preaching
KLEISER, Grenville . . . . How to Speak in Public
KLEISER, Grenville . . . . The World's Great Sermons
KUYPER, A. . . . . The Work of the Holy Spirit

Lewis, E. H. . . . Specimens of the Forms of Discourse
Little, C. E. . . . . . . Biblical Lights and Side-Lights
Little, C. E. . . . . Historical Lights
Loisette, A. . . . . Assimilative Memory

McIlvaine, J. H. . . . . Elocution
Mahaffy, J. P. . . . Principles of the Art of Conversation
Meyers, F. B. . . . . Hints for Lay Preachers
Momerie,, A. W. . . . . Preaching and Hearing
Monks, G. . . . . Preacher's Guide

Newman, J. P. . . . . Idea of a University

O'Connor, J. V. . . . . Hints on Preaching

Patterson, C. B. . . . . Measure of a Man
Phelps, Austin . . . . English Style in Public Discourse
Phelps, Austin . . . . The Theory of Preaching
Pierson, A. T. . . . . . Seed Thoughts for Public Speakers
Piner, H. L. . . . . Builders of the Beautiful
Pinkley, V. A. . . . Essentials of Elocution and Oratory
Pittenger, William . . . . Oratory Sacred and Secular

Quintilian . . . . Institutes of Oratory

Raymond, G. L. . . . . The Orator's Manual
Raymond, G. L. . . . . . . The Psychology of Inspiration
Ringwalt, R. C. . . . . Modern American Oratory
Robinson, E. G. . . . . . . Yale Lectures on Preaching
Robinson, W. C. . . . . Forensic Oratory
Russel, W. . . . . Pulpit Elocution

Schenck, F. S. . . . . Modern Practical Theology
Schofield, A. T. . . . . The Springs of Character
Sewart, T. . . . . Don't Worry
Sewart, T. . . . . Spiritual Knowing
Shairp, J. C. Culture and Religion in Some of Their Relations

SHEDD, W. G. T. . . . . Treatise on Homiletics
SHEPPARD, N. . . . . Before an Audience
SIMPSON, M. . . . . Lectures on Preaching
SPENCE, Exell and Neil . . . . Thirty Thousand Thoughts
SPENCER, Herbert . . . . Philosophy of Style
SPURGEON, C. H. . . . . Art of Illustration
STORRS, R. S. . . . . Preaching Without Notes

TAYLOR, W. . . . . Model Preacher
THWING, E. P. . . . Drill Book in Vocal Culture and Gestures
TRINE, R. W. . . . . In Tune with the Infinite
TUCKER, W. J. . . Making and Unmaking of the Preacher

VIZETELLY, F. H. . . . . . A Desk-Book of Errors in English

WATSON, John . . . . The Cure of Souls
WEBSTER, Daniel . . . . Orations
WIDE, Anders . . . . Home Gymnastics
WILLARD, F. E. . . . . How to Win
WILSON, F. B. . . . . Paths to Power

PART II

SELECTIONS FOR PRACTISE

SELECTIONS FOR STUDY AND PRACTISE

PUBLIC OPINION

BY WENDELL PHILLIPS

The age of bullets is over. The age of men armed in mail is over. The age of thrones has gone by. The age of thinking men has come. The age of the masses has come.

What I want to impress you with is the great weight that is attached to the opinion of everything that can call itself a man. Give me anything that walks erect and can read, and he shall count one in the millions of the Lord's sacramental host which is yet to come up and trample all oppression in the dust. The weeds poured forth in nature's lavish luxuriance—give them but time, and their tiny roots shall rend asunder the foundations of palaces and crumble the pyramids to the earth.

We may be weeds in comparison with these marked men; but in the lavish luxuriance of that nature which has at least allowed us to be thinking, reading men, I learn, Webster being my witness, that there is no throne potent enough to stand against us. It is morbid enthusiasm this that I have. Grant it. But they tell us that this heart of mine, which beats unintermittently in the bosom, if its force could be directed against a granite pillar, would wear it to dust in the course of a man's life.

There is nothing stronger than human prejudice. A crazy sentimentalism like that of Peter the Hermit hurled half of Europe upon Asia, and changed the destinies of kingdoms. We may be crazy. Would to God He would make us all crazy enough to forget for one moment the cold deductions of intellect, and let these hearts of ours beat, beat, beat, under the promptings of a common humanity!

They have put wickedness into the statute-book, and its destruction is just as certain as if they had gunpowder under the capitol. That is my faith. That it is which turns my eye from the ten thousand newspapers, from the forty thousand pulpits, from the millions of Whigs, from the millions of Democrats, from the might of sect, from the marble government, from the iron army, from the navy riding at anchor, from all that we are accustomed to deem great and potent—turns it back to the simplest child or woman, to the first murmured protest that is heard against bad laws. I recognize in it the great future, the first rumblings of that volcano destined to overthrow these mighty preparations, and bury in the hot lava of its full excitement all this laughing prosperity which now rests so secure on its side.

THE LIGHT OF KNOWLEDGE

BY ELIHU BURRITT

Knowledge can not be stolen from you, it can not be bought or sold. You may be poor, and the sheriff may come into your house and sell your furniture at auction, or drive away your cow or take your lamb, and leave you homeless and penniless; but he can not lay the law's hand upon the jewelry of your mind. This can not be taken for debt; neither can you give it away, tho you give enough of it to fill a million minds.

I will tell you what such giving is like. Suppose, now, that there were no sun nor stars in the heavens, nor anything that shone in the black brow of night; and suppose that a lighted lamp were put into your hand, which should burn, wasteless and clear, amid all the tempests that should brood upon this lower world. Suppose, next, that there were a thousand millions of human beings on the earth with you, each holding in his hand an unlighted lamp filled with the same oil as yours, and capable of giving as much light. Suppose these millions should come one by one to you, and light each his lamp by yours; would they rob you of any light? Would less of it shine on your own path? Would your lamp burn more dimly for lighting a thousand millions?

Thus it is, young friends. In getting rich in the things which perish with the using, men have often obeyed to the letter that first commandment of selfishness: "Keep what you can get, and get what you can." In filling your minds with the wealth of knowledge, you must reverse this rule and obey this law: "Keep what you give, and give what you can."

The fountain of knowledge is filled by its outlets, not by its inlets. You can learn nothing which you do not teach; you can acquire nothing of intellectual wealth except by giving. In the illustration of the lamps which I have given you, was not the light of the thousands of millions which were lighted at yours as much your light as if it all came from your solitary lamp? Did you not dispel darkness by giving away light?

Remember this parable. And, whenever you fall in with an unlighted mind in your walk of life, drop a kind and glowing thought upon it from yours, and set it a burning in the world with a light that shall shine in some dark place to beam on the benighted.

PAUL BEFORE AGRIPPA

ACTS XXVI

Then Agrippa said unto Paul, Thou art permitted to speak for thyself. Then Paul stretched forth the hand, and answered for himself:

I think myself happy, King Agrippa, because I shall answer for myself this day before thee touching all the things whereof I am accused of the Jews: especially because I know thee to be expert in all customs and questions which are among the Jews: wherefore I beseech thee to hear me patiently.

My manner of life from my youth, which was at the first among mine own nation at Jerusalem, know all the Jews; which knew me from the beginning, if they would testify, that after the most straitest sect of our religion I lived a Pharisee. And now I stand and am judged for the hope of the promise made of God unto our fathers: unto which promise our twelve tribes, instantly serving God day and night, hope to come. For which hope's sake, King Agrippa, I am accused of the Jews.

Why should it be thought a thing incredible with you, that God should raise the dead? I verily thought with myself, that I ought to do many things contrary to the name of Jesus of Nazareth. Which thing I also did in Jerusalem: and many of the saints did I shut up in prison, having received authority from the chief priests; and when they were put to death, I gave my voice against them. And I punished them oft in every synagog, and compelled them to blaspheme; and being exceedingly mad against them, I persecuted them even unto strange cities. Whereupon as I went to Damascus with authority and commission from the chief priests, at midday, O king, I saw in the way a light from heaven, above the brightness of the sun, shining round about me and them which journeyed with me. And when we were all fallen to the earth, I heard a voice speaking unto me, and saying in the Hebrew tongue, Saul, Saul, why persecutest thou me? it is hard for thee to kick against the pricks.

And I said, Who art thou, Lord? And he said, I am Jesus whom thou persecutest. But rise, and stand upon thy feet: for I have appeared unto thee for this purpose, to make thee a minister and a witness both of these things which thou hast seen, and of those things in the which I will appear unto thee; delivering thee from the people, and from the Gentiles, unto whom now I send thee, to open their eyes, and to turn them from darkness to light, and from the power of Satan unto God, that they may receive forgiveness of sins, and inheritance among them which are sanctified by faith that is in me.

Whereupon, O King Agrippa, I was not disobedient unto the heavenly vision: but showed first unto them of Damascus, and at Jerusalem, and throughout all the coasts of Judea, and then to the Gentiles, that they should repent and turn to God, and do works meet for repentance. For these causes the Jews caught me in the temple, and went about to kill me. Having therefore obtained help of God, I continue unto this day, witnessing both to small and great, saying none other things than those which the prophets and Moses did say should come: That Christ should suffer, and that he should be the first that should rise from the dead, and should show light unto the people, and to the Gentiles.

And as he thus spake for himself, Festus said with a loud voice, Paul, thou art beside thyself; much learning doth make thee mad. But he said, I am not mad, most noble Festus; but speak forth the words of truth, before soberness. For the king knoweth of these things, before whom also I speak freely: for I am persuaded that none of these things are hidden from him; for this thing was not done in a corner. King Agrippa, believest thou the prophets? I know that thou believest. Then Agrippa said unto Paul, Almost thou persuadest me to be a Christian.

And Paul said, I would to God that not only thou, but also all that hear me this day, were both almost, and altogether such as I am, except these bonds. And when he had thus spoken, the king rose up, and the governor, and Bernice, and they that sat with them: and when they were gone aside, they talked between themselves, saying, This man doeth nothing worthy of death or of bonds. Then said Agrippa unto Festus, this man might have been set at liberty, if he had not appealed unto Cæsar.

THE FIGHT WITH APOLLYON

FROM JOHN BUNYAN'S "THE PILGRIM'S PROGRESS"

Now Christian bethought himself of setting forward, and they were willing he should. But first, said they, let us go again into the armory. So they did; and when he came there, they harnessed him from head to foot with what was of proof, lest perhaps he should meet with assaults in the way. He, being therefore thus accoutered, walked out with his friends to the gate; and there he asked the Porter if he saw any pilgrim pass by. Then the Porter answered, Yes.

Chr. Pray did you know him?

Port. I asked his name and he told me it was Faithful.

Oh, said Christian, I know him: he is my townsman, my near neighbor; he comes from the place where I was born: how far do you think he may be before?

Port. He is got by this time below the hill.

Well, said Christian, good Porter, the Lord be with thee, and all to all thy blessings much increase, for the kindness that thou hast showed to me.

Then he began to go forward; but Discretion, Piety, Charity, and Prudence would accompany him down to the foot of the hill. So they went on together, reiterating their former discourses, till they came to go down the hill. Then said Christian, As it was *difficult* coming up, so, so far as I can see, it is *dangerous* going down. Yes, said Prudence, so it is; for it is a hard matter for a man to go down into the valley of Humiliation, as thou art now, and to catch no slip by the way; therefore, said they, are we come out to accompany thee down the hill. So he began to go down, but very warily; yet he caught a slip or two.

Then I saw in my dream, that these good companions, when Christian was gone down to the bottom of the hill, gave him a loaf of bread, a bottle of wine, and a cluster of raisins; and then he went his way.

But now, in this Valley of Humiliation, poor Christian was hard put to it; for he had gone but a little way before he espied a foul fiend coming over the field to meet him: his name is Apollyon. Then did Christian begin to be afraid, and to cast in his mind whether to go back or stand his ground. But he considered again, that he had no armor for his back, and therefore thought that to turn the back to him might give him greater advantage with ease to pierce him with his darts; therefore he resolved to venture and stand his ground: for, thought he, had I no more in mine eye than the saving of my life, it would be the very best way to stand.

So he went on, and Apollyon met him. Now the monster was hideous to behold: he was clothed with scales like a fish (and they are his pride); he had wings like a dragon, and feet like a bear, and out of his belly came fire and smoke; and his mouth was as the mouth of a lion. When he was come up to Christian, he beheld him with a disdainful countenance, and thus began to question with him.

Apol. Whence come you? and whither are you bound?

Chr. I am come from the City of Destruction, which is the place of all evil, and am going to the City of Zion.

Apol. By this I perceive that thou art one of my subjects; for all that country is mine, and I am the prince and god of it. How is it then that thou hast run away from thy king? Were it not for that I hope thou mayst do me more service, I would strike thee now at one blow to the ground.

Chr. I was indeed born in your dominions; but your service was hard, and your wages such as a man could not live on; "for the wages of sin is death;" therefore when I was come to years, I did as other considerate persons do, look out, if perhaps I might mend myself.

Apol. There is no prince that will thus lightly lose his subjects, neither will I as yet lose thee; but, since thou complainest of thy service and wages, be content to go back; what our country will afford, I do here promise to give thee.

Chr. But I have let myself to another, even to the King of princes; and how can I with fairness go back with thee?

Apol. Thou hast done in this according to the proverb, "*Changed a bad for a worse*": but it is ordinary for those that have profest themselves his servants, after a while to give him the slip, and return again to me. Do thou so too, and all shall be well.

Chr. I have given him my faith, and sworn my allegiance to him: how then can I go back from this, and not be hanged as a traitor?

Apol. Thou didst the same to me; and yet I am willing to pass by all, if now thou wilt yet turn again and go back.

Chr. What I promised thee was in my nonage; and besides, I count that the Prince under whose banner I now stand, is able to absolve me; yea, and to pardon also what I did as to my compliance with thee: and, besides, O thou destroying Apollyon, to speak truth, I like his service, his wages, his servants, his government, his company, and country, better than thine; therefore leave off to persuade me further; I am his servant and I will follow him.

Apol. Consider again when thou art in cold blood, what thou art likely to meet with in the way that thou goest. Thou knowest that, for the most part, his servants come to an ill end, because they are transgressors against me and my ways. How many of them have been put to shameful deaths! And besides, thou countest his service better than mine; whereas he never came yet from the place where he is, to deliver any that served him out of their hands: but, as for me, how many times, as all the world very well knows, have I delivered, either by power or fraud, those that have faithfully served me, from him and his, tho taken by them! And so I will deliver thee.

Chr. His forbearing at present to deliver them is on purpose to try their love, whether they will cleave to him to the end: and, as for the ill end thou sayst they come to, that is most glorious in their account; for, for present deliverance, they do not much expect it; for they stay for their glory, and then they shall have it, when their Prince comes in his and the glory of the angels.

Apol. Thou hast already been unfaithful in thy service to him; and how dost thou think to receive wages of him?

Chr. Wherein, O Apollyon, have I been unfaithful to him?

Apol. Thou didst faint at first setting out, when thou wast almost choked in the Gulf of Despond; thou didst attempt wrong ways to be rid of thy burden, whereas thou shouldst have stayed till thy Prince had taken it off: thou didst sinfully sleep, and lose thy choice things: thou wast almost persuaded to go back at the sight of the lions: and when thou talkest of thy journey, and of what thou hast seen and heard, thou art inwardly desirous of vainglory in all that thou sayest or doest.

Chr. All this is true and much more which thou hast left out: but the Prince, whom I serve and honor, is merciful and ready to forgive. But besides, these infirmities possest me in thy country: for there I sucked them in, and I have groaned under them, being sorry for them, and have obtained pardon of my Prince.

Then Apollyon broke out into a grievous rage, saying,

I am an enemy to this Prince; I hate his person, his laws, and people: I am come out on purpose to withstand thee.

Chr. Apollyon, beware what you do; for I am in the King's highway, the way of holiness; therefore take heed to yourself.

Then Apollyon straddled quite over the whole breadth of the way, and said, I am void of fear in this matter; prepare thyself to die; for I swear by my infernal den, that thou shalt go no farther; here will I spill thy soul.

And with that he threw a flaming dart at his breast; but Christian had a shield in his hand, with which he caught it, and so prevented the danger of that.

Then did Christian draw; for he saw it was time to bestir him; and Apollyon as fast made at him, throwing darts as thick as hail; by the which, notwithstanding all that Christian could do to avoid it, Apollyon wounded him in his head, his hand, and foot. This made Christian give a little back: Apollyon, therefore, followed his work amain, and Christian again took courage and resisted as manfully as he could. This sore combat lasted for above half a day, even till Christian was almost quite spent; for you must know that Christian, by reason of his wounds, must needs grow weaker and weaker.

Then Apollyon, espying his opportunity, began to gather up close to Christian, and wrestling with him, gave him a dreadful fall; and with that Christian's sword flew out of his hand. Then said Apollyon, I am sure of thee now: and with that he had almost prest him to death; so that Christian began to despair of life. But, as God would have it, while Apollyon was fetching his last blow, thereby to make a full end of this good man, Christian nimbly reached out his hand for his sword, and caught it, saying,

"Rejoice not against me, O mine enemy! when I fall, I shall arise," and with that he gave a deadly thrust, which made him give back as one that had received his mortal wound. Christian, perceiving that, made at him again, saying, "Nay, in all these things we are more than conquerors, through Him that loved us." And, with that, Apollyon, spread forth his dragon's wings and sped him away that Christian saw him no more.

In this combat no man can imagine, unless he had seen and heard, as I did, what yelling and hideous roaring Apollyon made all the time of the fight; he spake like a dragon: and on the other side, what sighs and groans burst from Christian's heart. I never saw him all the while give so much as one pleasant look, till he perceived that he had wounded Apollyon with his two-edged sword; then indeed he did smile and look upward! But it was the dreadfulest fight that ever I saw.

So when the battle was over, Christian said, I will here give thanks to Him that hath delivered me out of the mouth of the lion, to Him that did help me against Apollyon. And so he did, saying,

"Great Beelzebub, the captain of this fiend,
Design'd my ruin: therefore to this end
He sent him harness'd out, and he with rage
That hellish was, did fiercely me engage.
But blessed Michael helped me and I,
By dint of sword, did quickly make him fly:
Therefore to Him let me give lasting praise
And thanks, and bless His holy name always."

Then there came to him a hand with some of the leaves of the tree of life; the which Christian took, and applied to the wounds that he had received in the battle, and was healed immediately. He also sat down in that place to eat bread, and to drink of the bottle that was given to him a little before: so, being refreshened, he addrest himself to his journey, with his sword drawn in his hand; for, he said, I know not but some other enemy may be at hand. But he met with no other affront from Apollyon quite through this valley.

THE FREEDOM OF A FLY

BY JOHN RUSKIN

I believe we can nowhere find a better type of a perfectly free creature than in the common house-fly. Nor free only, but brave: and irreverent to a degree which I think no human republican could by any philosophy exalt himself to do. There is no courtesy in him; he does not care whether it is a king or a clown whom he teases; and in every step of his swift mechanical march, and in every pause of his resolute observation, there is one and the same expression of perfect egotism, perfect independence and self-confidence, and conviction of the world's having been made for flies.

Strike at him with your hand; and to him the mechanical fact and external aspect of the matter is, what to you it would be if an acre of red clay, ten feet thick, tore itself up from the ground in one massive field, hovered over you in the air for a second, and came crashing down with an aim. That is the external aspect of it; the inner aspect, to his fly's mind, is of quite natural and unimportant occurrence—one of the momentary conditions of his active life. He steps out of the way of your hand, and alights on the back of it. You can not terrify him nor govern him nor persuade him nor convince him. He has his own positive opinion on all matters; not an unwise one, usually, for his own ends; and will ask no advice of yours.

He has no work to do—no tyrannical instinct to obey. The earthworm has his digging; the bee, her gathering and building; the spider, her cunning network; the ant, her treasury and accounts. All these are comparative slaves, or people of vulgar business. But your fly, free in the air, free in the chamber—a black incarnation of caprice—wandering, investigating, flitting, flirting, feasting at his will, with rich variety of choice in feast, from the heaped sweets in the grocer's window to those of the butcher's back-yard, and from the galled place on your cab-horse's back to the brown spot on the road, from which, as the hoof disturbs him, he rises with angry, republican buzz—what freedom is like his?

DOCTOR MARIGOLD

BY CHARLES DICKENS

I am a Cheap Jack, and my own father's name was Willum Marigold. It was in his lifetime supposed by some that his name was William, but my own father always consistently said, No, it was Willum. On which point I content myself with looking at the argument this way: If a man is not allowed to know his own name in a free country, how much is he allowed to know in a land of slavery?

I was born on the Queen's highway, but it was the King's at that time. A doctor was fetched to my own mother by my own father, when it took place on a common; and in consequence of his being a very kind gentleman, and accepting no fee but a tea-tray, I was named Doctor, out of gratitude and compliment to him. There you have me. Doctor Marigold.

The doctor having accepted a tea-tray, you'll guess that my father was a Cheap Jack before me. You are right. He was. And my father was a lovely one in his time at the Cheap Jack work. Now I'll tell you what. I mean to go down into my grave declaring that, of all the callings ill-used in Great Britain, the Cheap Jack calling is the worst used. Why ain't we a profession? Why ain't we endowed with privileges? Why are we forced to take out a hawker's license, when no such thing is expected of the political hawkers? Where's the difference betwixt us? Except that we are Cheap Jacks and they are Dear Jacks, I don't see any difference but what's in our favor.

For look here! Say it's election-time. I am on the footboard of my cart in the market-place on a Saturday night. I put up a general miscellaneous lot. I say: "Now here, my free and independent voters, I'm going to give you such a chance as you never had in all your born days, nor yet the days preceding. Now I'll show you what I am a going to do with you. Here's a pair of razors that'll shave you closer than the Board of Guardians; here's a flat-iron worth its weight in gold; here's a frying-pan artificially flavored with essence of beefsteaks to that degree that you've only got for the rest of your lives to fry bread and dripping in it, and there you are complete with animal food; here's a genuine chronometer watch in such a solid silver case that you may knock at the door with it when you come home late from a social meeting, and rouse your wife and family and save up your knocker for the postman; and here's half a dozen dinner-plates that you may play the cymbals with to charm the baby when it's fractious. Stop. I'll throw you in another article, and I'll give you that, and it's a rolling-pin, and if the baby can only get it well into its mouth when its teeth are coming, and rub the gums once with it, they'll come through double, in a fit of laughter equal to be tickled. Stop again! I'll throw you in another article, because I don't like the looks of you, for you haven't the appearance of buyers unless I lose by you, and because I'd rather lose than not take money to-night, and that article's a looking-glass in which you may see how ugly you look when you don't bid. What do you say now? Come! Do you say a pound? Not you, for you haven't got it. Do you say ten shillings? Not you, for you owe more to the tallyman. Well, then, I'll tell you what I'll do with you. I'll heap 'em all on the footboard of the cart—there they are! razors, flat-iron, frying-pan, chronometer watch, dinner-plates, rolling-pin, and looking-glass—take 'em all away for four shillings, and I'll give you sixpence for your trouble!" This is me, the Cheap Jack.

But on Monday morning, in the same market-place, comes the Dear Jack on the hustings—*his* cart—and what does *he* say? "Now, you free and independent voters, I am going to give you such a chance" (he begins just like me) "as you never had in all your born days, and that's the chance of sending myself to Parliament. Now I'll tell you what I am a going to do for you. Here's the interests of this magnificent town promoted above all the rest of the civilized and uncivilized earth. Here's your railways carried, and your neighbors' railways jockeyed. Here's all your sons in the Post Office. Here's Britannia smiling on you. Here's the eyes of Europe on you. Here's uniwersal prosperity for you, repletion of animal food, golden corn-fields, gladsome homesteads, and rounds of applause from your own hearts, all in one lot, and that's myself. Will you take me as I stand? You won't! Well, then, I'll tell you what I'll do with you. Come now! I'll throw you in anything you ask for. There! Church-rates, abolition of church-rates, more malt tax, no malt tax, uniwersal education to the highest mark, or uniwersal ignorance to the lowest, total abolition of flogging in the army, or a dozen for every private once a month all round, Wrongs of Men or Rights of Women—only say which it shall be, take 'em or leave 'em, and I'm of your opinion altogether, and the lot's your own on your own terms. There! You won't take it yet? Well, then, I'll tell you what I'll do with you. Come! You *are* such free and independent woters, and I *am* so proud of you—you *are* such a noble and enlightened constituency, and I *am* so ambitious of the honor and dignity of being your member, which is by far the highest level to which the wings of the human mind can soar—that I'll tell you what I'll do with you. I'll throw you in all public-houses in your magnificent town for nothing. Will that content you? It won't? You won't take the lot yet? Well, then, before I put the horse in and drive away, and make the offer to the next most magnificent town that can be discovered, I'll tell you what I'll do. Take the lot, and I'll drop two thousand pound in the streets of your magnificent town for them to pick up that can. Not enough? Now look here. This is the very furthest that I'm a going to. I'll make it two thousand five hundred. And still you won't? Here, missis! Put the horse—No, stop half a moment, I shouldn't like to turn my back upon you, neither, for a trifle, I'll make it two thousand seven hundred and fifty pound. There! Take the lot on your own terms, and I'll count out two thousand seven hundred and fifty pound on the footboard of the cart, to be dropt in the streets of your magnificent town for them to pick up that can. What do you say? Come now! You won't do better, and you may do worse. You take it? Hooray! Sold again, and got the seat!"

THOUGHTS IN WESTMINSTER ABBEY

BY JOSEPH ADDISON

When I am in a serious humor, I very often walk by myself in Westminster Abbey; where the gloominess of the place, and the use to which it is applied, with the solemnity of the building, and the condition of the people who lie in it, are apt to fill the mind with a kind of melancholy, or rather thoughtfulness, that is not disagreeable. I yesterday passed a whole afternoon in the churchyard, the cloisters, and the church, amusing myself with the tombstone and inscriptions that I met with in those several regions of the dead. Most of them recorded nothing else of the buried person, but that he was born upon one day, and died upon another: the whole history of his life being comprehended in those two circumstances, that are common to all mankind. I could not but look upon these registers of existence, whether of brass or marble, as a kind of satire upon the departed persons; who had left no other memorial but that they were born and that they died. They put me in mind of several persons mentioned in the battles of heroic poems, who have sounding names given them, for no other reason but that they may be killed, and are celebrated for nothing but being knocked on the head. The life of these men is finely described in Holy Writ by "the path of an arrow," which is immediately closed up and lost.

Upon my going into the church, I entertained myself with the digging of a grave; and saw in every shovelful of it that was thrown up, the fragment of a bone or skull intermixt with a kind of fresh moldering earth, that some time or other had a place in the composition of a human body. Upon this I began to consider with myself what innumerable multitudes of people lay confused together under the pavement of that ancient cathedral; how men and women, friends and enemies, priests and soldiers, monks and prebendaries, were crumbled amongst one another, and blended together in the same common mass; how beauty, strength, and youth, with old age, weakness, and deformity, lay undistinguished in the same promiscuous heap of matter.

After having thus surveyed this great magazine of mortality, as it were in the lump, I examined it more particularly by the accounts which I found on several of the monuments which are raised in every quarter of that ancient fabric. Some of them were covered with such extravagant epitaphs, that, if it were possible for the dead person to be acquainted with them, he would blush at the praises which his friends have bestowed upon him. There are others so excessively modest, that they deliver the character of the person departed in Greek or Hebrew, and by that means are not understood once in a twelvemonth. In the poetical quarter, I found there were poets who had no monuments, and monuments which had no poets. I observed, indeed, that the present war had filled the church with many of these uninhabited monuments, which had been erected to the memory of persons whose bodies were perhaps buried in the plains of Blenheim or in the bosom of the ocean.

I could not but be very much delighted with several modern epitaphs, which are written with great elegance of expression and justness of thought, and therefore do honor to the living as well as to the dead. As a foreigner is very apt to conceive an idea of the ignorance or the politeness of a nation from the turn of their public monuments and inscriptions, they should be submitted to the perusal of men of learning and genius, before they are put in execution. Sir Cloudsly Shovel's monument has very often given me great offense: instead of the brave rough English Admiral, which was the distinguishing character of that plain gallant man, he is represented on his tomb by the figure of a beau, drest in a long periwig, and reposing himself upon velvet cushions under a canopy of state. The inscription is answerable to the monument; for instead of celebrating the many remarkable actions he had performed in the service of his country, it acquaints us only with the manner of his death, in which it was impossible for him to reap any honor. The Dutch, whom we are apt to despise for want of genius, show an infinitely greater taste of antiquity and politeness in their buildings and works of this nature than what we meet with in those of our own country. The monuments of their admirals, which have been erected at the public expense, represent them like themselves; and are adorned with rostral crowns and naval ornaments, with beautiful festoons of sea-weed, shells, and coral.

But to return to our subject. I left the repository of our English kings for the contemplation of another day, when I shall find my mind disposed for so serious an amusement. I know that entertainments of this nature are apt to raise dark and dismal thoughts in timorous minds and gloomy imaginations; but for my own part, tho I am always serious, I do not know what it is to be melancholy; and can therefore take a view of nature in her deep and solemn scenes, with the same pleasure as in her most gay and delightful ones. By this means I can improve myself with those objects which others consider with terror. When I look upon the tombs of the great, every emotion of envy dies in me; when I read the epitaphs of the beautiful, every inordinate desire goes out; when I meet with the grief of parents upon a tombstone, my heart melts with compassion; when I see the tomb of the parents themselves, I consider the vanity of grieving for those whom we must quickly follow; when I see kings lying by those who deposed them, when I consider rival wits placed side by side, or the holy men that divided the world with their contests and disputes, I reflect with sorrow and astonishment on the little competitions, factions, and debates of mankind. When I read the several dates on the tombs, of some that died yesterday, and some six hundred years ago, I consider that great day when we shall all of us be contemporaries, and make our appearance together.

A CHRISTMAS INVITATION

BY CHARLES DICKENS

The door of Scrooge's counting-house was open, that he might keep his eye upon his clerk, who, in a dismal little cell beyond, a sort of tank, was copying letters. Scrooge had a very small fire, but the clerk's fire was so very much smaller that it looked like one coal. But he couldn't replenish it, for Scrooge kept the coal-box in his own room; and, so surely as the clerk came in with the shovel, the master predicted that it would be necessary for them to part. Wherefore the clerk put on his white comforter, and tried to warm himself at the candle; in which effort, not being a man of strong imagination, he failed.

"A merry Christmas, uncle! God save you!" cried a cheerful voice. It was the voice of Scrooge's nephew, who came upon him so quickly that this was the first intimation he had of his approach.

"Bah!" said Scrooge. "Humbug!"

He had so heated himself with rapid walking in the fog and frost, this nephew of Scrooge's, that he was all in a glow; his face was ruddy and handsome; his eyes sparkled, and his breath smoked again.

"Christmas a humbug, uncle!" said Scrooge's nephew, "You don't mean that, I am sure?"

"I do," said Scrooge. "Merry Christmas! What right have you to be merry? What reason have you to be merry? You're poor enough. . . . Out upon merry Christmas! What's Christmas time to you but a time for paying bills without money; a time for finding yourself a year older and not an hour richer; a time for balancing your books, and having every item in 'em through a round dozen of months presented dead against you? If I could work my will," said Scrooge indignantly, "every idiot who goes about with 'Merry Christmas' on his lips should be boiled with his own pudding, and buried with a stake of holly through his heart. He should!"

"Uncle!" pleaded the nephew.

"Nephew!" returned the uncle, sternly, "keep Christmas in your own way, and let me keep it in mine."

"Keep it!" repeated Scrooge's nephew. "But you don't keep it."

"Let me leave it alone, then," said Scrooge. "Much good may it do you! Much good it has ever done you!"

"There are many things from which I might have derived good, by which I have not profited, I dare say," returned the nephew, "Christmas among the rest. But I am sure I have always thought of Christmas time, when it has come round—apart from the veneration due to its sacred name and origin, if anything belonging to it can be apart from that—as a good time; a kind, forgiving, charitable, pleasant time; the only time I know of, in the long calendar of the year, when men and women seem by one consent to open their shut-up hearts freely, and to think of people below them as if they really were fellow passengers to the grave, and not another race of creatures bound on other journeys. And therefore, uncle, tho it has never put a scrap of gold or silver in my pocket, I believe that it *has* done me good, and *will* do me good; and I say, God bless it!"

The clerk in the tank involuntarily applauded. Becoming immediately sensible of the impropriety, he poked the fire, and extinguished the last spark forever.

"Let me hear another sound from *you*," said Scrooge, "and you'll keep your Christmas by losing your situation! You're quite a powerful speaker, sir," he added, turning to his nephew. "I wonder you don't go into Parliament."

"Don't be angry, uncle. Come! Dine with us to-morrow."

Scrooge said that he would see him—Yes, indeed he did. He went the whole length of the expression, and said that he would see him in that extremity first.

"But why?" cried Scrooge's nephew. "Why?"

"Why did you get married?" said Scrooge.

"Because I fell in love."

"Because you fell in love!" growled Scrooge, as if that were the only one thing in the world more ridiculous than a merry Christmas. "Good-afternoon!"

"Nay, uncle, but you never came to see me before that happened. Why give it as a reason for not coming now?"

"Good-afternoon," said Scrooge.

"I want nothing from you; I ask nothing of you; why can not we be friends?"

"Good-afternoon," said Scrooge.

"I am sorry, with all my heart, to find you so resolute. We have never had any quarrel to which I have been a party. But I have made the trial in homage to Christmas, and I'll keep my Christmas humor to the last. So a merry Christmas, uncle!"

"Good-afternoon," said Scrooge.

"And a happy New Year!"

"Good-afternoon," said Scrooge.

His nephew left the room without an angry word, notwithstanding.

THE BATTLE OF TRAFALGAR

BY ROBERT SOUTHEY

It had been part of Nelson's prayer that the British fleet might be distinguished by humanity in the victory which he expected. Setting an example himself, he twice gave orders to cease firing upon the *Redoubtable*, supposing that she had struck, because her great guns were silent; for, as he carried no flag, there was no means of instantly ascertaining the fact. From this ship, which he had twice spared, he received his death. A ball fired from her mizzen-top, which in the then situation of the two vessels was not more than fifteen yards from that part of the deck where he was standing, struck the epaulet on his left shoulder, about a quarter after one, just in the heat of action. He fell upon his face, on the spot which was covered with his poor secretary's blood. Hardy, who was a few steps from him, turning round, saw three men raising him up. "They have done for me at last, Hardy!" said he. "I hope not!" cried Hardy. "Yes," he replied, "my back-bone is shot through!" Yet even now, not for a moment losing his presence of mind, he observed, as they were carrying him down the ladder, that the tiller-ropes, which had been shot away, were not yet replaced, and ordered that new ones should be rove immediately. Then, that he might not be seen by the crew, he took out his handkerchief, and covered his face and his stars. Had he but concealed those badges of honor from the enemy, England perhaps would not have had cause to receive with sorrow the news of the battle of Trafalgar.

The cockpit was crowded with wounded and dying men,

over whose bodies he was with some difficulty conveyed, and laid upon a pallet in the midshipmen's berth. It was soon perceived upon examination that the wound was mortal. This, however, was concealed from all except Captain Hardy, the chaplain, and the medical attendants. He himself being certain, from the sensation in his back and the gush of blood he felt momently within his breast, that no human care could avail him, insisted that the surgeon should leave him, and attend to those to whom he might be useful; "for," said he, "you can do nothing for me." All that could be done was to fan him with paper, and frequently to give him lemonade to alleviate his intense thirst. He was in great pain, and exprest much anxiety for the event of the action, which now began to declare itself. As often as a ship struck, the crew of the *Victory* hurrahed, and at every hurrah a visible expression of joy gleamed in the eyes and marked the countenance of the dying hero. But he became impatient to see Captain Hardy; and as that officer, tho often sent for, could not leave the deck, Nelson feared that some fatal cause prevented him, and repeatedly cried: "Will no one bring Hardy to me? He must be killed! He is surely dead!" An hour and ten minutes elapsed from the time Nelson received his wound before Hardy could come to him. They shook hands in silence; Hardy in vain struggling to suppress the feelings of that most painful and yet sublimest moment. "Well, Hardy," said Nelson, "how goes the day with us?" "Very well," replied Hardy, "ten ships have struck, but five of the van have tacked, and show an intention to bear down upon the *Victory*. I have called two or three of our fresh ships round, and have no doubt of giving them a drubbing." "I hope," said Nelson, "none of our ships have struck?" Hardy answered, "There was no fear of that." Then, and not till then, Nelson spoke of himself. "I am a dead man, Hardy," said he; "I am going fast; it will be all over with me soon. Come nearer to me. Let my dear Lady Hamilton have my hair and all other things belonging to me." Hardy observed that he hoped Mr. Beatty could yet hold out some prospect of life. "Oh, no!" he replied, "it is impossible; my back is shot through. Beatty will tell you so." Captain Hardy then once more shook hands with him, and with a heart almost bursting hastened upon deck.

By this time all feeling below the breast was gone; and Nelson, having made the surgeon ascertain this, said to him: "You know I am gone. I know it. I feel something rising in my breast"—putting his hand on his left side—"which tells me so." And upon Beatty's inquiring whether his pain was very great, he replied, "So great that I wish I were dead. Yet," said he in a lower voice, "one would like to live a little longer too!" And after a few minutes, in the same undertone he added, "What would become of poor Lady Hamilton if she knew my situation?" Next to his country, she occupied his thoughts. Captain Hardy, some fifty minutes after he has left the cockpit, returned, and again taking the hand of his dying friend and commander, congratulated him on having gained a complete victory. How many of the enemy were taken he did not know, as it was impossible to perceive them distinctly, but fourteen or fifteen at least. "That's well!" cried Nelson, "but I bargained for twenty." And then in a stronger voice he said: "Anchor, Hardy, anchor." Hardy upon this hinted that Admiral Collingwood would take upon himself the direction of affairs. "Not while I live,

Hardy," said the dying Nelson, ineffectually endeavoring to raise himself from the bed. "Do you anchor?" His previous order for preparing to anchor had shown how clearly he foresaw the necessity of this. Presently, calling Hardy back, he said to him in a low voice: "Don't throw me overboard!" and he desired that he might be buried by his parents unless it should please the king to order otherwise. Then, reverting to private feelings, "Take care of my dear Lady Hamilton, Hardy; take care of poor Lady Hamilton. Kiss me, Hardy!" said he. Hardy knelt down and kissed his cheek, and Nelson said: "Now I am satisfied. Thank God, I have done my duty!" Hardy stood over him in silence for a moment or two, then knelt again, and kissed his forehead. "Who is that?" said Nelson; and being informed he replied: "God bless you, Hardy!" And Hardy then left him forever.

Nelson now desired to be turned upon his right side, and said: "I wish I had not left the deck, for I shall soon be gone." Death was indeed rapidly approaching. He said to the chaplain: "Doctor, I have *not* been a *great* sinner." And after a short pause: "Remember that I leave Lady Hamilton and my daughter Horatia as a legacy to my country." His articulation now became difficult, but he was distinctly heard to say: "Thank God, I have done my duty!" These words he repeatedly pronounced, and they were the last words which he uttered. He expired at thirty minutes after four, three hours and a quarter after he had received his wound.

THE MAN IN BLACK

BY OLIVER GOLDSMITH

Tho fond of many acquaintances, I desire an intimacy only with a few. The man in black whom I have often mentioned, is one whose friendship I could wish to acquire, because he possesses my esteem. His manners, it is true, are tinctured with some strange inconsistencies; and he may be justly termed a humorist in a nation of humorists. Tho he is generous even to profusion, he affects to be thought a prodigy of parsimony and prudence; tho his conversation be replete with the most sordid and selfish maxims, his heart is dilated with the most unbounded love. I have known him profess himself a man-hater, while his cheek was glowing with compassion; and while his looks were softened into pity, I have heard him use the language of the most unbounded ill-nature. Some affect humanity and tenderness, others boast of having such dispositions from nature; but he is the only man I ever knew who seemed ashamed of his natural benevolence. He takes as much pains to hide his feelings as any hypocrite would to conceal his indifference; but on every unguarded moment the mask drops off and reveals him to the most superficial observer.

In one of our late excursions into the country, happening to discourse upon the provision that was made for the poor in England, he seemed amazed how any of his countrymen could be so foolishly weak as to relieve occasional objects of charity, when the laws had made such ample provision for their support. In every parish-house, says he, the poor are supplied with food, clothes, fire, and a bed to lie on; they want no more, I desire no more myself; yet still they seem discontented. I'm surprized at the inactivity of our magistrates in not taking up such vagrants, who are only a weight upon the industrious; I'm surprized that the people are found to relieve them, when they must be at the same time sensible that it in some measure encourages idleness, extravagance, and imposture. Were I to advise any man for whom I had the least regard, I would caution him by all means not to be imposed upon by their false pretences: let me assure you, sir, they are impostors, every one of them; and rather merit a prison than relief.

He was proceeding in this strain earnestly, to dissuade me from an imprudence of which I am seldom guilty, when an old man who still had about him the remnants of tattered finery, implored our compassion. He assured us that he was no common beggar, but forced into the shameful profession, to support a dying wife and five hungry children. Being prepossest against such falsehoods, his story had not the least influence upon me; but it was quite otherwise with the man in black; I could see it visibly operate upon his countenance and effectually interrupt his harangue. I could easily perceive that his heart burned to relieve the five starving children, but he seemed ashamed to discover his weakness to me. While he thus hesitated between compassion and pride, I pretended to look another way, and he seized this opportunity to give the poor petitioner a piece of silver, bidding him at the same time, in order that I should not hear, go work for his bread, and not tease passengers with such impertinent falsehoods for the future.

As he fancied himself quite unperceived, he continued, as we proceeded, to rail against beggars with as much animosity as before; he threw in some episodes on his own amazing prudence and economy, with his profound skill in discovering impostors; he explained the manner in which he would deal with beggars were he a magistrate, hinted at enlarging some of the prisons for their reception, and told two stories of ladies that were robbed by beggar-men. He was beginning a third to the same purpose, when a sailor with a wooden leg once more crossed our walks, desiring our pity, and blessing our limbs. I was for going on without taking any notice, but my friend looking wistfully upon the poor petitioner, bid me stop, and he would show me with how much ease he could at any time detect an impostor.

He now therefore assumed an air of importance, and in an angry tone began to examine the sailor, demanding in what engagement he was thus disabled and rendered unfit for service. The sailor replied in a tone as angrily as he, that he had been an officer on board a private ship of war, and that he had lost his leg abroad in defense of those who did nothing at home. At this reply all my friend's importance vanished in a moment; he had not a single question more to ask; he now studied what method he should take to relieve him unobserved. He had, however, no easy part to act, as he was obliged to preserve the appearance of ill-nature before me, and yet relieve himself by relieving the sailor. Casting therefore a furious look upon some bundles of chips which the fellow carried in a string at his back, my friend demanded how he sold his matches; but not waiting for a reply, desired in a surly tone to have a shilling's worth. The sailor seemed at first surprized at his demand, but soon recollected himself, and presenting his whole bundle, "Here master," says he, "take all my cargo, and a blessing into the bargain."

It is impossible to describe with what an air of triumph my friend marched off with his new purchase: he assured me that he was firmly of the opinion that those fellows must have stolen their goods, who could thus afford to sell them for half value: he informed me of several different uses to which those chips might be applied; he expatiated largely upon the savings that would result from lighting candles with a match instead of thrusting them into the fire. He averred, that he would as soon have parted with a tooth as his money to those vagabonds, unless for some valuable consideration. I can not tell how long this panegyric upon frugality and matches might have continued, had not his attention been called off by another object more distressful than either of the former. A woman in rags, with one child in her arms and another on her back, was attempting to sing ballads, but with such a mournful voice that it was difficult to determine whether she was singing or crying. A wretch, who in the deepest distress still aimed at good humor, was an object my friend was by no means capable of withstanding: his vivacity and his discourse were instantly interrupted; upon this occasion his very dissimulation had forsaken him. Even in my presence he immediately applied his hands to his pockets, in order to relieve her; but guess his confusion when he found he had already given away all the money he carried about him to former objects. The misery painted in the woman's visage was not half so strongly exprest as the agony in his. He continued to search for some time, but to no purpose, till, at length recollecting himself, with a face of ineffable good-nature, as he had no money, he put into her hands his shilling's worth of matches.

THE GETTYSBURG SPEECH

BY ABRAHAM LINCOLN

Fourscore and seven years ago, our fathers brought forth upon this continent a new nation, conceived in liberty and dedicated to the proposition that all men are created equal. Now we are engaged in a great civil war, testing whether that nation—or any nation so conceived and so dedicated—can long endure.

We are met on a great battle-field of that war. We are met to dedicate a portion of it as the final resting-place of those who have given their lives that that nation might live. It is altogether fitting and proper that we should do this.

But, in a larger sense, we can not dedicate, we can not consecrate, we can not hallow this ground. The brave men, living and dead, who struggled here, have consecrated it, far above our power to add or to detract. The world will very little note nor long remember what we say here; but it can never forget what they did here.

It is for us, the living, rather, to be dedicated here, to the unfinished work they have thus far so nobly carried on. It is rather for us to be here dedicated to the great task remaining before us; that from these honored dead we take increased devotion to that cause for which they here gave the last full measure of devotion; that we here highly resolve that these dead shall not have died in vain; that the nation shall, under God, have a new birth of freedom, and that government of the people, by the people, and for the people, shall not perish from the earth.

Lesson talk. First note the simplicity of the thought, the words and the style. Then observe the quality of directness in the speaker. He addresses himself immediately to his hearers, without a long introduction, explanation, or going around his subject. The quality of deliberateness pervades the thought itself, and consequently finds appropriateness in the expression. Carefully consider the speech as a whole, its unity, its thoroughness, its brevity, and its genuineness, all suggesting deep sincerity. These four qualities of simplicity, directness, deliberateness, and earnestness, should be carefully analyzed, and the speech read aloud for each of these separately. As the speech progresses in delivery the voice should grow in fulness and intensity. Lincoln took three minutes in which to deliver it. It made a profound impression, despite the fact that Everett, who had a national reputation as an orator, preceded him in a speech of great elaborateness.

THE MURDER OF LOVEJOY

BY WENDELL PHILLIPS

A comparison has been drawn between the events of the Revolution and the tragedy at Alton. We have heard it asserted here in Faneuil Hall, that Great Britain had a right to tax the Colonies; and we have heard the mob at Alton, the drunken murderers of Lovejoy, compared to those patriot fathers who threw the tea overboard! Fellow citizens, is this Faneuil Hall doctrine? The mob at Alton were met to wrest from a citizen his just rights—met to resist the laws. We have been told that our fathers did the same; and the glorious mantle of Revolutionary precedent has been thrown over the mobs of our day. To make out their title to such defense the gentleman says that the British Parliament had a right to tax these Colonies.

It is manifest that, without this, his parallel falls to the ground; for Lovejoy had stationed himself within constitutional bulwarks. He was not only defending the freedom of the press, but he was under his own roof, in arms with the sanction of the civil authority. The men who assailed him went against and over the laws. The mob, as the gentleman terms it—mob, forsooth! certainly we sons of the tea-spillers are a marvelously patient generation!—the "orderly mob" which assembled in the Old South to destroy the tea were met to resist, not the laws, but illegal exactions! Shame on the American who calls the tea tax and Stamp Act laws! Our fathers resisted, not the king's prerogative, but the king's usurpation. To find any other account, you must read our Revolutionary history upside down. Our State archives are loaded with arguments of John Adams to prove the taxes laid by the British Parliament unconstitutional—beyond its power. It was not till this was made out that the men of New England rushed to arms. The arguments of the council-chamber and the House of Representatives preceded and sanctioned the contest.

To draw the conduct of our ancestors into a precedent for mobs, for a right to resist laws we ourselves have enacted, is an insult to their memory. The difference between the excitements of those days and our own, which the gentlemen in kindness to the latter has overlooked, is simply this: the men of that day went for the right, as secured by the laws. They were the people rising to sustain the laws and Constitution of the province. The rioters of our day go for their own wills, right or wrong. Sir, when I heard the gentleman lay down principles which place the murderers of Alton side by side with Otis and Hancock, with Quincy and Adams, I thought those pictured lips [pointing to the portraits in the Hall] would have broken into voice to rebuke the recreant American—the slanderer of the dead. The gentleman said that he should sink into insignificance if he dared not gainsay the principles of these resolutions. Sir, for the sentiments he has uttered, on soil consecrated by the prayers of Puritans and the blood of patriots, the earth should have yawned him up.

Fellow citizens, I can not take back my words. Surely, the attorney-general, so long and well known here, needs not the aid of your hisses against one so young as I am—my voice never before heard within these walls!

Another ground has been taken to excuse the mob, and throw doubt and discredit on the conduct of Lovejoy and his associates. Allusion has been made to what lawyers understand very well—the "conflict of laws." We are told that nothing but the Mississippi River rolls between St. Louis and Alton; and the conflict of laws somehow or other gives the citizens of the former a right to find fault with the defender of the press for publishing his opinions so near their limits. Will the gentleman venture that argument before lawyers? How the laws of the two States could be said to come into conflict in such circumstances I question whether any lawyer in this audience can explain or understand. No matter whether the line that divides one sovereign State from another be an imaginary one or ocean-wide, the moment you cross it, the State you leave is blotted out of existence, so far as you are concerned. The Czar might as well claim to control the deliberations of Faneuil Hall, as the laws of Missouri demand reverence, or the shadow of obedience, from an inhabitant of Illinois.

I must find some fault with the statement which has been made of the events at Alton. It has been asked why Lovejoy and his friends did not appeal to the executive—trust their defense to the police of the city. It has been hinted that, from hasty and ill-judged excitement, the men within the building provoked a quarrel, and that he fell in the course of it—one mob resisting another. Recollect, sir, that they did act with the approbation and sanction of the mayor. In strict truth there was no executive to appeal to for protection. The mayor acknowledged that he could not protect them. They asked him if it was lawful for them to defend themselves. He told them it was, and sanctioned their assembling in arms to do so. They were not, then, a mob; they were not merely citizens defending their own property, they were in some sense the *posse comitatus*, adopted for the occasion into the police of the city, acting under the order of a magistrate. It was civil authority resisting lawless violence. Where, then, was the imprudence? Is the doctrine to be sustained here that it is imprudent for men to aid magistrates in executing the laws?

Men are continually asking each other, had Lovejoy a right to resist? Sir, I protest against the question instead of answering it. Lovejoy did not resist, in the sense they mean. He did not throw himself back on the natural right of self-defense. He did not cry anarchy, and let slip the dogs of civil war, careless of the horrors which would follow.

Sir, as I understand this affair, it was not an individual protecting his property; it was not one body of armed men resisting another, and making the streets of a peaceful city run blood with their contentions. It did not bring back the scenes in old Italian cities, where family met family, and faction met faction, and mutually trampled the laws under foot. No! the men in that house were regularly enrolled under the sanction of the mayor. There being no militia in Alton, about seventy men were enrolled with the approbation of the mayor. These relieved each other every other night. About thirty men were in arms on the night of the 6th, when the press was landed. The next evening it was not thought necessary to summon more than half that number: among these was Lovejoy. It was, therefore, you perceive, sir, the police of the city resisting rioters—civil government breasting itself to the shock of lawless men.

Here is no question about the right of self-defense. It is in fact simply this: Has the civil magistrate a right to put down a riot?

It has been stated, perhaps inadvertently, that Lovejoy or his comrades fired first. This is denied by those who have the best means of knowing. Guns were first fired by the mob. After being twice fired on, those within the building consulted together and deliberately returned the fire. But suppose they did fire first. They had a right so to do—not only the right which every citizen has to defend himself, but the further right which every civil officer has to resist violence. Even if Lovejoy fired the first gun, it would not lessen his claim to our sympathy or destroy his title to be considered a martyr in defense of a free press. The question now is, did he act within the Constitution and the laws? The men who fell in State Street on the 5th of March, 1770, did more than Lovejoy is charged with. They were the first assailants. Upon some slight quarrel they pelted the troops with every missile within reach. Did this bate one jot of the eulogy with which Hancock and Warren hallowed their memory, hailing them as the first martyrs in the cause of American liberty?

If, sir, I had adopted what are called peace principles, I might lament the circumstances of this case. But all you who believe, as I do, in the right and duty of magistrates to execute the laws, join with me and brand as base hypocrisy the conduct of those who assemble year after year on the Fourth of July to fight over the battles of the Revolution, and yet "damn with faint praise" or load with obloquy the memory of this man who shed his blood in defense of life, liberty, property, and the freedom of the press!

Imagine yourself present when the first news of Bunker Hill battle reached a New England town. The tale would have run thus: "The patriots are routed—the redcoats victorious—Warren lies dead upon the field." With what scorn would that Tory have been received who should have charged Warren with imprudence! who should have said that, bred a physician, he was "out of place" in that battle, and "died as the fool dieth!" How would the intimation have been received that Warren and his associates should have waited a better time? But, if success be indeed the only criterion of prudence, *Respice finem*—Wait till the end.

Mr. Chairman, from the bottom of my heart I thank that brave little band at Alton for resisting. We must remember that Lovejoy had fled from city to city; suffered the destruction of three presses patiently. At length he took counsel with friends; men of character, of tried integrity, of wide views, of Christian principle. They thought the crisis had come. It was full time to assert the laws. They saw around them, not a community like our own, of fixt habits, of character molded and settled, but one "in the gristle, not yet hardened into the bone of manhood." The people there, children of our older States, seem to have forgotten the blood-tried principles of their fathers the moment they lost sight of our New England hills. Something was to be done to show them the priceless value of the freedom of the press, to bring back and set right their wandering and confused ideas. He and his advisers looked out on a community staggering like a drunken man, indifferent to their rights and confused in their feelings. Deaf to argument, haply they might be stunned into sobriety. They saw that of which we can not judge: the necessity of resistance. Insulted law called for it. Public opinion, fast hastening on the downward course, must be arrested.

Does not the event show they judged rightly? Absorbed in a thousand trifles, how has the nation all at once come to a stand! Men begin, as in 1776 and 1640, to discuss principles, to weigh characters, to find out where they are. Haply we may awake before we are borne over the precipice.

I am glad, sir, to see this crowded house. It is good for us to be here. When liberty is in danger, Faneuil Hall has the right, it is her duty, to strike the key-note for these United States. I am glad, for one reason, that remarks such as those to which I have alluded have been uttered here. The passage of these resolutions, in spite of this opposition, led by the attorney-general of the commonwealth, will show more clearly, more decisively, the deep indignation with which Boston regards this outrage.

BUNKER HILL MONUMENT

BY DANIEL WEBSTER

This uncounted multitude before me and around me proves the feeling which the occasion has excited. These thousands of human faces, glowing with sympathy and joy, and from the impulses of a common gratitude turned reverently to heaven in this spacious temple of the firmament, proclaim that the day, the place and the purpose of our assembling have made a deep impression on our hearts.

If, indeed, there be anything in local association fit to affect the mind of man, we need not strive to repress the emotions which agitate us here. We are among the sepulchers of our fathers. We are on ground distinguished by their valor, their constancy and the shedding of their blood. We are here, not to fix an uncertain date in our annals, nor draw into notice an obscure and unknown spot. If our humble purpose had never been conceived, if we ourselves had never been born, the 17th of June, 1775, would have been a day on which all subsequent history would have poured its light, and the eminence where we stand a point of attraction to the eyes of successive generations. But we are Americans. We live in what may be called the early age of this great continent; and we know that our posterity, through all time, are here to enjoy and suffer the allotments of humanity. We see before us a probable train of great events; we know that our own fortunes have been happily cast; and it is natural, therefore, that we should be moved by the contemplation of occurrences which have guided our destiny before many of us were born, and settled the condition in which we should pass that portion of our existence which God allows to men on earth.

But the great event in the history of the continent, which we are now met here to commemorate, that prodigy of modern times, at once the wonder and blessing of the world, is the American Revolution. In a day of extraordinary prosperity and happiness, of high national honor, distinction, and power, we are brought together, in this place, by our love of country, by our admiration of exalted character, by our gratitude for signal services and patriotic devotion.

The society whose organ I am was formed for the purpose of rearing some honorable and durable monument to the memory of the early friends of American Independence. They have thought that for this object no time could be more propitious than the present prosperous and peaceful period; that no place could claim preference over this memorable spot; and that no day could be more auspicious to the undertaking, than the anniversary of the battle which was here fought. The foundation of that monument we have now laid. With solemnities suited to the occasion, with prayers to Almighty God for His blessing, and in the midst of this cloud of witnesses, we have begun the work. We trust it will be prosecuted, and that springing from a broad foundation, rising high in massive solidity and unadorned grandeur, it may remain as long as heaven permits the works of man to last, a fit emblem, both of the events in memory of which it is raised and of the gratitude of those who have reared it.

We know, indeed, that the record of illustrious actions is most safely deposited in the universal remembrance of mankind. We know that if we could cause this structure to ascend, not only till it reached the skies, but till it pierced them, its broad surfaces could still contain but part of that which, in an age of knowledge, hath already been spread over the earth, and which history charges itself with making known to all future times. We know that no inscription on entablatures less broad than the earth itself can carry information of the events we commemorate where it has not already gone; and that no structure, which shall not outlive the duration of letters and knowledge among men, can prolong the memorial. But our object is, by this edifice, to show our own deep sense of the value and importance of the achievements of our ancestors; and, by presenting this work of gratitude to the eye, to keep alive similar sentiments, and to foster a constant regard for the principles of the Revolution. Human beings are composed, not of reason only, but of imagination also, and sentiment; and that is neither wasted nor misapplied which is appropriated to the purpose of giving right direction to sentiments and opening proper springs of feeling in the heart.

Let it not be supposed that our object is to perpetuate national hostility, or even to cherish a mere military spirit. It is higher, purer, nobler. We consecrate our work to the spirit of national independence, and we cherish the hope that the light of peace may rest upon it forever. We rear a memorial of our conviction of that unmeasured benefit which has been conferred on our own land, and of the happy influences which have been produced, by the same events, on the general interests of mankind. We come, as Americans, to mark a spot which must forever be dear to us and our posterity. We wish that whosoever, in all coming time, shall turn his eye hither, may behold that the place is not undistinguished where the first great battle of the Revolution was fought. We wish that this structure may proclaim the magnitude and importance of that event to every class and every age. We wish that infancy may learn the purpose of its erection from maternal lips, and that weary and withered age may behold it, and be solaced by the recollections which it suggests. We wish that labor may look up here, and be proud, in the midst of its toil. We wish that, in those days of disaster, which, as they come upon all nations, must be expected to come upon us also, desponding patriotism may turn its eyes hitherward, and be assured that the foundations of our national power are still strong. We wish that this column, rising toward heaven among the pointed spires of so many temples dedicated to God, may contribute also to produce, in all minds, a pious feeling of dependence and gratitude. We wish, finally, that the last object to the sight of him who leaves his native shore, and the first to gladden him who revisits it, may be something which shall remind him of the liberty and glory of his country. Let it rise! Let it rise, till it meet the sun in his coming; let the earliest light of the morning gild it, and parting day linger and play on its summit.

THE RESPONSIBILITY OF WAR

BY WILLIAM E. CHANNING

Nothing in the whole compass of legislation is so solemn as a declaration of war. By nothing do a people incur such tremendous responsibility. Unless justly waged, war involves a people in the guilt of murder. The state which, without the command of justice and God, sends out fleets and armies to slaughter fellow creatures, must answer for the blood it sheds, as truly as the assassin for the death of his victim. Oh, how loudly does the voice of blood cry to heaven from the field of battle! Undoubtedly the men whose names have come down to us with the loudest shouts of ages stand now before the tribunal of eternal justice condemned as murderers; and the victories which have been thought to encircle a nation with glory have fixt the same brand on multitudes in the sight of the final and almighty Judge. How essential is it to a nation's honor that it should engage in war with a full conviction of rectitude!

But there is one more condition of an honorable war. A nation should engage in it with unfeigned sorrow. It should beseech the throne of grace with earnest supplication that the dreadful office of destroying fellow beings may not be imposed on it. War concentrates all the varieties of human misery, and a nation which can inflict these without sorrow contracts deeper infamy than from cowardice. It is essentially barbarous, and will be looked back upon by enlightened and Christian ages with the horror with which we recall the atrocities of savage tribes. Let it be remembered that the calamities of war, its slaughter, famine, and desolation, instead of being confined to its criminal authors, fall chiefly on multitudes who have had no share in provoking and no voice in proclaiming it; and let not a nation talk of its honor which has no sympathy with woes, which is steeled to the most terrible sufferings of humanity.

When recently the suggestion of war was thrown out to this people, what reception did it meet? Was it viewed at once in the light in which a Christian nation should immediately and most earnestly consider it? Was it received as a proposition to slaughter thousands of our fellow creatures? Did we feel as if threatened with a calamity more fearful than earthquakes, famine, or pestilence? The blight which might fall on our prosperity drew attention; but the thought of devoting as a people, our power and resources to the destruction of mankind, of those whom a common nature, whom reason, conscience, and Christianity command us to love and save—did this thrill us with horror? Did the solemn inquiry break forth through our land: Is the dreadful necessity indeed laid upon us to send abroad death and wo? No. There was little manifestation of the sensibility with which men and Christians should look such an evil in the face.

As a people we are still seared and blinded to the crimes and miseries of war. The principles of honor, to which the barbarism and infatuation of dark ages gave birth, prevail among us. The generous, merciful spirit of our religion is little understood. The law of love preached from the cross and written in the blood of the Savior is trampled upon by public men. The true dignity of man, which consists in breathing and cherishing God's spirit of justice and philanthropy toward every human being, is counted folly in comparison with that spirit of vindictiveness and self-aggrandizement which turns our earth into an image of the abodes of the damned. How long will the friends of humanity, of religion, of Christ, silently, passively, uncomplainingly suffer the men of this world, the ambitious, vindictive, and selfish, to array them against their brethren in conflicts which they condemn and abhor? Shall not truth, humanity, and the mild and holy spirit of Christianity find a voice to rebuke and awe the wickedness which precipitates nations into war, and to startle and awaken nations to their fearful responsibility in taking arms against the children of their Father in heaven? Prince of Peace! Savior of men! speak in Thine own voice of love, power, and fearful warning; and redeem the world, for which Thou hast died, from lawless and cruel passions, from the spirit of rapine and murder, from the powers of darkness and hell!

CARRYING A MESSAGE TO GARCIA

BY ELBERT HUBBARD

In all this Cuban business there is one man who stands out on the horizon of my memory like Mars at perihelion. When war broke out between Spain and the United States, it was very necessary to communicate quickly with the leader of the insurgents. Garcia was somewhere in the mountain fastnesses of Cuba—no one knew where. No mail nor telegraph message could reach him. The President must secure his cooperation, and quickly.

What to do!

Some one said to the President, "There is a fellow by the name of Rowan will find Garcia for you, if anybody can."

Rowan was sent for and given a letter to be delivered to Garcia. How the "fellow by the name of Rowan" took the letter, sealed it up in an oil-skin pouch, strapped it over his heart, in four days landed by night off the coast of Cuba from an open boat, disappeared into the jungle, and in three weeks came out on the other side of the island, having traversed a hostile country on foot, and delivered his letter to Garcia—are things I have no special desire now to tell in detail. The point I wish to make is this: McKinley gave

Rowan a letter to be delivered to Garcia; Rowan took the letter and did not ask, "Where is he?"

By the Eternal! there is a man whose form should be cast in deathless bronze and the statue placed in every college of the land. It is not book-learning young men need, nor instruction about this and that, but a stiffening of the vertebræ which will cause them to be loyal to a trust, to act promptly, concentrate their energies: do the thing—"Carry a message to Garcia."

General Garcia is dead now, but there are other Garcias. No man who has endeavored to carry out an enterprise where many hands were needed, but has been well-nigh appalled at times by the imbecility of the average man—the inability or unwillingness to concentrate on a thing and do it.

Slipshod assistance, foolish inattention, dowdy indifference and half-hearted work seem the rule; and no man succeeds, unless by hook or crook or threat he forces or bribes other men to assist him or, mayhap, God in His goodness performs a miracle and sends him an angel of light for an assistant.

You, reader, put this matter to a test: You are sitting now in your office—six clerks are within call. Summon any one and make this request: "Please look in the encyclopedia and make a brief memorandum for me concerning the life of Correggio."

Will the clerk quietly say, "Yes, sir," and go do the task? On your life he will not. He will look at you out of a fishy eye and ask one or more of the following questions:

Who was he?

Which encyclopedia?

Where is the encyclopedia?

Was I hired for that?

Don't you mean Bismarck?

What's the matter with Charlie doing it?

Is he dead?

Is there any hurry?

Sha'n't I bring you the book and let you look it up yourself?

What do you want to know for?

And I will lay you ten to one that after you have answered the questions, and explained how to find the information, and why you want it, the clerk will go off and get one of the other clerks to help him try to find Garcia—and then come back and tell you there is no such man. Of course I may lose my bet, but according to the law of average I will not.

Now if you are wise, you will not bother to explain to your "assistant" that Correggio in indexed under the C's, not in the K's, but you will smile sweetly and say, "Never mind," and go look it up yourself. And this incapacity for independent action, this moral stupidity, this infirmity of the will, this unwillingness to cheerfully catch hold and lift—these are the things that put pure socialism so far into the future. If men will not act for themselves, what will they do when the benefit of their effort is for all?

A first mate with knotted club seems necessary; and the dread of getting "the bounce" Saturday night holds many a worker to his place. Advertise for a stenographer, and nine out of ten who apply can neither spell nor punctuate—and do not think it necessary to. Can such a one write a letter to Garcia? "You see that bookkeeper," said the foreman to me in a large factory.

"Yes, what about him?"

"Well, he's a fine accountant, but if I'd send him up-town on an errand, he might accomplish the errand all right, and, on the other hand, might stop at four saloons on the way, and when he got to Main Street, would forget what he had been sent for."

Can such a man be entrusted to carry a message to Garcia?

We have recently been hearing much maudlin sympathy exprest for the "down-trodden denizen of the sweat-shop" and the "homeless wanderer searching for honest employment," and with it all often go many hard words for the men in power.

Nothing is said about the employer who grows old before his time, in a vain attempt to get frowzy ne'er-do-wells to do intelligent work; and his long, patient striving after "help" that does nothing but loaf when his back is turned. In every store and factory there is a constant weeding-out process going on. The employer is constantly sending away "help" that have shown their incapacity to further the interests of the business, and others are being taken on. No matter how good times are, this sorting continues: only, if times are hard and work is scarce, the sorting is done finer—but out, and forever out, the incompetent and unworthy go. It is the survival of the fittest. Self-interest prompts every employer to keep the best—those who can carry a message to Garcia.

I know one man of really brilliant parts who has not the ability to manage a business of his own, and yet who is absolutely worthless to any one else, because he carries with him constantly the insane suspicion that his employer is oppressing, or intending to oppress him. He can not give orders, and he will not receive them. Should a message be given him to take to Garcia, his answer would probably be, "Take it yourself."

To-night this man walks the streets looking for work, the wind whistling through his threadbare coat. No one who knows him dare employ him, for he is a regular firebrand of discontent. He is impervious to reason, and the only thing that can impress him is the toe of a thicksoled No. 9 boot.

Of course I know that one so morally deformed is no less to be pitied than a physical cripple, but in our pitying, let us drop a tear, too, for the men who are striving to carry on a great enterprise, whose working hours are not limited by the whistle, and whose hair is fast turning white through the struggle to hold in line dowdy indifference, slipshod imbecility, and the heartless ingratitude which, but for their enterprise, would be both hungry and homeless.

Have I put the matter too strongly? Possibly I have; but when all the world has gone a-slumming I wish to speak a word of sympathy for the man who succeeds—the man who, against great odds, has directed the efforts of others, and having succeeded, finds there's nothing in it: nothing but bare board and clothes. I have carried a dinner-pail and worked for day's wages, and I have also been an employer of labor, and I know there is something to be said on both sides. There is no excellence, *per se,* in poverty; rags are no recommendation; and all employers are not rapacious and high-handed, any more than all poor men are virtuous. My heart goes out to the man who does his work when the "boss" is away as well as when he is at home. And the man who, when given a letter for Garcia, quietly takes the missive, without asking any idiotic questions, and with no lurking intention of chucking it into the nearest sewer, or of doing aught else but deliver it, never gets "laid off," nor has to go on a strike for higher wages. Civilization is one long anxious search for just such individuals. Anything such a man asks shall be granted. He is wanted in every city, town and village—in every office, shop, store and factory. The world cries out for such: he is needed, and needed badly—the man who can carry a message to Garcia.

THE DYING ALCHYMIST

BY NATHANIEL P. WILLIS

The night wind with a desolate moan swept by;
And the old shutters of the turret swung
Screaming upon their hinges; and the moon,
As the torn edges of the clouds flew past,
Struggled aslant the stain'd and broken panes
So dimly, that the watchful eye of death
Scarcely was conscious when it went and came.

. . . .

The fire beneath his crucible was low;
Yet still it burn'd; and ever as his thoughts
Grew insupportable, he raised himself
Upon his wasted arm, and stirr'd the coals
With difficult energy, and when the rod
Fell from his nerveless fingers, and his eye
Felt faint within its socket, he shrank back
Upon his pallet, and with unclosed lips
Mutter'd a curse on death! The silent room,
From its dim corners, mockingly gave back
His rattling breath; the humming in the fire

Had the distinctness of a knell; and when
Duly the antique horologe beat one,
He drew a vial from beneath his head,
And drank. And instantly his lips comprest,
And, with a shudder in his skeleton frame,
He rose with supernatural strength, and sat
Upright, and communed with himself:—

I did not think to die
Till I had finished what I had to do;
I thought to pierce th' eternal secret through
With this my mortal eye;
I felt—O God, it seems even now
This can not be the death-dew on my brow!

And yet it is—I feel,
Of this dull sickness at my heart, afraid!
And in my eyes the death-sparks flash and fade;
And something seems to steal
Over my bosom like a frozen hand—
Binding its pulses with an icy band.

And this is death! But why
Feel I this wild recoil? It can not be
Th' immortal spirit shuddereth to be free!
Would it not leap to fly,
Like a chain'd eaglet at its parent's call?
I fear—I fear—that this poor life is all!

Yet thus to pass away!—
To live but for a hope that mocks at last—
To agonize, to strive, to watch, to fast,

To waste the light of day,
Night's better beauty, feeling, fancy, thought,
All that we have and are—for this—are naught!

Grant me another year,
God of my spirit!—but a day—to win
Something to satisfy this thirst within!
I would *know* something here!
Break for me but one seal that is unbroken!
Speak for me but one word that is unspoken!

Vain!—vain!—my brain is turning
With a swift dizziness, and my heart grows sick,
And these hot temple-throbs come fast and thick,
And I am freezing—burning—
Dying! O God! if I might only live!
My vial— Ha! it thrills me—I revive!

. . . .

Ay—were not man to die,
He were too mighty for this narrow sphere!
Had he but time to brood on knowledge here—
Could he but train his eye—
Might he but wait the mystic word and hour—
Only his Maker would transcend his power!

Earth has no mineral strange—
Th' illimitable air no hidden wings—
Water no quality in covert springs,
And fire no power to change—
Seasons no mystery, and stars no spell,
Which the unwasting soul might not compel.

Oh, but for time to track
The upper stars into the pathless sky—
To see th' invisible spirits, eye to eye—
To hurl the lightning back—
To tread unhurt the sea's dim-lighted halls—
To chase Day's chariot to the horizon-walls—

And more, much more—for now
The life-seal'd fountains of my nature move—
To nurse and purify this human love—
To clear the godlike brow
Of weakness and mistrust, and bow it down,
Worthy and beautiful, to the much-loved one—

This were indeed to feel
The soul-thirst slaken at the living stream—
To live—O God! that life is but a dream!
And death— Aha! I reel—
Dim—dim—I faint—darkness comes o'er my eye—
Cover me! save me!—God of heaven! I die!

'Twas morning, and the old man lay alone.
No friend had closed his eyelids, and his lips,
Open and ashy pale, th' expression wore
Of his death-struggle. His long silvery hair
Lay on his hollow temples thin and wild,
His frame was wasted, and his features wan
And haggard as with want, and in his palm
His nails were driven deep, as if the throe
Of the last agony had wrung him sore.

The storm was raging still. The shutter swung
Screaming as harshly in the fitful wind,
And all without went on—as ay it will,
Sunshine or tempest, reckless that a heart
Is breaking, or has broken, in its change.

The fire beneath the crucible was out;
The vessels of his mystic art lay round,
Useless and cold as the ambitious hand
That fashion'd them, and the small rod,
Familiar to his touch for threescore years,
Lay on th' alembic's rim, as if it still
Might vex the elements at its master's will.

And thus had pass'd from its unequal frame
A soul of fire—a sun-bent eagle stricken
From his high soaring down—an instrument
Broken with its own compass. Oh, how poor
Seems the rich gift of genius, when it lies,
Like the adventurous bird that hath outflown
His strength upon the sea, ambition-wreck'd—
A thing the thrush might pity, as she sits
Brooding in quiet on her lowly nest!

Lesson talk. Read this poem first as a whole. Then read it a second time carefully, endeavoring to grasp each thought in detail. Underscore emphatic words, and indicate in margin the changes of feeling and movement throughout. Look up all unfamiliar words. Carefully note the shades of pausing and transitions.

OPPORTUNITY[1]

BY BISHOP JOHN LANCASTER SPALDING

How shall I live? How shall I make the most of my life and put it to the best use? How shall I become a man and do a man's work? This, and not politics or trade or war or pleasure, is the question. The primary consideration is not how shall one get a living, but how shall he live; for if he live rightly, whatever is needful he shall easily find. Life is opportunity, and therefore its whole circumstance may be made to serve the purpose of those who are bent on self-improvement, on making themselves capable of doing thorough work. Opportunity is a word which, like so many others that are excellent, we get from the Romans. It means near port, close to haven. It is a favorable occasion, time, or place for learning or saying or doing a thing. It is an invitation to seek safety and refreshment, an appeal to make escape from what is low and vulgar and to take refuge in high thoughts and worthy deeds, from which flow increase of strength and joy. It is omnipresent. What we call evils, as poverty, neglect, and suffering, are, if we are wise, opportunities for good. Death itself teaches life's value not less than its vanity. It is the background against which its worth and beauty stand forth in clear relief. Its dark form follows us like our shadow, to bid us win the prize while yet there is time; to teach that if we live in what is permanent, the destroyer can not blight what we know and love; to urge us, with a

[1] Reprinted by permission of the author, and the publishers, A. C. McClurg & Co., Chicago.

power that belongs to nothing else, to lay the stress of all our hoping and doing on the things that can not pass away. "Poverty," says Ouida, "is the north wind that lashes men into Vikings." "Lowliness is young ambition's ladder." What is more pleasant than to read of strong-hearted youths who, in the midst of want and hardships of many kinds, have clung to books, feeding, like bees to flowers? By the light of pine logs, in dim-lit garrets, in the fields following the plow, in early dawns when others are asleep, they ply their blest task, seeking nourishment for the mind, athirst for truth, yearning for full sight of the high worlds of which they have caught faint glimpses; happier now, lacking everything save faith and a great purpose, than in after years when success shall shower on them applause and gold.

Life is good, and opportunities of becoming and doing good are always with us. Our house, our table, our tools, our books, our city, our country, our language, our business, our profession—the people who love us and those who hate, they who help and they who oppose, what is all this but opportunity? Wherever we be there is opportunity of turning to gold the dust of daily happenings. If snow and storm keep me at home is not here an invitation to turn to the immortal silent ones who never speak unless they are addrest? If loss or pain or wrong befall me, shall they not show me the soul of good there is in things evil? Good fortune may serve to persuade us that the essential good is a noble mind and a conscience without flaw. Success will make plain the things in which we fail; failure shall spur us on to braver hope and striving. If I am left alone, yet God and all the heroic dead are with me still. If a great city is my dwelling-place, the superficial life of noise and haste shall teach me how blest a thing it is to live within in the company of true thoughts and high resolves.

Whatever can help me to think and love, whatever can give me strength and patience, whatever can make me humble and serviceable, tho it be a trifle light as air, is opportunity, whose whim it is to hide in unconsidered things, in chance acquaintance and casual speech, in the falling of an apple, in floating weeds, or the accidental explosion in a chemist's mortar. Wisdom is habited in plainest garb, and she walks modestly, unheeded of the gaping and wondering crowd. She rules over the kingdom of little things, in which the lowly minded hold the places of privilege. Her secrets are revealed to the careful, the patient, and the humble. They may be learned from the ant, or the flower that blooms in some hidden spot, or from the lips of husbandmen and housewives. He is wise who finds a teacher in every man, an occasion to improve in every happening, for whom nothing is useless or in vain. If one whom he has trusted prove false, he lays it to the account of his own heedlessness and resolves to become more observant. If men scorn him, he is thankful that he need not scorn himself. If they pass him by, it is enough for him that truth and love still remain. If he is thrown with one who bears himself with ease and grace, or talks correctly in pleasantly modulated tones, or utters what can spring only from a sincere and generous mind—there is opportunity. If he chance to find himself in the company of the rude, their vulgarity gives him a higher estimate of the worth of breeding and behavior. The happiness and good fortune of his fellows add to his own. If they are beautiful or wise or strong, their beauty, wisdom, and strength shall in some way help him. The merry voices of children bring gladness to his heart; the songs of birds wake melody there. Whoever anywhere, in any age, spoke noble words or performed heroic deeds, spoke and wrought for him. For him Moses led the people forth from bondage; for him the three hundred perished at Thermopylæ; for him Homer sang; for him Demosthenes denounced the tyrant; for him Columbus sailed the untraveled sea; for him Galileo gazed on the starry vault; for him the blest Savior died. He knows that whatever diminishes his good will to men, his sympathy with them, even in their blindness and waywardness, makes him poorer, and he therefore finds means to convert their faults even into opportunities for loving them more. The rivalries of business and politics, the shock of conflicting aims and interests, the prejudices and perversities of men, shall not cheat him of his own good by making him less just or kind. He stands with the Eternal for righteousness, and will not suffer that fools or criminals divert him to lower ends. If we have but the right mind, all things, even those that hurt, help us. "That which befits us," says Emerson, "embosomed in beauty and wonder as we are, is cheerfulness and courage, and the endeavor to realize our aspirations. The life of man is the true romance which, when it is valiantly conducted, yields the imagination a higher joy than any fiction." May we not make the stars and the mountains and the all-enduring earth minister to tranquillity of soul, to elevation of mind, and to patient striving? Have not the flowers, and the human eye, and the look of heaven when the sun first appears or departs, power to show us that God is beautiful and good?

Since life is great, nay, of inestimable value, no opportunity by which it may be improved can be small. Higher things remain to be done than have yet been accomplished. God and His universe still wait on each individual soul, offering opportunity. In the midst of the humble and inevitable realities of daily life each one must seek out for himself the way to better worlds. Our power, our worth will be proportionate to the industry and perseverance with which we make right use of the ever-recurring minor occasions, whether for becoming or for doing good. Opportunity is not wanting—there is place and means for all—but we lack will, we lack faith, hope, and desire, we lack watchfulness, meditation, and earnest striving, we back aim and purpose. Do we imagine that it is not possible to lead a high life in a lowly room? That one may not be hero, sage, or saint in a factory or a coalpit, at the handle of the plow or the throttle of the engine? We are all in the center of the same world, and whatever happens to us is great, if there be greatness in us. The disbelievers in opportunity are voluble with excuses. They can not; they have no leisure; they have not the means. But they can if they will; leisure to improve oneself is never wanting, and they who seek find the means. There is always opportunity to do right, tho he who does it stands alone, like Abdiel,

> Among innumerable false, unmoved,
> Unshaken, unseduced, unterrified.

Let a man but have an aim, a purpose, and opportunities to attain his end shall start forth like buds at the kiss of spring. If we do not know what we want, how shall anything be made to serve us? The heedless walk through deserts in which the observant find the most precious things. Little is to be hoped for from the weavers of pretexts, from those who tell us what they should do, if circumstances were other. What hinders helps, where souls are alive. Say not thou lackest talent. What talent had any of the great ones better than their passionate trust in the efficacy of labor?

The important thing is to have an aim and to pursue it with perseverance. What is the aim the wise should propose to themselves? Not getting and possessing, but becoming and being. Man is not only more than anything that can belong to him: he is greater than planets and solar systems. We easily persuade ourselves that were circumstances more favorable we should be better and happier. It may be so, but the mood is weak and foolish. There is never a question of what might have been where true men think and act. The past is irrevocable. It is our business to do what we can here now, and regrets serve but to enfeeble and distract us. The boundless good lies near each one, and tho a thousand times it has eluded us, let us believe that now we shall hold it fast. From failure to failure we rise toward truth and love. The ascent is possible even for the lowliest of God's creatures. When, indeed, we look backward through long years of life, lost opportunities rise before us like mocking fiends crying, "Too late, too late! Nevermore, nevermore!" but the wise heed no voice that bids them lose heart. They look ever forward, they press toward the mark, knowing that the present is the only opportunity. Now is the day of salvation, now is the day of doom. The individual is but as a bubble that rises from out of the infinite ocean of being and bursts in the inane; but his life is nevertheless enrooted in the Absolute, and all the circumstances by which his existence is surrounded and attended are but meant to awaken in him a knowledge and appreciation of his abiding and inestimable worth. They all, therefore, are or may be made opportunities. The paramount consideration is not what will procure for him more money, finer houses, better machines, more rapid or more destructive engines, but what will make him wiser, stronger, holier, more loving, more godlike.

What innumerable blessings we miss through lack of sensibility, of openness to light, of fair-mindedness, of insight, of teachableness—virtues which it is possible for all to cultivate! The best is not ours, not because it is far away and unattainable, but because we ourselves are indifferent, narrow, short-sighted and unsympathetic. To make our world larger and fairer it is not necessary to discover or acquire new objects, but to grow into conscious and loving harmony with the good which is ever-present and inviting. How much of life's joy we lose from want of a fearless and cheerful spirit! The brave and glad-hearted, like the beautiful, are welcome in all companies.

It is our own fault if beauty is not ours. A fair and luminous mind creates a body after its own image. With health and a soul, nor man nor woman can be other than beautiful, whatever the features. The most potent charm is that of expression. As the moonlight clothes the rugged and jagged mountain with loveliness, so a noble mind transfigures its vesture.

The man himself is the best part of the opportunity. The starlit heaven is not sublime when there is no soul capable of awe; the spring is not fair where there is no glad heart to see and feel. Opportunity is living correspondence with one's environment. Where there is no correspondence there is no opportunity. For ages the exhaustless resources of America lay unknown and unutilized because the right kind of a man was not here. The Kimberley diamonds were but worthless pebbles, the playthings of the children of savages, until it chanced they fell under the eye of one who knew how to look.

. . . .

Opportunity in the highest sense of the word is opportunity for education, for making ourselves men. This end every occasion should serve, since for this we are born. "We should, as far as it is possible," says Aristotle, "make ourselves immortal, and strive to live by that part of ourselves which is more excellent." Now, the testimony of the wise of all ages agrees that a virtuous life is the best and the happiest. Choose and follow it then, tho thou find it hard; for custom will make it easy and pleasant. Piety nourishes faith, hope, and love, and therefore sustains life. If thou seekest for what is new and also permanently interesting, live with the old truths, until they strike root in thy being and break into new light and power. The happenings of the day and year are but novelties, but bubbles that burst in the vacant air; that which is forever new is ancient as God. It is that whereby the soul lives. It was with the first man when first he blossomed forth from eternity; it is with thee now and shall be with all men until the end. It is the source whence thy being springs; its roots dip into infinity; its flowers make the universe glad and sweet; it is the power which awakens the soul to the consciousness of its kinship with Him who is all in all, who is life and truth and love, who the more He is sought and loved doth seem to be the more divinely beautiful and good. Learn to live with the thoughts which are symbols of His Eternal Being, and thou shalt come to feel that nothing else is so fresh or fair. As a sound may suggest light and color, a perfume recall forgotten worlds; as a view, disclosed by a turn in the road, may carry us across years and oceans to scenes and friends long unvisited; as a bee, weaving his winding path from flower to flower, may bring back the laughter of children, the songs of birds, and the visionary clouds fallen asleep in the voluptuous sky of June; so the universe will come to utter for us the voice of the Creator, who is our Father. Nothing touches the soul but leaves its impress, and thus, little by little, we are fashioned into the image of all we have seen and heard, known and meditated; and if we learn to live with all that is fairest and purest and best, the love of it all will in the end become our very life.

THE DEFINITION OF A GENTLEMAN

BY CARDINAL JOHN HENRY NEWMAN

It is almost a definition of a gentleman to say that he is one who never inflicts pain. This description is both refined, and, so far as it goes, accurate. He is mainly occupied in merely removing the obstacles which hinder the free and unembarrassed action of those about him, and he concurs with their movements rather than takes the initiative himself. His benefits may be considered as parallel to what are called the comforts or conveniences in arrangements of a personal nature—like an easy chair or a good fire, which do their best in dispelling cold and fatigue, tho nature provides both means of rest and animal heat without them. The true gentleman in like manner carefully avoids whatever may cause a jar or a jolt in the mind of those with whom he is cast—all clashing of opinion or collision of feeling, all restraint or suspicion or gloom or resentment, his great concern being to make every one at ease and at home. He has his eyes on all his company, he is tender toward the bashful, gentle toward the distant, and merciful toward the absurd. He can recollect to whom he is speaking; he guards against unseasonable allusions or topics which may irritate; he is seldom prominent in conversation, and never wearisome. He makes light of favors when he does them, and seems to be receiving when he is conferring. He never speaks of himself except when compelled, never defends himself by a mere retort; he has no ears for slander or gossip, is scrupulous in imputing motives to those who interfere with him, and interprets everything for the best. He is never mean or little in his disputes, never takes unfair advantage, never mistakes personalities or sharp sayings for arguments, or insinuates evil which he dare not say out. From a long-sighted prudency, he observes the maxim of the ancient sage, that we should ever conduct ourselves toward our enemy as if he were one day to be our friend. He has too much good sense to be affronted at insults. He is too well employed to remember injuries and too indolent to bear malice. He is patient, forbearing, and resigned on philosophical principle; he submits to pain because it is inevitable, to bereavement because it is irreparable, and to death because it is his destiny. If he engages in controversy of any kind, his disciplined intellect preserves him from the blundering discourtesy of better, perhaps, but less educated minds, who, like blunt weapons, tear and hack instead of cutting clean, who mistake the point in argument, waste their strength on trifles, misconceive their adversary, and leave the question more involved than they find it. He may be right or wrong in his opinion, but he is too clear-headed to be unjust; he is as simple as he is forcible, and as brief as he is decisive. Nowhere shall we find greater candor, consideration, indulgence; he throws himself into the minds of his opponents, he accounts for their mistakes. He knows the weakness of human reason as well as its strength, its province, and its limits. If he can be an unbeliever, he will be too profound and large-minded to ridicule religion or to act against it; he is too wise to be a dogmatist or fanatic in his infidelity. He respects piety and devotion; he even supports institutions as venerable, beautiful or useful, to which he does not assent; he honors the ministers of religion, and it contents him to decline its mysteries without assailing or denouncing them. He is a friend of religious toleration, and that not only because his philosophy has taught him to look on all forms of faith with an impartial eye, but also from the gentleness and effeminacy of feeling which is attendant on civilization. Not that he may not hold a religion, too, in his own way, even when he is not a Christian. In that case his religion is one of imagination and sentiment; it is the embodiment of those ideas of the sublime, majestic, and beautiful without which there can be no large philosophy. Sometimes he acknowledges the being of God, sometimes he invests an unknown principle or qualities with the attributes of perfection. And this deduction of his reason or creation of his fancy he makes the occasion of such excellent thoughts, and the starting-point of so varied and systematic a teaching, that he even seems like a disciple of Christianity itself. From the very accuracy and steadiness of his logical powers he is able to see what sentiments are consistent in those who hold any religious doctrine at all, and he appears to others to feel and to hold a whole circle of theological truths, which exist in his mind otherwise than as a number of deductions. Such are some of the lineaments of the ethical character which the cultivated intellect will form, apart from the religious principle. They are seen within the pale of the Church and without it, in holy men and in profligate; they form the the beau-ideal of the world; they partly assist and partly distort the development of the Catholic. They may subserve the education of a St. Francis de Sales or a Cardinal Pole; they may be the limits of contemplations of a Shaftesbury or a Gibbon. Basil and Julian were fellow students at the schools of Athens; and one became the saint and doctor of the Church, the other a scoffing and relentless foe.

FIVE EVIDENCES OF AN EDUCATION[1]

BY NICHOLAS MURRAY BUTLER

"If you had children, sir," said Boswell, "would you have taught them anything?" "I hope," replied Dr. Johnson, "that I should have willingly lived on bread and water to obtain instruction for them; but I would not have set their future friendship to hazard, for the sake of thrusting into their heads knowledge of things for which they might not perhaps have either taste or necessity. You teach your daughters the diameters of the planets, and wonder

[1] An address delivered before the Phi Beta Kappa Society of Vassar College, June 10, 1901. Reprinted by permission.

when you have done that they do not delight in your company." From which it appears that Dr. Johnson, by a sort of prolepsis, was moved to contribute to the discussion of one of the vexed questions of our time. Who is the educated man? By what signs shall we know him?

"In the first golden age of the world," Erasmus observes, in his *Praise of Folly*, "there was no need of these perplexities. There was then no other sort of learning but what was naturally collected from every man's common-sense, improved by an easy experience. What use could there have been of grammar, when all men spoke the same mother-tongue, and aimed at no higher pitch of oratory than barely to be understood by each other? What need of logic, when they were too wise to enter into any dispute? Or what occasion for rhetoric, where no difference arose to require any laborious decision?" Surely, in contrasting this picture of a far-off golden age with our present-day strenuous age of steel, we must be moved to say, with the preacher, "in much wisdom is grief; and he that increaseth knowledge increaseth sorrow."

It is only 250 years ago that Comenius urged, with ardent zeal, the establishment in London of a college of learned men who should bring together in one book the sum total of human wisdom, so exprest as to meet the needs of both the present and all future generations. This scheme for a pansophia, or repository of all learning proved very attractive in the seventeenth century, for it easily adjusted itself to the notions of a period which looked upon learning as a substantial and measurable quantity, to be acquired and possest. Unfortunately, this quantitative ideal of education, with its resultant processes and standards, is still widely influential, and it tempts us to seek the evidences of an education in the number of languages learned, in the variety of sciences studied, and generally in the quantity of facts held in the memory reserve. But, on the other hand, any serious attempt to apply quantitative standards to the determination of education quickly betrays their inadequacy and their false assumptions. If to be educated means to know nature in systematic fashion and to be able to interpret it, then nearly every man of letters, ancient or modern, must be classed with the uneducated. Or if to be educated means to have sympathetic, almost affectionate, insight into the great masterpieces of art and of literature, then innumerable great men of action, who have fully represented the ideals and the power of their time and who manifested most admirable qualities of mind and of character, were uneducated. The case is even worse to-day. A host of knowledges compass us about on every side and bewilder by their variety and their interest. We must exclude the many to choose the one. The penalty of choice is deprivation; the price of not choosing is shallowness and incapacity. The quantitative method of estimating education breaks down, then, of its own weight. A true standard is to be sought in some other direction.

A full analysis of the facts of life as they confront us to-day would show, I feel confident, that all knowledges and all influences are not on a single plane of indifference toward the human mind that would be educated. All parts of the spiritual machine are not mutually interchangeable. There are needs to be met and longings to be satisfied that will not accept any vicarious response to their demands. The scientific, the literary, the esthetic, the institutional, and the religious aspects of life and of civilization, while interdependent, are yet independent of each other, in the sense that no one of them can be reduced to a function of another or can be stated in terms of another. Therefore, each of these five aspects must, I think, be represented in some degree in every scheme of training which has education for its end. Nevertheless, this training when it arrives at education will not suffer itself to be measured and estimated quantitatively in terms either of science, of letters, of art, of institutions, or of religion. It will have produced certain traits of intellect and of character which find expression in ways open to the observation of all men, and it is toward these traits of habits, not toward external and substantial acquisition or accomplishment, that one must turn to find the true and sure evidences of an education, as education is conceived to-day.

First among the evidences of an education I name correctness and precision in the use of the mother-tongue. Important as this power is, and is admitted to be, it is a comparatively new thing in education. The modern European languages took on educational significance only when the decentralization of culture began at the close of the Middle Ages. So late as 1549 Jacques de Ballay supported the study of French with the very mild assertion that it is "not so poor a tongue as many may think it." Mulcaster, writing a little later, found it necessary to tell why his book on education was put in English rather than in Latin, and to defend the vernacular when he referred to its educational usefulness. Melanchthon put German in a class with Greek and Hebrew and contrasted all three unfavorably with Latin. Indeed, it was not until the present German Emperor plainly told the Berlin School Conference of 1890 that a national basis was lacking in

German education, that the foundation of the gymnasium course of study must be German; that the duty of the schoolmasters was to train the young to become Germans, not Greeks and Romans, and that the German language must be made the center around which all other subjects revolved, that a revision of the official school program was brought about that made place for the really serious study of the German language and literature. And to-day, where the influence of the English universities and of not a few American colleges is potent, the study of English is slight and insignificant indeed. The superstition that the best gate to English is through the Latin is anything but dead.

But for the great mass of the people the vernacular is not only the established medium of instruction, but fortunately also an important subject of study. A chief measure of educational accomplishment is the ease, the correctness, and the precision with which one uses this instrument.

It is no disrespect to the splendid literatures which are embodied in the French and the German tongues, and no lack of appreciation of the services of those great peoples to civilization and to culture, to point out that of modern languages the English is easily the first and the most powerful, for "it is the greatest instrument of communication that is now in use among men upon the earth." It is the speech of an aggressive people among whom individual liberty and personal initiative are highly prized.

It falls short, no doubt, of the philosophical pliability of the Greek and of the scientific ductility of the German; but what is there in the whole field of human passion and human action that it can not express with freedom and with a power all its own? Turn *Othello* into German or compare the verse of Shelley or of Keats with the graceful lines of some of their French contemporaries, and learn the peculiar power of the English speech. In simple word or sonorous phrase it is unequalled as a medium to reveal the thoughts, the feelings, and the ideals of humanity.

One's hold upon the English tongue is measured by his choice of words and by his use of idiom. The composite character of modern English offers a wide field for apt and happy choice of expression. The educated man, at home with his mother-tongue, moves easily about in its Saxon, Romanic, and Latin elements, and has gained by long experience and wide reading a knowledge of the mental incidence of words as well as of their artistic effect. He is hampered by no set formulas, but manifests in his speech, spoken and written, the characteristic powers and appreciation of his nature. The educated man is of necessity, therefore, a constant reader of the best written English. He reads not for conscious imitation, but for unconscious absorption and reflection. He knows the wide distinction between correct English on the one hand and pedantic, or as it is sometimes called, "elegant," English on the other. He is more likely to "go to bed" than to "retire," to "get up" than to "arise," to have "legs" rather than "limbs," to "dress" than to "clothe himself," and to "make a speech" rather than to "deliver an oration." He knows that "if you hear poor English and read poor English, you will pretty surely speak poor English and write poor English," and governs himself accordingly. He realizes the power and place of idiom and its relation to grammar, and shows his skill by preserving a balance between the two in his style. He would follow with intelligent sympathy the scholarly discussions of idiom and of grammar by Professor Earle and would find therein the justification of much of his best practise. In short, in his use of his mother-tongue he would give sure evidence of an education.

As a second evidence of education I name those refined and gentle manners which are the expression of fixt habits of thought and of action. "Manners are behavior and good breeding," as Addison said, but they are more. It is not without significance that the Latin language has but a single word *(mores)* both for usages, habits, manners, and for morals. Real manners, the manners of a truly educated man or woman, are an outward expression of intellectual and moral conviction. Sham manners are a veneer which falls away at the dampening touch of the first selfish suggestion. Manners have a moral significance, and find their basis in that true and deepest self-respect which is built upon respect for others. An infallible test of character is to be found in one's manners toward those whom, for one reason or another, the world may deem his inferiors.

A man's manners toward his equals or his superiors are shaped by too many motives to render their interpretation either easy or certain. Manners do not make the man, but manners reveal the man. It is by the amount of respect, deference, and courtesy shown to human personality as such that we judge whether one is on dress parade or whether he is so well-trained, well-educated, and so habitually ethical in thought and action that he realizes his proper relation to his fellows and reveals his realization in his manners. As Kant insisted more than a century ago, a man exists as an end in himself, and not merely as a means to be arbitrarily used by this or that will; and in all his actions, whether they concern himself alone or other rational beings, he must always be regarded as an end. True manners are based upon a recognition of this fact, and that is a poor education indeed which fails to inculcate the ethical principle and the manners that embody it.

As a third evidence of education I name the power and habit of reflection. It is a frequent charge against us moderns, particularly against Americans, that we are losing the habit of reflection and the high qualities which depend upon it. We are told that this loss is a necessary result of our hurried and busy lives, of our diverse interests, and of the annihilation of space and time by steam and electricity. The whole world and its happenings are brought to our very doors by the daily newspaper. Our attention leaps from Manila to Peking, from Peking to the Transvaal, and from the Transvaal to Havana. We are torn by conflicting or unconnected emotions, and our minds are occupied by ideas following each other with such rapidity that we fail to get a firm and deep hold of any one of the great facts that come into our lives. This is the charge which even sympathetic critics bring against us.

If it be true—and there are some counts in the indictment which it is difficult to deny—then one of the most precious evidences of an education is slipping from us, and we must redouble our efforts to keep fast hold upon it. The life which asks no questions of itself, which traces events back to no causes and forward to no purposes, which raises no vital issues of principle, and which seeks no interpretation of what passes within and without, is not a human life at all; it is the life of an animal. The trained and the untrained mind are perhaps in sharpest contrast at this very point. An armory of insights and convictions always ready for applications to new conditions, and invincible save by deeper insights and more rational convictions, is a mark of a trained and educated mind. The educated man has standards of truth, of human experience, and of wisdom by which new proposals are judged. These standards can be gained only through reflection. The undisciplined mind is a prey to every passing fancy and the victim of every plausible doctrinaire. He has no permanent forms of judgment which give him character.

Renan was right when he held that the first condition for the development of the mind is that it shall have liberty; and liberty for the mind means freedom from the control of the unreasonable, and freedom to choose the reasonable in accordance with principle. A body of principles is a necessary possession of the educated man. His development is always with reference to his principles, and proceeds by evolution, not revolution.

Philosophy is, of course, the great single study by which the power of reflection is developed until it becomes a habit, but there is a philosophic study of literature, of politics, of natural science, which makes for the same end. The question how, whose answer is science, and the question why, whose answer is philosophy, are the beginnings of reflection. A truly educated man asks both questions continually, and as a result is habituated to reflection.

As a fourth evidence of an education I name the power of growth. There is a type of mind which, when trained to a certain point, crystallizes, as it were, and refuses to move forward thereafter. This type of mind fails to give one of the essential evidences of an education. It has perhaps acquired much and promised much; but somehow or other the promise is not fulfilled. It is not dead, but in a trance. Only such functions are performed as serve to keep it where it is; there is no movement, no development, no new power or accomplishment. The impulse to continuous, and to that self-education which are the conditions of permanent, intellectual growth, is wanting. Education has so far failed of one of its chief purposes.

A human mind continuing to grow and to develop throughout a long life is a splendid and impressive sight. It was that characteristic in Mr. Gladstone which made his personality so attractive to young and ambitious men. They were fired by his zeal and inspired by his limitless intellectual energy. To have passed from being "the rising hope of the stern and unbending Tories" in 1838 to the unchallenged leadership of the anti-Tory party in Great Britain a generation later, and to have continued to grow throughout an exceptionally long life, is no mean distinction, and it is an example of what, in less conspicuous ways, is the lot of every mind whose training is effective. Broadened views, widened sympathies, deepened insights, are the accompaniments of growth.

For this growth a many-sided interest is necessary, and this is why growth and intellectual and moral narrowness are eternally at war. There is much in our modern education which is uneducational because it makes growth difficult, if not impossible. Early specialization, with its attendant limited range both of information and of interest, is an enemy of growth. Turning from the distasteful before it is understood, is an enemy of growth. Failure to see the relation of the subject of one's special interest to other subjects is an enemy of growth. The pretense of investigation and discovery before mastering existent knowledge is an enemy of growth. The habit of cynical indifference toward men and things and of aloofness from them, sometimes supposed to be peculiarly academic, is an enemy of growth. These, then, are all to be shunned while formal education is going on, if it is to carry with it the priceless gift of an impulse to continuous growth. "Life," says Bishop Spalding in an eloquent passage, "is the unfolding of a mysterious power, which in man rises to self-consciousness, and through self-consciousness to the knowledge of a world of truth and order and love, where action may no longer be left wholly to the sway of matter or to the impulse of instinct, but may and should be controlled by reason and conscience. To further this process by deliberate and intelligent effort is to educate"—and, I add, to educate so as to sow the seed of continuous growth, intellectual and moral.

And as a fifth evidence of an education I name efficiency, the power to do. The time has long since gone by, if it ever was, when contemplation pure and simple, withdrawal from the world and its activities, or intelligent incompetence was a defensible ideal of education. To-day the truly educated man must be, in some sense, efficient. With brain, tongue, or hand he must be able to express his knowledge and so leave the world other than he found it. Mr. James is simply summing up what physiology and psychology both teach when he exclaims: "No reception without reaction, no impression without correlative expression—this is the great maxim which the teacher ought never to forget. An impression which simply flows in the pupil's eyes or ears, and in no way modifies his active life, is an impression gone to waste. It is physiologically incomplete. It leaves no fruits behind it in the way of capacity acquired. Even as a mere impression it fails to produce its proper effect upon the memory; for, to remain fully among the acquisitions of the latter faculty, it must be wrought into the whole cycle of our operations. Its motor consequences are what clinch it." This is just as true of knowledge in general as of impressions. Indefinite absorption without production is fatal both to character and to the highest intellectual power. Do something and be able to do it well; express what you know in some helpful and substantial form; produce, and do not everlastingly feel only and revel in feelings—these are counsels which make for a real education and against that sham form of it which is easily recognized as well-informed incapacity. Our colleges and universities abound in false notions, notions as unscientific as they are unphilosophical, of the supposed value of knowledge, information, for its own sake. It has none. The date of the discovery of America is in itself as meaningless as the date of the birth of the youngest blade of grass in the neighboring field; it means something because it is part of a larger knowledge-whole, because it has relations, applications, uses; and for the student who sees none of these and knows none of them, America was discovered in 1249 quite as much as it was in 1492.

High efficiency is primarily an intellectual affair, and only *longo intervallo* does it take on anything approaching a mechanical form. Its mechanical form is always wholly subordinate to its springs in the intellect. It is the outgrowth of an established and habitual relationship between intellect and will, by means of which knowledge is constantly made power. For knowledge is not power, Bacon to the contrary notwithstanding, unless it is made so, and it can be made so only by him who possesses the knowledge. The habit of making knowledge power is efficiency. Without it education is incomplete.

These five characteristics, then, I offer as evidences of

an education—correctness and precision in the use of the mother-tongue; refined and gentle manners, which are the expression of fixt habits of thought and action; the power and habit of reflection; the power of growth; and efficiency, or the power to do. On this plane the physicist may meet with the philologian and the naturalist with the philosopher, and each recognize the fact that his fellow is an educated man, tho the range of their information is widely different and the centers of their highest interests are far apart. They are knit together in a brotherhood by the close tie of those traits which have sprung out of the reaction of their minds and wills upon that which has fed them and brought them strength. Without these traits men are not truly educated and their erudition, however vast, is of no avail; it furnishes a museum, not a developed human being.

It is these habits, of necessity made by ourselves alone, begun in days of school and college, and strengthened with maturer years and broader experience, that serve to show to ourselves and to others that we have discovered the secret of gaining an education.

Lesson talk. This selection is inserted here for its suggestive value to the student rather than for practise in reading. It should be noted that Dr. Butler places "correctness and precision in the use of the mother-tongue" first in his five evidences of an education. President Eliot, of Harvard, has given expression to a similar opinion when he says: "I recognize but one mental acquisition as an essential part of the education of a lady or gentleman, namely, an accurate and refined use of the mother-tongue."

THE PRINCE OF PEACE

BY WILLIAM JENNINGS BRYAN

I offer no apology for speaking upon a religious theme, for it is the most universal of all themes. If I addrest you upon the subject of law I might interest the lawyers; if I discust the science of medicine I might interest the physicians; in like manner merchants might be interested in a talk on commerce, and farmers in a discussion of agriculture; but none of these subjects appeals to all. Even the science of government, tho broader than any profession or occupation, does not embrace the whole sum of life, and those who think upon it differ so among themselves that I could not speak upon the subject so as to please a part without offending others. While to me the science of government is intensely absorbing, I recognize that the most important things in life lie outside of the realm of government and that more depends upon what the individual does for himself than upon what the government does or can do for him. Men can be miserable under the best government and they can be happy under the worst government.

Government affects but a part of the life which we live here and does not touch at all the life beyond, while religion touches the infinite circle of existence as well as the small arc of that circle which we spend on earth. No greater theme, therefore, can engage our attention.

Man is a religious being; the heart instinctively seeks for a God. Whether he worships on the banks of the Ganges, prays with his face upturned to the sun, kneels toward Mecca, or, regarding all space as a temple, communes with the heavenly Father according to the Christian creed, man is essentially devout.

There are honest doubters whose sincerity we recognize and respect, but occasionally I find young men who think it smart to be skeptical; they talk as if it were an evidence of larger intelligence to scoff at creeds and refuse to connect themselves with churches. They call themselves "liberal," as if a Christian were narrow minded. To these young men I desire to address myself.

Even some older people profess to regard religion as a superstition, pardonable in the ignorant but unworthy of the educated—a mental state which one can and should outgrow. Those who hold this view look down with mild contempt upon such as give to religion a definite place in their thoughts and lives. They assume an intellectual superiority and often take little pains to conceal the assumption. Tolstoy administers to the "Cultured crowd" (the words quoted are his) a severe rebuke when he declares that the religious sentiment rests not upon a superstitious fear of the invisible forces of nature, but upon man's consciousness of his finiteness amid an infinite universe and of his sinfulness; and this consciousness, the great philosopher adds, man can never outgrow. Tolstoy is right; man recognizes how limited are his own powers and how vast is the universe, and he leans upon the arm that is stronger than his. Man feels the weight of his sins and looks for One who is sinless.

Religion has been defined as the relation which man fixes between himself and his God, and morality as the outward manifestation of this relation. Every one, by the time he reaches maturity, has fixt some relation between himself and God and no material change in this relation can take place without a revolution in the man, for this relation is the most potent influence that acts upon a human life.

Religion is the basis of morality in the individual and in the group of individuals. Materialists have attempted to build up a system of morality upon the basis of enlightened self-interest. They would have man figure out by mathematics that it pays him to abstain from wrong doing; they would even inject an element of selfishness into altruism; but the moral system elaborated by the materialists has several defects. First, its virtues are borrowed from moral systems based upon religion; second, as it rests upon argument rather than upon authority, it does not appeal to the young, and by the time the young are able to follow their reason they have already become set in their ways. Our laws do not permit a young man to dispose of real estate until he is twenty-one—Why this restraint? Because his reason is not mature; and yet a man's life is largely molded by the environment of his youth. Third, one never knows just how much of his decision is due to reason and how much is due to passion or to selfish interest. We recognize the bias of self-interest when we exclude from the jury every man, no matter how reasonable or upright he may be, who has a pecuniary interest in the result of the trial. And, fourth, one whose morality is based upon a nice calculation of benefits to be secured spends time figuring that he should spend in action. Those who keep a book account of their good deeds seldom do enough good to justify keeping books.

Morality is the power of endurance in man; and a religion which teaches personal responsibility to God gives strength to morality. There is a powerful restraining influence in the belief that an all-seeing eye scrutinizes every thought and word and act of the individual.

There is a wide difference between the man who is trying to conform to a standard of morality about him and the man who is endeavoring to make his life approximate to a divine standard. The former attempts to live up to the standard if it is above him and down to it if it is below him—and if he is doing right only when others are looking he is sure to find a time when he thinks he is unobserved, and then he takes a vacation and falls. One needs the inner strength which comes with the conscious presence of a personal God. If those who are thus fortified sometimes yield to temptation how helpless and hopeless must those be who rely upon their own strength alone!

There are difficulties to be encountered in religion, but there are difficulties to be encountered everywhere. I passed through a period of skepticism when I was in college and I have been glad ever since that I became a member of the Church before I left home for college, for it helped me during those trying days. The college days cover the dangerous period in the young man's life; it is when he is just coming into possession of his powers—when he feels stronger than he ever feels afterward and thinks he knows more than he ever does know.

It was at this period that I was confused by the different theories of creation. But I examined these theories and found that they all assumed something to begin with. The nebular hypothesis, for instance, assumes that matter and force existed—matter in particles infinitely fine and each particle separated from every other particle by space infinitely great. Beginning with this assumption, force working on matter—according to this hypothesis—creates a universe. Well, I have a right to assume, and I prefer to assume a Designer back of the design—a Creator back of creation; and no matter how long you draw out the process of creation, so long as God stands back of it you can not shake my faith in Jehovah. In Genesis it is written that, in the beginning, God created the heavens and the earth, and I can stand on that proposition until I find some theory of creation that goes farther back than "the beginning."

I do not carry the doctrine of evolution as far as some do; I have not yet been able to convince myself that man is a lineal descendant of the lower animals. I do not mean to find fault with you if you want to accept it; all I mean to say is that while you may trace your ancestry back to the monkey, if you find pleasure or pride in doing so, you shall not connect me with your family tree without more evidence than has yet been produced. It is true that man, in some physical qualities, resembles the beast, but man has a mind as well as a body and a soul as well as a mind. The mind is greater than the body and the soul is greater than the mind, and I object to having man's pedigree traced on one-third of him only—and that the lowest third. Fairbairn lays down a sound proposition when he says that it is not sufficient to explain man as an animal; it is necesary to explain man in history—and the Darwinian theory does not do this. The ape, according to this theory, is older than man and yet he is still an ape, while man is the author of the marvelous civilization which we see about us.

One does not escape from mystery, however, by accepting this theory, for it does not explain the origin of life. When the follower of Darwin has traced the germ of life back to the lowest form in which it appears—and to follow him one must exercise more faith than religion calls for—he finds that scientists differ. Some believe that the first germ of life came from another planet, and others hold that it was the result of spontaneous generation.

If I were compelled to accept one of these theories I would prefer the first, for if we can chase the germ of life off this planet and get it out into space we can guess the rest of the way and no one can contradict us, but if we accept the doctrine of spontaneous generation we can not explain why spontaneous generation ceased to act after the first germ was created.

Go back as far as we may, we can not escape from the creative act, and it is just as easy for me to believe that God created man as he is, as to believe that, millions of years ago, He created a germ of life and endowed it with power to develop into all that we see to-day. But I object to the Darwinian theory, until more conclusive proof is produced, because I fear we shall lose the consciousness of God's presence in our daily life, if we must assume that through all the ages no spiritual force has touched the life of man or shaped the destiny of nations. But there is another objection. The Darwinian theory represents man as reaching his present perfection by the operation of the law of hate—the merciless law by which the strong crowd out and kill off the weak. If this is the law of our development then, if there is any logic that can bind the human mind, we shall turn backward toward the beast in proportion as we substitute the law of love. How can hatred be the law of development when nations have advanced in proportion as they have departed from that law and adopted the law of love?

But while I do not accept the Darwinian theory I shall not quarrel with you about it; I only refer to it to remind you that it does not solve the mystery of life or explain human progress. I fear that some have accepted it in the hope of escaping from the miracle, but why should the miracle frighten us? It bothered me once, and I am inclined to think that it is one of the test questions with the Christian.

Christ can not be separated from the miraculous; His birth, His ministrations, and His resurrection, all involve the miraculous, and the change which His religion works in the human heart is a continuing miracle. Eliminate the miracles and Christ becomes merely a human being and His gospel is stript of divine authority.

The miracle raises two questions: "Can God perform a miracle?" and, "Would He want to?" The first is easy to answer. A God who can make a world can do anything He wants to do with it. The power to perform miracles is necessarily implied in the power to create. But would God want to perform a miracle?—this is the question which has given most of the trouble. The more I have considered it the less inclined I am to answer in the negative. To say that God would not perform a miracle is to assume a more intimate knowledge of God's plans and purposes than I can claim to have. I will not deny that God does perform a miracle or may perform one merely because I do not know how or why He does it. The fact that we are constantly learning of the existence of new forces suggests the possibility that God may operate through forces yet unknown to us, and the mysteries with which we deal every day warn me that faith is as necessary as sight. Who would have credited a century ago the stories that are now told of the wonder-working electricity? For ages man had known the lightning, but only to fear it; now, this invisible current is generated by a man-made machine, imprisoned in a man-made wire and made to do the bidding of man. We are even able to dispense with the wire and hurl words through space, and the X-ray has enabled us to look through substances which were supposed, until recently, to exclude all light. The miracle is not more mysterious than many of the things with which man now deals—it is simply different. The immaculate conception is not more mysterious than any other conception—it is simply unlike; nor is the resurrection of Christ more mysterious than the myriad resurrections which mark each annual seed-time.

It is sometimes said that God could not suspend one of His laws without stopping the universe, but do we not suspend or overcome the law of gravitation every day? Every time we move a foot or lift a weight, we temporarily interfere with the operation of the most universal of natural laws and yet the world is not disturbed.

Science has taught us so many things that we are tempted to conclude that we know everything, but there is really a great unknown which is still unexplored and that which we have learned ought to increase our reverence rather than our egotism. Science has disclosed some of the machinery of the universe, but science has not yet revealed to us the great secret—the secret of life. It is to be found in every blade of grass, in every insect, in every bird and in every animal, as well as in man. Six thousand years of recorded history and yet we know no more about the secret of life than they knew in the beginning. We live, we plan; we have our hopes, our fears; and yet in a moment a change may come over any one of us and this body will become a mass of lifeless clay. What is it that, having, we live, and, having not, we are as the clod? We know not and yet the progress of the race and the civilization which we now behold are the work of men and women who have not solved the mystery of their own lives.

And our food, must we understand it before we eat it? If we refused to eat anything until we could understand the mystery of its growth, we would die of starvation. But mystery does not bother us in the dining-room; it is only in the church that it is an obstacle.

I was eating a piece of watermelon some months ago and was struck with its beauty. I took some of the seed and dried them and weighed them, and found that it would require some five thousand seed to weigh a pound. And then I applied mathematics to that forty-pound melon. One of these seeds, put into the ground, when warmed by the sun and moistened by the rain, goes to work; it gathers from somewhere two hundred thousand times its own weight and, forcing this raw material through a tiny stem, constructs a watermelon. It covers the outside with a coating of green; inside of the green it puts a layer of white, and within the white a core of red, and all through the red it scatters seeds, each one capable of continuing the work of reproduction. Where did that little seed get its tremendous power? Where did it find its coloring matter? How did it collect its flavoring extract? How did it build a watermelon? Until you can explain a watermelon, do not be too sure that you can set limits to the power of the Almighty or say just what He would do or how He would do it. I can not explain the watermelon but I eat it and enjoy it.

Everything that grows tells a like story of infinite power. Why should I deny that a divine hand fed a multitude with a few loaves and fishes when I see hundreds of millions fed every year by a hand which converts the seeds scattered over the field into an abundant harvest? We know that food can be multiplied in a few months' time; shall we deny the power of the Creator to eliminate the element of time, when we have gone so far in eliminating the element of space?

But there is something even more wonderful still—the mysterious change that takes place in the human heart when the man begins to hate the things he loved and to love the things he hated—the marvelous transformation that takes place in the man who, before the change, would have sacrificed the world for his own advancement but who, after the change, would give his life for a principle and esteem it a privilege to make sacrifice for his convictions. What greater miracle than this, that converts a selfish, self-centered, human being into a center from which good influences flow out in every direction! And yet this miracle has been wrought in the heart of each one of us—or may be wrought—and we have seen it wrought in the hearts of those about us. No, living in the midst of mystery and miracles I shall not allow either to deprive me of the benefits of the Christian religion.

Some of those who question the miracle also question the theory of atonement; they assert that it does not accord with their idea of justice for one to die for others. Let each one bear his own sins and the punishments due for them, they say. The doctrine of vicarious suffering is not a new one; it is as old as the race. That one should suffer for others is one of the most familiar of principles and we see the principle illustrated every day of our lives. Take the family, for instance; from the day the mother's first child is born, for twenty-five or thirty years they are scarcely out of her waking thoughts. She sacrifices for them, she surrenders herself to them. Is it because she expects them to pay her back? Fortunate for the parent and fortunate for the child if the latter has an opportunity to repay in part the debt it owes. But no child can compensate a parent for a parent's care. In the course of nature the debt is paid, not to the parent, but to the next generation, each generation suffering and sacrificing for the one following.

Nor is this confined to the family. Every step in advance has been made possible by those who have been willing to sacrifice for posterity. Freedom of speech, freedom of the press, freedom of conscience and free government have all been won for the world by those who were willing to make sacrifices for their fellows. So well established is this doctrine that we do not regard any one as great unless he recognizes how unimportant his life is in comparison with the problems with which he deals.

I find proof that man was made in the image of his Creator in the fact that, throughout the centuries, man has been willing to die that blessings denied to him might be enjoyed by his children, his children's children and the world.

The seeming paradox: "He that saveth his life shall lose it and he that loseth his life for my sake shall find it," has an application wider than that usually given to it; it is an epitome of history. Those who live only for themselves live little lives, but those who give themselves for the advancement of things greater than themselves find a larger life than the one surrendered. Wendell Phillips gave expression to the same idea when he said: "How prudently most men sink into nameless graves, while now and then a few forget themselves into immortality."

Instead of being an unnatural plan, the plan of salvation is in perfect harmony with human nature as we understand it. Sacrifice is the language of love, and Christ, in suffering for the world, adopted the only means of reaching the heart, and this can be demonstrated, not only by theory but by experience, for the story of His life, His teachings, His sufferings and His death has been translated into every language and everywhere it has touched the heart.

But if I were going to present an argument in favor of the divinity of Christ, I would not begin with miracles or mystery or theory of atonement. I would begin as Carnegie Simpson begins in his book entitled, "The Fact of Christ." Commencing with the fact that Christ lived, he points out that one can not contemplate this undisputed fact without feeling that in some way this fact is related to those now living. He says that one can read of Alexander, of Cæsar, or of Napoleon, and not feel that it is a matter of personal concern; but that when one reads that Christ lived and how He lived and how He died he feels that somehow there is a chord that stretches from that life to his. As he studies the character of Christ he becomes conscious of certain virtues which stand out in bold relief—purity, humility, a forgiving spirit and an unfathomable love. The author is correct. Christ presents an example of purity in thought and life, and man, conscious of his own imperfections and grieved over his shortcomings, finds inspiration in One who was tempted in all points like as we are, and yet without sin. I am not sure but that we can find just here a way of determining whether one possesses the true spirit of a Christian. If he finds in the sinlessness of Christ an inspiration and a stimulus to greater effort and higher living, he is indeed a follower; if, on the other hand, he resents the reproof which the purity of Christ offers he is likely to question the divinity of Christ in order to excuse himself for not being a follower.

Humility is a rare virtue. If one is rich he is apt to

be proud of his riches; if he has distinguished ancestry, he is apt to be proud of his lineage; if he is well educated, he is apt to be proud of his learning. Some one has suggested that if one becomes humble, he soon becomes proud of his humility. Christ, however, possest of all power, was the very personification of humility.

The most difficult of all the virtues to cultivate is the forgiving spirit. Revenge seems to be natural to the human heart; to want to get even with an enemy is a common sin. It has even been popular to boast of vindictiveness; it was once inscribed on a monument to a hero that he had repaid both friends and enemies more than he had received. This was not the spirit of Christ. He taught forgiveness and in that incomparable prayer which He left as a model for our petitions He made our willingness to forgive the measure by which we may claim forgiveness. He not only taught forgiveness, but He exemplified His teachings in His life. When those who persecuted Him brought Him to the most disgraceful of all deaths, His spirit of forgiveness rose above His sufferings and He prayed, "Father, forgive them, for they know not what they do!"

But love is the foundation of Christ's creed. The world had known love before; parents had loved children and children, parents; husband had loved wife and wife husband; and friends had loved friends; but Jesus gave a new definition of love. His love was as boundless as the sea; its limits were so far-flung that even an enemy could not travel beyond it. Other teachers sought to regulate the lives of their followers by rule and formula, but Christ's plan was, first to purify the heart and then to leave love to direct the footsteps.

What conclusion is to be drawn from the life, the teachings and the death of this historic figure? Reared in a carpenter shop; with no knowledge of literature, save Bible literature; with no acquaintance with philosophers living or with the writings of sages dead, this young man gathered disciples about Him, promulgated a higher code of morals than the world had ever known before, and proclaimed Himself the Messiah. He taught and performed miracles for a few brief months and then was crucified; His disciples were scattered and many of them put to death; His claims were disputed, His resurrection denied and His followers persecuted, and yet from this beginning His religion has spread until millions take His name with reverence upon their lips and thousands have been willing to die rather than surrender the faith which He put into their hearts. How shall we account for Him? "What think ye of Christ?" It is easier to believe Him divine than to explain in any other way what He said and did and was. And I have greater faith even than before since I have visited the Orient and witnessed the successful contest which Christianity is waging against the religions and philosophies of the East.

I was thinking a few years ago of the Christmas which was then approaching and of Him in whose honor the day is celebrated. I recalled the message, Peace on earth, good will to men, and then my thoughts ran back to the prophecy uttered centuries before His birth, in which He was described as the Prince of Peace. To reenforce my memory I reread the prophecy and found immediately following a verse which I had forgotten—a verse which declares that of the increase of His peace and government there shall be no end, for adds Isaiah, "He shall judge his people with justice and with judgment." Thinking of the prophecy, I have selected this theme that I may present some of the reasons which lead me to believe that Christ has fully earned the title, The Prince of Peace, and that in the years to come it will be more and more applied to Him. Faith in Him brings peace to the heart and His teachings, when applied, will bring peace between man and man. And if He can bring peace to each heart, and if His creed will bring peace throughout the earth who will deny His right to be called the Prince of Peace?

All the world is in search of peace; every heart that ever beat has sought for peace, and many have been the methods employed to secure it. Some have thought to purchase it with riches and they have labored to secure wealth, hoping to find peace when they were able to go where they pleased and buy what they liked. Of those who have endeavored to purchase peace with money, the large majority have failed to secure the money. But what has been the experience of those who have been successful in accumulating money? They all tell the same story; viz., that they spent the first half of their lives trying to get money from others and the last half trying to keep others from getting their money, and that they found peace in neither half. Some have even reached the point where they find difficulty in getting people to accept their money; and I know of no better indication of the ethical awakening in this country than the increasing tendency to scrutinize the methods of money making. A long step in advance will have been taken when religious, educational and charitable institutions refuse to condone immoral methods in business and leave the possessor of ill-gotten gains to learn the loneliness of life when one prefers money to morals.

Some have sought peace in social distinction, but whether they have been within the charmed circle and fearful lest they might fall out, or outside and hopeful that they might get in, they have not found peace.

Some have thought, vain thought! to find peace in political prominence; but whether office comes by birth, as in monarchies, or by election, as in republics, it does not bring peace. An office is conspicuous only when few can occupy it. Only when few in a generation can hope to enjoy an honor do we call it a great honor. I am glad that our heavenly Father did not make the peace of the human heart depend upon the accumulation of wealth, or upon the securing of social or political distinction, for in either case but few could have enjoyed it, but when He made peace the reward of a conscience void of offense toward God and man, He put it within the reach of all. The poor can secure it as easily as the rich, the social outcast as freely as the leader of society and the humblest citizen equally with those who wield political power.

To those who have grown gray in the faith I need not speak of the peace to be found in the belief in an overruling Providence. Christ taught that our lives are precious in the sight of God, and poets have taken up the theme and woven it into immortal verse. No uninspired writer has exprest the idea more beautifully than William Cullen Bryant in the "Ode to a Waterfowl." After following the wanderings of the bird of passage as it seeks first its northern and then its southern home, he concludes:

> Thou art gone; the abyss of heaven
>   Hath swallowed up thy form, but on my heart
> Deeply hath sunk the lesson thou hast given,
>   And shall not soon depart.

He who, from zone to zone,
  Guides through the boundless sky thy certain flight,
In the long way that I must tread alone,
  Will lead my steps aright.

Christ promoted peace by giving us assurance that a line of communication can be established between the Father above and the child below. And who will measure the consolation that has been brought to troubled hearts by the hour of prayer?

And immortality! Who will estimate the peace which a belief in a future life has brought to the sorrowing? You may talk to the young about death ending all, for life is full and hope is strong, but preach not this doctrine to the mother who stands by the death-bed of her babe or to one who is within the shadow of a great affliction. When I was a young man I wrote to Colonel Ingersoll and asked him for his views on God and immortality. His secretary answered that the great infidel was not at home, but enclosed a copy of a speech which covered my question. I scanned it with eagerness and found that he had exprest himself about as follows: "I do not say that there is no God, I simply say I do not know. I do not say that there is no life beyond the grave, I simply say I do not know." And from that day to this I have not been able to understand how any one could find pleasure in taking from any human heart a living faith and substituting therefor the cold and cheerless doctrine, "I do not know."

Christ gave us proof of immortality and yet it would hardly seem necessary that one should rise from the dead to convince us that the grave is not the end. To every created thing God has given a tongue that proclaims a resurrection.

If the Father deigns to touch with divine power the cold and pulseless heart of the buried acorn and to make it burst forth from its prison walls, will He leave neglected in the earth the soul of man, made in the image of his Creator? If He stoops to give to the rose-bush, whose withered blossoms float upon the autumn breeze, the sweet assurance of another springtime, will He refuse the words of hope to the sons of men when the frosts of winter come? If matter, mute and inanimate, tho changed by the forces of nature into a multitude of forms, can never die, will the spirit of man suffer annihilation when it has paid a brief visit like a royal guest to this tenement of clay? No, I am as sure that there is another life as I am that I live to-day!

In Cairo I secured a few grains of wheat that had slumbered for more than three thousand years in an Egyptian tomb. As I looked at them this thought came into my mind: If one of those grains had been planted on the banks of the Nile the year after it grew, and all its lineal descendants planted and replanted from that time until now, its progeny would to-day be sufficiently numerous to feed the teeming millions of the world. There is in the grain of wheat an invisible something which has power to discard the body that we see, and from earth and air fashion a new body so much like the old one that we can not tell the one from the other. If this invisible germ of life in the grain of wheat can thus pass unimpaired through three thousand resurrections, I shall not doubt that my soul has power to clothe itself with a body suited to its new existence when this earthly frame has crumbled into dust.

A belief in immortality not only consoles the individual, but it exerts a powerful influence in bringing peace between individuals. If one really thinks that man dies as the brute dies, he may yield to the temptation to do injustice to his neighbor when the circumstances are such as to promise security from detection. But if one really expects to meet again, and live eternally with, those whom he knows to-day, he is restrained from evil deeds by the fear of endless remorse. We do not know what rewards are in store for us or what punishments may be reserved, but if there were no other punishment it would be enough for one who deliberately and consciously wrongs another to have to live forever in the company of the person wronged and have his littleness and selfishness laid bare. I repeat, a belief in immortality must exert a powerful influence in establishing justice between men and thus laying the foundation for peace.

Again, Christ deserves to be called the Prince of Peace because He has given us a measure of greatness which promotes peace. When His disciples disputed among themselves as to which should be greatest in the kingdom of heaven, He rebuked them and said: "Let him who would be chiefest among you be the servant of all." Service is the true measure of greatness; it always has been true; it is true to-day, and it always will be true, that he is greatest who does the most of good. And yet, what a revolution it will work in this old world when this standard becomes the standard of life. Nearly all of our controversies and combats arise from the fact that we are trying to get something from each other—there will be peace when our aim is to do something for each other. Our enmities and animosities arise from our efforts to get as much as possible out of the world—there will be peace when our endeavor is to put as much as possible into the world. Society will take an immeasurable step toward peace when it estimates a citizen by his output rather than by his income, and gives the crown of its approval to the one who makes the largest contribution to the welfare of all. It is the glory of the Christian ideal that, while it is within sight of the weakest and the lowliest, it is yet so high that the best and the noblest are kept with their faces turned ever upward.

Christ has also led the way to peace by giving us a formula for the propagation of good. Not all of those who have really desired to do good have employed the Christian method—not all Christians even. In all the history of the human race but two methods have been employed. The first is the forcible method. A man has an idea which he thinks is good; he tells his neighbors about it and they do not like it. This makes him angry and seizing a club, he attempts to make them like it. One trouble about this rule is that it works both ways; when a man starts out to compel his neighbors to think as he does, he generally finds them willing to accept the challenge and they spend so much time in trying to coerce each other that they have no time left to be of service to each other.

The other is the Bible plan—be not overcome of evil but overcome evil with good. And there is no other way of overcoming evil. I am not much of a farmer—I get more credit for my farming than I deserve, and my little farm receives more advertising than it is entitled to. But I am farmer enough to know that if I cut down weeds they will spring up again, and I know that if I plant something there which has more vitality than the weeds I shall not only get rid of the constant cutting but have the benefit of the crop besides.

In order that there might be no mistake about His plan

of propagating good, Christ went into detail and laid emphasis upon the value of example—"so live that others seeing your good works may be constrained to glorify your Father which is in heaven." There is no human influence so potent for good as that which goes out from an upright life. A sermon may be answered; the arguments presented in a speech may be disputed, but no one can answer a Christian life—it is the unanswerable argument in favor of our religion.

It may be a slow process—this conversion of the world by the silent influence of a noble example, but it is the only sure one, and the doctrine applies to nations as well as to individuals. The gospel of the Prince of Peace gives us the only hope that the world has—and it is an increasing hope—of the substitution of reason for the arbitrament of force in the settlement of international disputes.

But Christ has given us a platform more fundamental than any political party has ever written. We are interested in platforms; we attend conventions, sometimes traveling long distances; we have wordy wars over the phraseology of various planks and then we wage earnest campaigns to secure the endorsement of these platforms at the polls. But the platform given to the world by the Nazarene is more far-reaching and more comprehensive than any platform ever written by the convention of any party in any country. When He condensed into one commandment those of the ten which relate to man's duty toward his fellows and enjoined upon us the rule, "Thou shalt love thy neighbor as thyself," He presented a plan for the solution of all the problems that now vex society or may hereafter arise. Other remedies may palliate or postpone the day of settlement, but this is all-sufficient and the reconciliation which it effects is a permanent one.

If I were to attempt to apply this thought to various questions which are at issue, I might be accused of entering the domain of partizan politics, but I may safely apply it to two great problems. First, let us consider the question of capital and labor. This is not a transient issue or a local one. It engages the attention of the people of all countries and has appeared in every age. The immediate need in this country is arbitration, for neither side to the controversy can be trusted to deal with absolute justice, if allowed undisputed control; but arbitration, like a court, is a last resort. It would be better if the relations between employer and employee were such as to make arbitration unnecessary. Just in proportion as men recognize their kinship to each other and deal with each other in the spirit of brotherhood will friendship and harmony be secured. Both employer and employee need to cultivate the spirit which follows from obedience to the great commandment.

The second problem to which I would apply this platform of peace is that which relates to the accumulation of wealth. We can not much longer delay consideration of the ethics of money-making. That many of the enormous fortunes which have been accumulated in the last quarter of a century are now held by men who have given to society no adequate service in return for the money secured is now generally recognized. While legislation can and should protect the public from predatory wealth, a more effective remedy will be found in the cultivation of a public opinion which will substitute a higher ideal than the one which tolerates the enjoyment of unearned gains. No man who really knows what brotherly love is will desire to take advantage of his neighbor, and the conscience when not seared will admonish against injustice. My faith in the future rests upon the belief that Christ's teachings are being more studied to-day than ever before, and that with this larger study will come an application of those teachings to the every-day life of the world. In former times men read that Christ came to bring life and immortality to light and placed the emphasis upon immortality; now they are studying Christ's relation to human life. In former years many thought to prepare themselves for future bliss by a life of seclusion here; now they are learning that they can not follow in the footsteps of the Master unless they go about doing good. Christ declared that He came that we might have life and have it more abundantly. The world is learning that Christ came not to narrow life but to enlarge it—to fill it with purpose, earnestness and happiness.

But this Prince of Peace promises not only peace but strength. Some have thought His teachings fit only for the weak and the timid and unsuited to men of vigor, energy and ambition. Nothing could be farther from the truth. Only the man of faith can be courageous. Confident that he fights on the side of Jehovah, he doubts not the success of his cause. What matters it whether he shares in the shouts of triumph? If every word spoken in behalf of truth has its influence and every deed done for the right weighs in the final account it is immaterial to the Christian whether his eyes behold victory or whether he dies in the midst of the conflict.

"Yea, tho thou lie upon the dust,
   When they who helped thee flee in fear,
Die full of hope and manly trust,
   Like those who fell in battle here.

"Another hand thy sword shall wield,
Another hand the standard wave,
Till from the trumpets mouth is pealed
The blast of triumph o'er thy grave."

Only those who believe attempt the seemingly impossible and, by attempting, prove that one with God can chase a thousand and two can put ten thousand to flight. I can imagine that the early Christians who were carried into the arena to make a spectacle for those more savage than the beasts, were entreated by their doubting companions not to endanger their lives. But, kneeling in the center of the arena, they prayed and sang until they were devoured. How helpless they seemed and, measured by every human rule, how hopeless was their cause! And yet within a few decades the power which they invoked proved mightier than the legions of the emperor and the faith in which they died was triumphant o'er all that land. It is said that those who went to mock their sufferings returned asking themselves, "What is it that can enter into the heart of man and make him die as these die?" They were greater conquerors in their death than they could have been had they purchased life by a surrender of their faith.

What would have been the fate of the Church if the early Christians had had as little faith as many of our Christians now have? And, on the other hand, if the Christians of to-day had the faith of the martyrs, how long would it be before the fulfilment of the prophecy that every knee shall bow and every tongue confess?

Our faith should be even stronger than the faith of those who lived two thousand years ago, for we see our religion spreading and supplanting the philosophies and creeds of the Orient.

As the Christian grows older he appreciates more and more the completeness with which Christ fills the requirements of the heart and, grateful for the peace which he enjoys and for the strength which he has received, he repeats the words of the great scholar, Sir William Jones:

"Before thy mystic altar, heavenly truth,
I kneel in manhood, as I knelt in youth,
Thus let me kneel, till this dull form decay,
And life's last shade be brightened by the ray."

HAMLET'S SOLILOQUY

BY WILLIAM SHAKESPEARE

To *be* or *not* to be: that is the question:
Whether 'tis nobler in the mind to suffer
The slings and arrows of outrageous fortune,
Or to take arms against a sea of troubles,
And by opposing end them? To *die:* to *sleep;*
No more; and by a sleep to say we end
The heartache and the thousand natural shocks
That flesh is heir to: 'tis a consummation
Devoutly to be wish'd. To die, to sleep;
To sleep: perchance to *dream!*—ay, there's the rub;
For in that sleep of death what dreams may come
When we have shuffled off this mortal coil,
Must give us pause: there's the respect
That makes calamity of so long life;

For who would bear the whips and scorns of time,
The oppressor's wrong, the proud man's contumely,
The pangs of despised love, the law's delay,
The insolence of office and the spurns
That patient merit of the unworthy takes,
When he himself might his quietus make
With a bare bodkin? who'd these fardels bear,
To grunt and sweat under a weary life
But that the dread of something after death,
The undiscover'd country from whose bourn
No traveler returns, puzzles the will
And makes us rather bear those ills we have
Than fly to others that we know not of?
Thus conscience does make cowards of us all;
And thus the native hue of resolution
Is sicklied o'er with the pale cast of thought,
And enterprises of great pith and moment
With this regard their currents turn awry,
And lose the name of action.

VIRGINIA

THOMAS BABINGTON MACAULAY

Ye good men of the Commons, with loving hearts and true,
Who stand by the bold Tribunes that still have stood by you,
Come, make a circle round me, and mark my tale with care,
A tale of what Rome once hath borne, of what Rome may
    yet bear.
This is no Grecian fable, of fountains running wine,
Of maids with snaky tresses, or sailors turned to swine;

Here, in this very Forum, under the noonday sun,
In sight of all the people, the bloody deed was done.
Old men still creep among us who saw that fearful day,
Just seventy years and seven ago, when the wicked Ten bare sway.

Of all the wicked Ten still the names are held accurst,
And of all the wicked Ten, Appius Claudius was the worst.
He stalked along the Forum like King Tarquin in his pride:
Twelve axes waited on him, six marching on each side;
The townsmen shrank to right and left, and eyed askance with fear
His lowering brow, his curling mouth, which always seemed to sneer.

Nor lacks he fit attendance; for close behind his heels,
With outstretched chin and crouching pace, the client Marcus steals.
Where'er ye shed the honey, the buzzing flies will crowd;
Where'er ye fling the carrion, the raven's croak is loud;
Where'er down Tiber garbage floats, the greedy pike you see;
And wheresoe'er such lord is found, such client still will be.

Just then, as through one cloudless chink in a black stormy sky
Shines out the dewy morning star, a fair young girl came by,
With her small tablets in her hand, and her satchel on her arm,
Home she went bounding from the school, nor dreamed of shame or harm;

And past those dreaded axes she innocently ran,
With bright, frank brow that had not learned to blush at gaze of man;

And up the Sacred Street she turned, and as she danced along,
She warbled gaily to herself lines of the good old song.
And Appius heard her sweet young voice and saw her sweet young face
And loved her with the accursèd love of his accursèd race,
And all along the Forum, and up the Sacred Street,
His vulture eye pursued the trip of those small glancing feet.

She crossed the Forum, shining with stalls in alleys gay,
And had just reached the very spot whereon I stand this day,
When up the varlet Marcus came; not such as when, erewhile,
He crouched behind his patron's heels, with the true client smile;
He came with lowering forehead, swollen features and clenched fist,
And strode across Virginia's path, and caught her by the wrist.

Hard strove the frightened maiden, and screamed with look aghast;
And at her scream, from right and left, the folks came running fast;
The money-changer Crispus, with his thin silver hairs,

And Hanno from the stately booth glittering with Punic wares,
And the strong, smith Muræna, grasping a half-forged brand,
And Volero, the flesher, his cleaver in his hand.
All came in wrath and wonder; for all knew that fair child;
And, as she passed them twice a day, all kissed their hands and smiled;
And the strong smith Muræna gave Marcus such a blow,
The caitiff reeled three paces back, and let the maiden go.
Yet glared he fiercely round him, and growled in harsh, fell tone,
"She's mine, and I will have her. I seek but for my own:
She is my slave, born in my house, and stolen away and sold,
The year of the sore sickness, ere she was twelve hours old.
I wait on Appius Claudius; I waited on his sire:
Let him who works the client wrong, beware the patron's ire!"

So spake the varlet Marcus; and dread and silence came
On all the people at the sound of the great Claudian name.
Straightway Virginius led his child a little space aside,
To where the reeking shambles stood, piled with horn and hide.
Hard by, a flesher on a block had laid his whittle down:
Virginius caught the whittle up, and hid it in his gown.
And then his eyes grew very dim, and his throat began to swell,
And in a hoarse, changed voice he spake, "Farewell, sweet child! Farewell!
The house that was the happiest within the Roman walls,

The house that envied not the wealth of Capua's marble halls,
Now, for the brightness of thy smile, must have eternal gloom,
And for the music of thy voice, the silence of the tomb.

"The time is come. See how he points his eager hand this way!
See how his eyes gloat on thy grief, like a kite's upon the prey!
With all his wit, he little deems, that, spurned, betrayed, bereft,
Thy father hath in his despair one fearful refuge left.
He little deems that in this hand I clutch what still can save
Thy gentle youth from taunts and blows, the portion of the slave;
Then clasp me round the neck once more, and give me one more kiss;
And now, mine own dear little girl, there is no way but this."

With that he lifted high the steel, and smote her in the side,
And in her blood she sank to earth, and with one sob she died.
Then for a little moment all the people held their breath;
And through the crowded Forum was stillness as of death;
And in another moment brake forth from one and all
A cry as if the Volscians were coming o'er the wall.
Some with averted faces shrieking fled home amain;
Some ran to call a leech, and some ran to lift the slain;
Some felt her lips and little wrist, if life might there be found:

And some tore up their garments fast, and strove to stanch
the wound.
In vain they ran, and felt, and stanched; for never truer
blow
That good right arm had dealt in fight against a Volscian
foe.

When Appius Claudius saw that deed he shuddered and
sank down,
And hid his face some little space with the corner of his
gown,
Till, with white lips and bloodshot eyes, Virginius tottered
nigh,
And stood before the judgment-seat, and held the knife on
high.
"Oh, dwellers in the nether gloom, avengers of the slain,
By this dear blood I cry to you, do right between us twain;
And even as Appius Claudius hath dealt by me and mine,
Deal you by Appius Claudius and all the Claudian line!"
So spake the slayer of his child, and turned, and went his
way;
But first he cast one haggard glance to where the body lay,
And writhed and groaned a fearful groan, and then with
stedfast feet,
Strode right across the market-place unto the Sacred Street.
Then up sprang Appius Claudius: "Stop him; alive or
dead!
Ten thousand pounds of copper to the man who brings his
head!"
He looked upon his clients, but none would work his will.
He looked upon his lictors, but they trembled and stood
still.

And as Virginius through the press his way in silence cleft,
Ever the mighty multitude fell back to right and left,
And he hath passed in safety into his woful home,
And there ta'en horse to tell the camp what deeds are done
in Rome.

RICHELIEU

BY EDWARD BULWER-LYTTON

The characters in this scene are: RICHELIEU, *the minister of France and Cardinal of the Church of Rome;* LOUIS, *the king;* BARADAS, *the chief conspirator; and* JULIE, *Richelieu's ward.*

The KING *and* BARADAS *plan the assassination of* RICHELIEU. *A false report of his death misleads them, and in the midst of their rejoicing* RICHELIEU *enters and says:*

Rich. (fiercely). Room, my lords, room.
The minister of France can need no intercession with the king.

Louis. What means this false report of death, Lord Cardinal?

Rich. Are you, then, angered, sire, that I live still?

Louis. No; but such artifice—

Rich. Not mine; look elsewhere,
Louis! My castle swarmed with the assassins.

Bar. (advancing). We have punished them already. Huguet is now
In the Bastile. Oh, my lord, we were prompt
To avenge you—we were.

Rich. We? Ha, ha! you hear
My liege! What page, man, in the last court grammar,
Made you a plural? Count, you have seized the *hireling;*
Sire, shall I name the master?

Louis. Tush, my lord,
The old contrivance; ever does your wit
Invent assassins, that ambition may
Slay rivals—

Rich. Rivals, sire, in what?
Service to France? I have none. Lives the man
Whom Europe deems rival to Armand Richelieu?

Louis. What, so haughty!
Remember, he who made, can unmake.

Rich. Never!
Never! Your anger can recall your trust,
Annul my office, despoil me of my lands,
Rifle my coffers—but my name, my deeds
Are loyal in a land beyond your scepter.
Pass sentence on me, if you will; from kings
Lo! I appeal to time!

Louis. (motions to Baradas and turns haughtily to the Cardinal).
Enough! Your Eminence must excuse a longer audience.
To your own palace: for our conference, this
Nor place, nor season.

Rich. Good, my liege, for Justice
All place a temple, and all seasons summer!
Do you deny me justice? Saints of heaven!
He turns from me! Do you deny me justice?
For fifteen years, while in these hands dwelt empire,
The humblest craftsman, the obscurest vassal,
The very leper shrinking from the sun,

Tho loathed by charity, might ask for justice!
Not with the fawning tone and crawling mien
Of some I see around you—counts and princes
Kneeling for favors; but erect and loud,
As men who ask man's rights!—My liege, my Louis,
Do you refuse me justice—audience even—
In the pale presence of the baffled murder?

Louis. Lord Cardinal, one by one you have severed from me
The bonds of human love; all near and dear
Marked out for vengeance—exile or the scaffold.
You find me now amidst my trustiest friends,
My closest kindred. You would tear them from me;
They murder you, forsooth, since me they love.
Enough of plots and treasons for one reign.
Home! home! and sleep away these fantoms.

Rich. Sire!
I—patience, Heaven! Sweet Heaven! Sire, from the foot
Of that great throne, these hands have raised aloft
On an Olympus, looking down on mortals
And worshiped by their awe—before the foot
Of that high throne, spurn you the gray-haired man
Who gave you empire—and now sues for safety?

Louis. No; when we see your Eminence in truth
At the foot of the throne, we'll listen to you.

Exeunt KING *and train.*

Rich. Goddess of bright dreams,
My country—shalt thou lose me now, when most
Thou need'st thy worshiper? My native land!
Let me but ward this dagger from thy heart,
And die—but on thy bosom.

Enter JULIE

Julie. Heaven! I thank thee!
It can not be, or this all-powerful man
Would not stand idly thus.

Rich. Julie de Mauprat, what dost thou here?
Home!

Julie. Home!—is Adrien there? You're dumb, yet strive
For words; I see them trembling on your lips,
But choked by pity. It was truth—all truth!
Seized—the Bastile—and in your presence, too!
Cardinal, where is Adrien? Think! he saved
Your life; your name is infamy, if wrong
Should come to his!

Rich. Be soothed, child.

Julie. Child no more!
I love, and I am woman! Hope and suffer:
Love, suffering, hope—what else doth make the strength
And majesty of woman?
I ask thee for my home, my fate, my all!
Where is my husband?

Rich. You are Richelieu's ward,
A soldier's bride; they who insist on truth
Must out-face fear: you ask me for your husband?
There, where the clouds of heaven look darkest o'er
The domes of the Bastile!

Julie. O, mercy, mercy!
Save him, restore him, father! Art thou not
The Cardinal King? the lord of life and death,
Art thou not Richelieu?

Rich. Yesterday I was;
To-day a very weak old man; to-morrow,
I know not what.

Enter CLERMONT

Cler. Madame de Mauprat!—
Pardon, your Eminence; even now I seek
This lady's home—commanded by the King
To pray her presence.

Rich. To those who sent you!
And say you found the virtue they would slay
Here, couched upon this heart, as at an altar,
And sheltered by the wings of sacred Rome!
Be gone!

Enter BARADAS

Bar. My lord, the king can not believe your Eminence
So far forgets your duty, and his greatness,
As to resist his mandate.—Pray you, madame,
Obey the king; no cause for fear.

Julie. My father!

Rich. She shall not stir!

Bar. You are not of her kindred;
An orphan—

Rich. And her country is her mother.

Bar. The country is the king.

Rich. Ay, is it so?
Then wakes the power which in the age of iron
Bursts forth to curb the great, and raise the low.
Mark where she stands: around her form I draw
The awful circle of our solemn Church!
Set but a foot within that holy ground,
And on thy head—yea, tho it wore a crown—
I launch the curse of Rome!

Bar. I dare not brave you;
I do but speak the orders of my king:
The Church, your rank, power, very word, my lord,

Suffice you for resistance; blame yourself,
If it should cost your power.
Rich. That's *my* stake. Ah!
Dark gamester! *what is thine?* Look to it well—
Lose not a trick. By this same hour to-morrow
Thou shalt have France, or I thy head!
Bar. In sooth, my lord,
You do need rest; the burdens of the state
O'ertask your health. *(Aside.)* His mind
And life are breaking fast.
Rich. *(Overhearing him.)* Irreverent ribald!
If so, beware the falling ruins! Hark!
I tell thee, scorner of these whitening hairs,
When this snow melteth there shall come a flood!
Avaunt! My name is Richelieu—I defy thee!

Lesson talk—Give the words of the introduction in a conversational tone. The scene proper is impersonation. The voice should be carefully differentiated to represent the various characters. The deepest and fullest voice should distinguish Richelieu. Except where an interruption is intended there should be a very distinct pause between each speaker. Richelieu's lines are marked by deep feeling and intensity throughout, with a gradual rising tendency, culminating toward the close in great dramatic power. All the other characters are to be subordinated to him. Aim more particularly at subjective effects, and do not use much gesture. The facial expression should accurately reflect the thought and emotion. This can be studied to advantage before a looking-glass. In pronunciation note: Artifice, Huguet, Bastile, Armand, Richelieu, mien, liege, Louis, Mauprat, iron, launch, sooth, ribald, whitening, avaunt.

THE BUILDING OF THE SHIP[1]

BY HENRY WADSWORTH LONGFELLOW

"Build me straight, O worthy Master!
  Stanch and strong, a goodly vessel,
That shall laugh at all disaster,
  And with wave and whirlwind wrestle!"

The merchant's word
Delighted the Master heard;
For his heart was in his work, and the heart
Giveth grace unto every art.

A quiet smile played round his lips,
As the eddies and dimples of the tide
Play round the bows of ships,
That steadily at anchor ride.
And with a voice that was full of glee,
He answered, "Ere long we will launch
A vessel as goodly, and strong, and stanch,
As ever weathered a wintry sea!"

And first with nicest skill and art,
Perfect and finished in every part,
A little model the Master wrought,
Which should be to the larger plan
What the child is to the man,
Its counterpart in miniature;
That with a hand more swift and sure
The greater labor might be brought

[1] *By permission of* Houghton, Mifflin & Co.

To answer to his inward thought.
And as he labored, his mind ran o'er
The various ships that were built of yore
And above them all, and strangest of all
Towered the Great Harry, crank and tall,
Whose picture was hanging on the wall,
With bows and stern raised high in air
And balconies hanging here and there,
And single lanterns and flags afloat,
And eight round towers, like those that frown
From some old castle, looking down
Upon the drawbridge and the moat,
And he said with a smile, "Our ship, I wish,
Shall be of another form than this!"

It was of another form, indeed;
Built for freight, and yet for speed,
A beautiful and gallant craft;
Broad in the beam, that the stress of the blast,
Pressing down upon sail and mast,
Might not the sharp bows overwhelm;
Broad in the beam, but sloping aft
With graceful curve, and slow degrees,
That she might be docile to the helm,
And that the currents of parted seas,
Closing behind, with mighty force,
Might aid and not impede her course.
In the ship-yard stood the Master
  With the model of the vessel
That should laugh at all disaster,
  And with wave and whirlwind wrestle!

Covering many a rood of ground,
Lay the timber piled around;
Timber of chestnut, and elm, and oak,
And scattered here and there, with these,
The gnarled and crooked cedar-knees;
Brought from regions far away,
From Pascagoula's sunny bay,
And the banks of the roaring Roanoke!
Ah! what a wondrous thing it is
To note how many wheels of toil
One thought, one word, can set in motion!
There's not a ship that sails the ocean,
But every climate, every soil,
Must bring its tribute, great or small,
And help to build the wooden wall!

The sun was rising o'er the sea,
And long the level shadows lay,
As if they, too, the beams would be
Of some great, airy argosy,
Framed and launched in a single day.
That silent architect, the sun,
Had hewn and laid them every one,
Ere the work of man was yet begun.
Beside the Master, when he spoke,
A youth, against an anchor leaning,
Listened, to catch his slightest meaning.
Only the long waves, as they broke
In ripples on the pebbly beach,
Interrupted the old man's speech.

Beautiful they were, in sooth,
The old man and the fiery youth!
The old man, in whose busy brain
Many a ship that sailed the main
Was modeled o'er and o'er again:—
The fiery youth, who was to be
The heir of his dexterity,
The heir of his house, and his daughter's hand,
When he had built and launched from land
What that elder head had planned.

"Thus," said he, "will we build this ship!
Lay square the blocks upon the slip,
And follow well this plan of mine.
Choose the timbers with greatest care:
Of all that is unsound beware;
For only what is sound and strong
To this vessel shall belong.
Cedar of Maine and Georgia pine
Here together shall combine.
A goodly frame, and a goodly fame,
And the UNION be her name!
For the day that gives her to the sea
Shall give my daughter unto thee!"

The Master's word
Enraptured the young man heard;
And as he turned his face aside,
With a look of joy and a thrill of pride,
Standing before
Her father's door,
He saw the form of his promised bride.

The sun shone on her golden hair,
And her cheek was glowing fresh and fair.
With the breath of morn and the soft sea air.
Like a beauteous barge was she,
Still at rest on the sandy beach,
Just beyond the billow's reach;
But he
Was the restless, seething, stormy sea.

Ah, how skilful grows the hand
That obeyeth Love's command!
It is the heart, and not the brain,
That to the highest doth attain,
And he who followeth Love's behest
Far excelleth all the rest!

Thus with the rising of the sun
Was the noble task begun,
And soon throughout the ship-yard's bounds
Were heard the intermingled sounds
Of axes and of mallets, plied
With vigorous arms on every side;
Plied so deftly and so well,
That, ere the shadows of evening fell,
The keel of oak for a noble ship,
Scarfed and bolted, straight and strong,
Was lying ready, and stretched along
To blocks, well placed upon the slip.
Happy, thrice happy, every one
Who sees his labor well begun,
And not perplexed and multiplied
By idly waiting for time and tide!

And when the hot, long day was o'er
The young man at the Master's door
Sat with the maiden calm and still.
And within the porch, a little more
Removed beyond the evening chill,
The father sat, and told them tales
Of wrecks in the great September gales,
Of pirates coasting the Spanish main,
And ships that never came back again,
The chance and change of a sailor's life,
Want and plenty, rest and strife,
His roving fancy, like the wind,
That nothing can stay and nothing can bind,
And the magic charm of foreign lands,
With shadows of palms, and shining sands,
Where the tumbling surf,
O'er the coral reefs of Madagascar,
Washes the feet of the swarthy Lascar,
As he lies alone and asleep on the turf.
And the trembling maiden held her breath
At the tales of that awful, pitiless sea,
With all its terror and mystery,
The dim, dark sea, so like unto death
That divides and yet unites mankind!
And whenever the old man paused, a gleam
From the bowl of his pipe would awhile illume
The silent group in the twilight gloom,
And thoughtful faces, as in a dream;
And for a moment one might mark
What had been hidden by the dark,
That the head of the maiden lay at rest,
Tenderly, on the young man's breast!

Day by day the vessel grew,
With timbers fashioned strong and true,
Stemson and keelson and sternson knee,
Till, framed with perfect symmetry,
A skeleton ship rose up to view!
And around the bows and along the side
The heavy hammers and mallets plied,
Till after many a week, at length,
Wonderful for form and strength,
Sublime in its enormous bulk,
Loomed aloft the shadowy hulk!
And around it columns of smoke upwreathing,
Rose from the boiling, bubbling, seething
Caldron, that glowed,
And overflowed
With the black tar, heated for the sheathing.
And amid the clamors
Of clattering hammers,
He who listened heard now and then
The song of the Master and his men:

"Build me straight, O worthy Master,
  Stanch and strong, a goodly vessel,
That shall laugh at all disaster,
  And with wave and whirlwind wrestle!"

With oaken brace and copper band,
Lay the rudder on the sand,
That, like a thought, should have control
Over the movement of the whole;
And near it the anchor whose giant hand
Would reach down and grapple with the land,

And immovable and fast
Hold the great ship agáinst the bellowing blast!
And at the bows an image stood,
By a cunning artist carved in wood,
With robes of white, that far behind
Seemed to be fluttering in the wind.
It was not shaped in a classic mold,
Not like a Nymph or Goddess of old,
Or Naiad rising from the water,
But modeled from the Master's daughter!
On many a dreary and misty night,
'Twill be seen by the rays of the signal light,
Speeding along through the rain and the dark,
Like a ghost in its snow-white sark,
The pilot of some fantom bark,
Guiding the vessel, in its flight,
By a path none other knows aright!
Behold, at last,
Each tall and tapering mast
Is swung into its place;
Shrouds and stays
Holding it firm and fast!

Long ago,
In the deer-haunted forests of Maine,
When upon mountain and plain
Lay the snow,
They fell—those lordly pines!
Those grand, majestic pines!
'Mid shouts and cheers
The jaded steers,
Panting beneath the goad,

Dragged down the weary, winding road
Those captive kings so straight and tall,
To be shorn of their streaming hair,
And, naked and bare,
To feel the stress and the strain
Of the wind and the reeling main,
Whose roar
Would remind them forevermore
Of their native forests they should not see again.

'And everywhere
The slender, graceful spars
Poise aloft in the air,
And at the mast-head,
White, blue, and red,
A flag unrolls the Stripes and Stars.
Ah! when the wanderer, lonely, friendless,
In foreign harbors shall behold
That flag unrolled,
'Twill be as a friendly hand
Stretched out from his native land,
Filling his heart with memories sweet and endless!

All is finished! and at length
Has come the bridal day
Of beauty and of strength.
To-day the vessel shall be launched!
With fleecy clouds the sky is blanched,
And o'er the bay,
Slowly, in all his splendors dight,
The great sun rises to behold the sight.

The ocean old,
Centuries old,
Strong as youth, and as uncontrolled,
Paces restless to and fro,
Up and down the sands of gold.
His beating heart is not at rest;
And far and wide,
With ceaseless flow,
His beard of snow
Heaves with the heaving of his breast.
He waits impatient for his bride.
There she stands,
With her foot upon the sands,
Decked with flags and streamers gay,
In honor of her marriage day,
Her snow-white signals fluttering, blending,
Round her like a veil descending,
Ready to be
The bride of the gray old sea.

On the deck another bride
Is standing by her lover's side.
Shadows from the flags and shrouds,
Like the shadows cast by clouds,
Broken by many a sunny fleck,
Fall around them on the deck.

The prayer is said,
The service read,
The joyous bridegroom bows his head;
And in tears the good old Master
Shakes the brown hand of his son,

Kisses his daughter's glowing cheek
In silence, for she can not speak,
And even faster
Down his own the tears begin to run.
The worthy pastor—
The shepherd of that wandering flock,
That has the ocean for its wold,
That has the vessel for its fold,
Leaping ever from rock to rock—
Spake, with accents mild and clear,
Words of warning, words of cheer,
But tedious to the bridegroom's ear.
He knew the chart
Of the sailor's heart,
All its pleasures and its griefs,
All its shallows and rocky reefs,
All those secret currents, that flow
With such resistless undertow,
And lift and drift, with terrible force,
The will from its moorings and its course.
Therefore he spake, and thus he said:

"Like unto ships far off at sea,
Outward or homeward bound, are we,
Before, behind, and all around,
Floats and swings the horizon's bound,
Seems at its distant rim to rise
And climb the crystal wall of the skies,
And then again to turn and sink,
As if we could slide from its outer brink.
Ah! it is not the sea,
It is not the sea that sinks and shelves,

But ourselves
That rock and rise
With endless and uneasy motion,
Now touching the very skies,
Now sinking into the depths of ocean.
Ah! if our souls but poise and swing
Like the compass in its brazen ring,
Ever level and ever true
To the toil and the task we have to do,
We shall sail securely, and safely reach
The Fortunate Isles, on whose shining beach
The sights we see, and the sounds we hear,
Will be those of joy and not of fear!"

Then the Master,
With a gesture of command,
Waved his hand;
And at the word,
Loud and sudden there was heard,
All around them and below,
The sound of hammers, blow on blow,
Knocking away the shores and spurs.
And see! she stirs!
She starts—she moves— she seems to feel
The thrill of life along her keel,
And, spurning with her foot the ground,
With one exulting, joyous bound,
She leaps into the ocean's arms!

And lo! from the assembled crowd
There rose a shout, prolonged and loud,
That to the ocean seemed to say,

"Take her, O bridegroom, old and gray,
Take her to thy protecting arms,
With all her youth and all her charms!"

How beautiful she is! How fair
She lies within those arms that press
Her form with many a soft caress
Of tenderness and watchful care!
Sail forth into the sea, O ship!
Through wind and wave, right onward steer!
The moistened eye, the trembling lip,
Are not the signs of doubt or fear.

Sail forth into the sea of life,
O gentle, loving, trusting wife,
And safe from all adversity
Upon the bosom of that sea
Thy comings and thy goings be!
For gentleness and love and trust
Prevail o'er angry wave and gust;
And in the wreck of noble lives
Something immortal still survives!

Thou, too, sail on, O Ship of State!
Sail on, O UNION, strong and great!
Humanity with all its fears,
With all the hopes of future years,
Is hanging breathless on thy fate!
We know what Master laid thy keel,
What workmen wrought thy ribs of steel,
Who made each mast, and sail, and rope,
What anvils rang, what hammers beat,

In what a forge and what a heat
Were shaped the anchors of thy hope!
Fear not each sudden sound and shock
'Tis of the wave and not the rock;
'Tis but the flapping of the sail,
And not a rent made by the gale!
Our hearts, our hopes, are all with thee,
Our hearts, our hopes, our prayers, our tears,
Our faith triumphant o'er our fears
Are all with thee—are all with thee!

THE TONGUE

BY WILLIAM COWPER

Words learned by rote a parrot may rehearse,
But talking is not always to converse;
Not more distinct from harmony divine
The constant creaking of a country sign.
As alphabets in ivory employ
Hour after hour the yet unlettered boy,
Sorting and puzzling with a deal of glee
Those seeds of science called his A B C;
So language in the mouth of the adult
(Witness its insignificant result),
Too often proves an implement of play,
A toy to sport with and pass time away.
Collect at evening what the day brought forth,
Compress the sum into its solid worth,
And if it weigh the importance of a fly,
The scales are false, or algebra a lie.

OPPORTUNITY[1]

BY WALTER MALONE

They do me wrong who say I come no more
  When once I knock and fail to find you in;
For every day I stand outside your door,
  And bid you wake, and rise to fight and win.

Wail not for precious chances passed away,
  Weep not for golden ages on the wane!
Each night I burn the records of the day:
  At sunrise every soul is born again.

Laugh like a boy at splendors that have sped,
  To vanished joys be blind and deaf and dumb;
My judgments seal the dead past with its dead,
  But never bind a moment yet to come.

Tho deep in mire wring not your hands and weep,
  I lend my arm to all who say "I can!"
No shamefaced outcast ever sank so deep
  But yet might rise and be again a man!

Dost thou behold thy lost youth all aghast?
  Dost reel from righteous retribution's blow?
Then turn from blotted archives of the past
  And find the future's pages white as snow

Art thou a mourner? Rouse thee from thy spell;
  Art thou a sinner? Sin may be forgiven;
Each morning gives thee wings to flee from hell,
  Each night a star to guide thy feet to heaven.

---

[1] *By permission of the author.*

ESSAY ON CRITICISM

BY ALEXANDER POPE

. . . But most by numbers judge a poet's song,
And smooth or rough, with them, is right or wrong.
In the bright muse, tho thousand charms conspire,
Her voice is all these tuneful fools admire;
Who haunt Parnassus but to please their ear,
Not mend their minds; as some to church repair,
Not for the doctrine, but the music there.
These equal syllables alone require,
Tho oft the ear the open vowels tire;
While expletives their feeble aid do join,
And ten low words oft creep in one dull line:
While they ring round the same unvaried chimes,
With sure returns of still expected rhymes.
Where'er you find "the cooling western breeze,"
In the next line "it whispers through the trees."
If crystal streams "with pleasing murmurs creep,"
The reader's threatened (not in vain) with "sleep."
Then at the last and only couplet fraught
With some unmeaning thing they call a thought,
A needless Alexandrine ends the song,
That, like a wounded snake, drags its slow length along.
Leave such to tune their own dull rimes and know
What's roundly smooth or languishingly slow,
And praise the easy vigor of a line
Where Denham's strength and Waller's sweetness join
True ease in writing comes from art, not chance,
As those move easiest who have learned to dance.

'Tis not enough no harshness gives offense,
The sound must seem an echo to the sense.
Soft is the strain when Zephyr gently blows,
And the smooth stream in smoother numbers flows;
But, when loud surges lash the sounding shore,
The hoarse, rough verse should like the torrent roar.
When Ajax strives some rock's vast weight to throw,
The line, too, labors, and the words move slow.
Not so when swift Camilla scours the plain,
Flies o'er the unbending corn, and skims along the main.
Hear how Timotheus' varied lays surprize,
And bid alternate passions fall and rise!
While, at each change, the son of Libyan Jove
Now burns with glory, and then melts with love.
Now his fierce eyes with sparkling fury glow,
Now sighs steal out, and tears begin to flow;
Persians and Greeks like turns of nature found,
And the world's victor stood subdued by sound.
The power of music all our hearts allow,
And what Timotheus was is Dryden now.
  Avoid extremes, and shun the fault of such
Who still are pleased too little or too much.
At every trifle scorn to take offense—
That always shows great pride and little sense.
Those heads, as stomachs, are not sure the best
Which nauseate all, and nothing can digest.
Yet let not each gay turn thy rapture move,
For fools admire, but men of sense approve.
As things seem large which we through mists descry,
Dulness is very apt to magnify.

GOD'S FIRST TEMPLES

BY WILLIAM CULLEN BRYANT

The groves were God's first temples. Ere man learn'd
To hew the shaft, and lay the architrave,
And spread the roof above them, ere he framed
The lofty vault, to gather and roll back
The sound of anthems, in the darkling wood,
Amidst the cool and silence, he knelt down
And offer'd to the Mightiest solemn thanks
And supplication. For his simple heart
Might not resist the sacred influences
That, from the stilly twilight of the place,
And from the gray old trunks, that, high in heaven,
Mingled their mossy boughs, and from the sound
Of the invisible breath, that sway'd at once
All their green tops, stole over him, and bow'd
His spirit with the thought of boundless power
And inaccessible Majesty. Ah, why
Should we, in the world's riper years, neglect
God's ancient sanctuaries, and adore
Only among the crowd, and under roofs
That our frail hands have raised? Let me, at least,
Here, in the shadow of the ancient wood,
Offer one hymn; thrice happy, if it find
Acceptance in His ear.

Father, thy hand
Hath reared these venerable columns: Thou didst look down
Upon the naked earth, and forthwith rose
All these fair ranks of trees. They in Thy sun
Budded, and shook their green leaves in Thy breeze,

And shot toward heaven. The century-living crow,
Whose birth was in their tops, grew old and died
Among their branches, till at last they stood,
As now they stand, massy and tall and dark,
Fit shrine for humble worshiper to hold
Communion with his Maker.
Here are seen
No traces of man's pomp or pride; no silks
Rustle, no jewels shine, nor envious eyes
Encounter; no fantastic carvings show
The boast of our vain race to change the form
Of Thy fair works. But Thou art here; Thou fill'st
The solitude. Thou art in the soft winds
That run along the summits of these trees
In music; Thou art in the cooler breath,
That, from the inmost darkness of the place,
Comes, scarcely felt; the barky trunks, the ground,
The fresh, moist ground, are all instinct with Thee.
Here is continual worship; Nature here,
In the tranquillity that Thou dost love,
Enjoys Thy presence. Noiselessly around,
From perch to perch the solitary bird
Passes; and yon clear spring, that, 'midst its herbs,
Wells softly forth, and visits the strong roots
Of half the mighty forests, tells no tale
Of all the good it does.
Thou hast not left
Thyself without a witness, in these shades,
Of Thy perfections. Grandeur, strength, and grace
Are here to speak of Thee. This mighty oak—
By whose immovable stem I stand, and seem
Almost annihilated—not a prince,

In all the proud old world beyond the deep,
Ere wore his crown as loftily as he
Wears the green coronal of leaves with which
Thy hand has graced him. Nestled at his root
Is beauty, such as blooms not in the glare
Of the broad sun. That delicate forest flower,
With scented breath, and looks so like a smile,
Seems, as it issues from the shapeless mold,
An emanation of th' indwelling life,
A visible token of the upholding love,
That are the soul of this wide universe.
My heart is awed within me when I think
Of the great miracle that still goes on,
In silence, round me—the perpetual work
Of Thy creation, finish'd, yet renew'd
Forever. Written on Thy work I read
The lesson of Thine own eternity.
Lo! all grow old and die; but see, again,
How, on the faltering footsteps of decay,
Youth presses—ever gay and beautiful youth—
In all its beautiful forms. These lofty trees
Wave not less proudly than their ancestors
Molder beneath them.

O, there is not lost
One of Earth's charms: upon her bosom yet,
After the flight of untold centuries,
The freshness of her far beginning lies,
And yet shall lie. Life mocks the idle hate
Of his arch enemy Death; yea, seats himself
Upon the sepulcher, and blooms and smiles,
And of the triumphs of his ghastly foe
Makes his own nourishment. For he came forth
From Thine own bosom, and shall have no end.

O God, when Thou
Dost scare the world with tempests, set on fire
The heavens with falling thunderbolts, or fill,
With all the waters of the firmament,
The swift, dark whirlwind, that uproots the woods
And drowns the villages; when, at Thy call,
Uprises the great deep, and throws himself
Upon the continent, and overwhelms
Its cities; who forgets not, at the sight
Of these tremendous tokens of Thy power,
His pride, and lays his strifes and follies by!
Oh, from these sterner aspects of Thy face
Spare me and mine; nor let us need the wrath
Of the mad, unchain'd elements, to teach
Who rules them. Be it ours to meditate,
In these calm shades, Thy milder majesty,
And to the beautiful order of Thy works
Learn to conform the order of our lives.

Lesson talk. This selection lends itself particularly to practise in deep-toned voice, in which the orotund quality prevails. The student should endeavor to realize the depth and majesty of the thought, as well as its spirit of praise and devotion. The general movement is dignified and stately, with occasional swelling and increasing intensity of the voice. The rate should not be so slow as to suggest tardiness, nor so uniform as to be monotonous. All the effects of variety, depth, fulness, animation, and intensity, should be brought to the reading aloud of this inspiring poem. Consult your dictionary for the pronunciation of all doubtful words, such as: architrave, boughs, sanctuaries, columns, humble, nature, solitude, solitary, herbs, grandeur.

GIVE US MEN!

BY BISHOP OF EXETER

Give us Men!
Men—from every rank,
Fresh and free and frank;
Men of thought and reading,
Men of light and leading,
Men of loyal breeding,
The nation's welfare speeding:
Men of faith and not of fiction,
Men of lofty aim in action;
Give us Men—I say again,
Give us Men!

Give us Men!
Strong and stalwart ones;
Men whom highest hope inspires,
Men whom purest honor fires,
Men who trample self beneath them,
Men who make their country wreath them
As her noble sons,
Worthy of their sires;
Men who never shame their mothers,
Men who never fail their brothers,
True, however false are others:
Give us Men—I say again,
Give us Men!

Give us Men!
Men who, when the tempest gathers,
Grasp the standard of their fathers
In the thickest fight:

Men who strike for home and altar,
(Let the coward cringe and falter),
    God defend the right!
True as truth tho lorn and lonely,
Tender, as the brave are only;
Men who tread where saints have trod,
Men for Country—Home—and God:
    Give us Men! I say again—again—
        Give us Men!

CASSIUS AGAINST CÆSAR

BY WILLIAM SHAKESPEARE

Honor is the subject of my story,
I can not tell what you and other men
Think of this life; but for my single self,
I had as lief not be, as live to be
In awe of such a thing as I myself.
I was born free as Cæsar; so were you;
We both have fed as well; and we can both
Endure the winter's cold as well as he.

For once, upon a raw and gusty day,
The troubled Tiber, chafing with her shores,
Cæsar said to me—"Darest thou, Cassius, now
Leap in with me, into this angry flood,
And swim to yonder point?" Upon the word,
Accoutered as I was, I plunged in,
And bade him follow; so, indeed, he did.
The torrent roared, and we did buffet it;
With lusty sinews, throwing it aside,

And stemming it, with hearts of controversy.
But ere we could arrive the point proposed,
Cæsar cried—"Help me, Cassius, or I sink."
I, as Æneas, our great ancestor,
Did from the flames of Troy, upon his shoulder
The old Anchises bear, so, from the waves of Tiber
Did I the tired Cæsar; and this man
Is now become a god; and Cassius is
A wretched creature, and must bend his body
If Cæsar carelessly but nod on him.

He had a fever when he was in Spain,
And when the fit was on him, I did mark
How he did shake: 'tis true, this god did shake;
His coward lips did from their color fly;
And that same eye, whose bend doth awe the world,
Did lose its luster; I did hear him groan:
Ay, and that tongue of his, that bade the Romans
Mark him, and write his speeches in their books,
"Alas!" it cried—"Give me some drink, Titinius,"
As a sick girl.—Ye gods! it doth amaze me,
A man of such a feeble temper should
So get the start of the majestic world,
And bear the palm alone.
Why, man, he doth bestride the narrow world
Like a Colossus; and we, petty men,
Walk under his huge legs, and peep about,
To find ourselves dishonorable graves.

Men, at some time, are masters of their fates:
The fault, dear Brutus, is not in our stars,
But in ourselves that we are underlings.

Brutus and Cæsar! What should be in that Cæsar?
Why should that name be sounded more than yours?
Write them together: yours is as fair a name;
Sound them: it doth become the mouth as well;
Weigh them: it is as heavy; conjure with them:
Brutus will start a spirit as soon as Cæsar.
Now, in the name of all the gods at once,
Upon what meat doth this our Cæsar feed,
That he is grown so great? Age, thou art shamed:
Rome, thou hast lost the breed of noble bloods.
When went there by an age, since the great flood,
But it was famed with more than one man?
When could they say, till now, that talked of Rome,
That her wide walks encompassed but one man?
Now is it Rome, indeed, and room enough,
When there is in it but one only man.
Oh! you and I have heard our fathers say,
There was a Brutus once, that would have brooked
The eternal devil, to keep his state in Rome,
As easily as a king.

THE BATTLE OF IVRY

BY THOMAS BABINGTON MACAULAY

Now glory to the Lord of hosts, from whom all glories are!
And glory to our sovereign liege, King Henry of Navarre!
Now let there be the merry sound of music and of dance,
Through thy corn-fields green, and sunny vines, O pleasant land of France!

And, thou, Rochelle! our own Rochelle! proud city of the waters,
Again let rapture light the eyes of all thy mourning daughters;
As thou wert constant in our ills, be joyous in our joy,
For cold and stiff and still are they who wrought thy walls' annoy.
Hurrah! hurrah! a single field hath turned the chance of war,
Hurrah! hurrah! for Ivry, and Henry of Navarre!

O how our hearts were beating when, at the dawn of day,
We saw the Army of the League drawn out in long array;
With all its priest-led citizens and all its rebel peers,
And Appenzel's stout infantry, and Egmont's Flemish spears!
There rode the brood of false Lorraine, the curses of our land;
And dark Mayenne was in the midst, a truncheon in his hand:
And as we looked on them we thought of Seine's empurpled flood,
And good Coligni's hoary hair, all dabbled with his blood;
And we cried unto the living God, who rules the fate of war,
To fight for his own holy name, and Henry of Navarre.

The king is come to marshal us, in all his armor drest,
And he has bound a snow-white plume upon his gallant crest.
He looked upon his people, and a tear was in his eye;
He looked upon the traitors, and his glance was stern and high.

Right graciously he smiled on us, as rolled from wing to
wing,
All down our line, a deafening shout, "God save our lord,
the king!"
"And, if my standard-bearer fall, as fall full well he may,
For never saw I promise yet of such a bloody fray,
Press where ye see my white plume shine, amidst the ranks
of war,
And be your oriflamme to-day the helmet of Navarre."

Hurrah! the foes are moving. Hark to the mingled din
Of fife and steed and trump and drum and roaring culverin.
The fiery duke is pricking fast across Saint Andre's plain,
With all the hireling chivalry of Guelders and Almayne.
Now by the lips of those ye love, fair gentlemen of France,
Charge for the golden lilies—upon them with the lance!
A thousand spurs are striking deep, a thousand spears in
rest,
A thousand knights are pressing close behind the snow-
white crest;
And in they burst, and on they rushed, while like a guiding-
star,
Amidst the thickest carnage blazed the helmet of Navarre.

Now God be praised, the day is ours! Mayenne hath turned
his rein;
D'Aumale hath cried for quarter; the Flemish count is
slain;
Their ranks are breaking like thin clouds before a Biscay
gale;
The field is heaped with bleeding steeds, and flags and cloven
mail;

And then we, tho on vengeance, and all along our van,
"Remember Saint Bartholomew!" was passed from man to man.
But out spake gentle Henry, "No Frenchman is my foe;
Down, down with every foreigner, but let your brethren go."
Oh, was there ever such a knight, in friendship or in war,
As our sovereign lord, King Henry, the soldier of Navarre?

Ho! maidens of Vienna; ho! matrons of Lucerne;
Weep, weep, and rend your hair for those who never shall return.
Ho! Philip, send for charity thy Mexican pistoles,
That Antwerp monks may sing a mass for thy poor spearmen's souls.
Ho! gallant nobles of the League, look that your arms be bright;
Ho! burghers of Saint Genevieve, keep watch and ward to-night;
For our God hath crusht the tyrant, our God hath raised the slave,
And mocked the counsel of the wise, and the valor of the brave.
Then glory to His holy name, from whom all glories are;
And glory to our sovereign lord, King Henry of Navarre!

SONNET ON HIS BLINDNESS

BY JOHN MILTON

When I consider how my light is spent
Ere half my days, in this dark world and wide,
And that one talent, which is death to hide,
Lodged with me useless, tho my soul more bent
To serve therewith my Maker, and present
My true account, lest he returning chide;
"Doth God exact day-labor, light denied?"
I fondly ask: but Patience, to prevent
That murmur, soon replies, "God doth not need
Either man's work or his own gifts; who best
Bear his mild yoke, they serve him best: his state
Is kingly; thousands at his bidding speed,
And post o'er land and ocean without rest;
They also serve who only stand and wait."

THE LAST HOUR

BY SUSAN COOLIDGE

If I were told that I must die to-morrow,
That the next sun
Which sinks should bear me past all fear and sorrow
For any one,
All the fight fought, all the short journey through,
What should I do?

I do not think that I should shrink or falter,
    But just go on,
Doing my work, nor change, nor seek to alter
    Aught that is gone;
But rise and move, and love and smile and pray
    For one more day.

And lying down at night for a last sleeping,
    Say in that ear
Which hearkens ever: "Lord, within Thy keeping,
    How should I fear?
And when to-morrow brings Thee nearer still,
    Do Thou Thy will."

I might not sleep for awe; but peaceful, tender,
    My soul would lie
All the night long; and when the morning splendor
    Flushed o'er the sky,
I think that I could smile—could calmly say,
    "It is His day."

But if a wondrous hand from the blue yonder
    Held out a scroll,
On which my life was writ, and I with wonder
    Beheld unroll
To a long century's end its mystic clue,
    What should I do?

What *could* I do, O blest Guide and Master,
    Other than this:
Still to go on as now, not slower, faster,
    Nor fear to miss
The road, altho so very long it be,
    While led by Thee?

Step after step, feeling Thee close beside me,
Altho unseen,
Through thorns, through flowers, whether the tempest hides thee,
Or heavens serene,
Assured Thy faithfulness can not betray,
Thy love decay.

I may not know, my God, no hand revealeth
Thy counsels wise;
Along the path a deepening shadow stealeth,
No voice replies
To all my questioning thought, the time to tell,
And it is well.

Let me keep on, abiding and unfearing
Thy will always,
Through a long century's ripening fruition,
Or a short day's;
Thou canst not come too soon; and I can wait,
If Thou come late.

THE HIGHER GOOD

BY THEODORE PARKER

Father, I will not ask for wealth or fame,
Tho once they would have joyed my carnal sense:
I shudder not to bear a hated name,
Wanting all wealth, myself my sole defense.
But give me, Lord, eyes to behold the truth;
A seeing sense that knows the eternal right;

A heart with pity filled, and gentlest ruth;
  A manly faith that makes all darkness light:
Give me the power to labor for mankind;
  Make me the mouth of such as can not speak;
Eyes let me be to groping men, and blind;
  A conscience to the base; and to the weak
Let me be hands and feet; and to the foolish, mind;
  And lead still farther on such as Thy kingdom seek.

THE CREEDS OF THE BELLS

BY GEORGE W. BUNGAY

How sweet the chime of the Sabbath bells!
Each one its creed of music tells
In tones that float upon the air
As soft as song, as pure as prayer;
And I will put in simple rime
The language of the golden chime;
My happy heart with rapture swells
Responsive to the bells, sweet bells.

"Ye purifying waters, swell!"
In mellow tones rang out a bell;
"Tho faith alone in Christ can save,
Man must be plunged beneath the wave,
To show the world unfaltering faith
In what the Sacred Scriptures saith;
O swell! ye rising waters, swell!"
Pealed out the clear-toned Baptist bell.

"Oh heed the ancient landmarks well!"
In solemn tones exclaimed a bell;
"No progress made by mortal man
Can change the just eternal plan;
With God there can be nothing new;
Ignore the false, embrace the true,
While all is well! is well! is well!"
Pealed out the good old Dutch church-bell.

"In deeds of love excel! excel!"
Chimed out from ivied towers a bell;
"This is the church not built on sands,
Emblem of one not built by hands;
Its forms and sacred rites revere,
Come worship here! come worship here!
In rituals and faith excel!"
Chimed out the Episcopalian bell.

"Not faith alone, but works as well,
Must test the soul!" said a soft bell!
"Come here and cast aside your load,
And work your way along the road,
With faith in God, and faith in man,
And hope in Christ, where hope began;
Do well! do well! do well! do well!"
Rang out the Unitarian bell.

"To all the truth we tell! we tell!"
Shouted in ecstasies a bell;
"Come all ye weary wanderers, see!
Our Lord has made salvation free!

Repent, believe, have faith, and then
Be saved, and praise the Lord, Amen!
Salvation's free, we tell! we tell!"
Shouted the Methodistic bell.

"Farewell! farewell! base world, farewell!"
In touching tones exclaimed a bell;
"Life is a boon, to mortals given,
To fit the soul for bliss in heaven;
Do not invoke the avenging rod,
Come here and learn the way to God;
Say to the world, farewell! farewell!"
Pealed forth the Presbyterian bell.

"In after life there is no hell!"
In raptures rang a cheerful bell;
"Look up to heaven this holy day,
Where angels wait to lead the way;
There are no fires, no fiends to blight
The future life; be just and right,
No hell! no hell! no hell! no hell!"
Rang out the Universalist bell.

"Ye workers who have toiled so well,
To save the race!" said a sweet bell;
"With pledge, and badge, and banner, come,
Each brave heart beating like a drum;
Be royal men of noble deeds,
For love is holier than creeds;
Drink from the well, the well, the well!"
In rapture rang the Temperance bell.

THE LEPER

BY NATHANIEL P. WILLIS

"Room for the leper! Room!" and as he came
The cry passed on. "Room for the leper! Room!"
And aside they stood—
Matron, and child, and pitiless manhood—all
Who met him on the way—and let him pass.
And onward through the open gate he came,
A leper, with the ashes on his brow.
Sackcloth about his loins, and on his lip
A covering—stepping painfully and slow,
And with difficult utterance, like one
Whose heart is with an iron nerve put down,
Crying, "Unclean! unclean!"
For Helon was a leper.

Day was breaking,
When at the altar of the temple stood
The holy priest of God. The incense lamp
Burned with a struggling light, and a low chant
Swelled through the hollow arches of the roof,
Like an articulate wail; and there, alone,
Wasted to ghastly thinness, Helon knelt.
The echoes of the melancholy strain
Died in the distant aisles, and he rose up,
Struggling with weakness; and bowed down his head
Unto the sprinkled ashes, and put off
His costly raiment for the leper's garb,
And with the sackcloth round him, and his lip
Hid in the loathsome covering, stood still,
Waiting to hear his doom:

"Depart! depart, O child
Of Israel, from the temple of thy God!
For He has smote thee with His chastening rod,
And to the desert wild,
From all thou lov'st, away thy feet must flee,
That from thy plague His people may be free.

"Depart! and come not near
The busy mart, the crowded city more;
Nor set thy foot a human threshold o'er;
And stay thou not to hear
Voices that call thee in the way; and fly
From all who in the wilderness pass by.

"Wet not thy burning lip
In streams that to human dwelling glide;
Nor rest thee where the covert fountains hide;
Nor kneel thee down to dip
The water where the pilgrim bends to drink,
By desert well, or river's grassy brink.

"And pass thou not between
The weary traveler and the cooling breeze;
And lie not down to sleep beneath the trees
Where human tracks are seen.
Nor milk the goat that browseth on the plain,
Nor pluck the standing corn, or yellow grain.

"And now depart! and when
Thy heart is heavy, and thine eyes are dim,
Lift up thy prayer beseechingly to Him

Who from the tribes of men,
Selected thee to feel His chastening rod:
Depart, O leper! and forget not God."

And he went forth—alone! Not one of all
The many whom he loved, nor she whose name
Was woven in the fibers of the heart,
Breaking within him, now to come and speak
Comfort unto him. Yea, he went his way—
Sick and heartbroken and alone—to die!
For God had curst the leper.

It was noon,
And Helon knelt beside a stagnant pool
In the lone wilderness, and bathed his brow,
Hot with the burning leprosy, and touched
The loathsome water to his fevered lips,
Praying he might be so blest—to die!
Footsteps approached, and with no strength to flee,
He drew the covering closer on his lip,
Crying, "Unclean! unclean!" and in the folds
Of the coarse sackcloth, shrouding up his face,
He fell upon the earth till they should pass.
Nearer the stranger came, and bending o'er
The leper's prostrate form, pronounced his name,
"Helon!" The voice was like the master-tone
Of a rich instrument—most strangely sweet;
And the dull pulses of disease awoke,
And for a moment beat beneath the hot
And leprous scales with a restoring thrill.
"Helon, arise!" And he forgot his curse,
And rose and stood before him. Love and awe
Mingled in the regard of Helon's eye

As he beheld the stranger. He was not
In costly raiment clad, nor on his brow
The symbol of a princely lineage wore;
No followers at his back, nor in his hand
Buckler, sword, or spear; yet in his mien
Command sat throned serene, and if he smiled,
A kingly condescension graced his lips,
The lion would have crouched to in his lair.
His garb was simple and his sandals worn;
His statue modeled with a perfect grace;
His countenance, the impress of a God,
Touched with the open innocence of a child;
His eye was blue and calm, as is the sky
In the serenest noon; his hair unshorn
Fell to his shoulders; and his curling beard
The fulness of perfected manhood bore.
He looked on Helon earnestly awhile,
As if his heart was moved, and stooping down,
He took a little water in his hand
And laid it on his brow, and said, "Be clean!"
And lo! the scales fell from him, and his blood
Coursed with delicious coolness through his veins,
And his dry palms grew moist, and on his brow
The dewy softness of an infant stole.
His leprosy was cleansed, and he fell down
Prostrate at Jesus' feet, and worshiped him.

THE SEA

BY BRYAN WALLER PROCTER

The sea! the sea! the open sea!
The blue, the fresh, the ever free!
Without a mark, without a bound,
It runneth the earth's wide regions round!
It plays with the clouds; it mocks the skies;
Or like a cradled creature lies.

I'm on the sea! I'm on the sea!
I am where I would ever be;
With the blue above, and the blue below,
And silence whereso'er I go;
If a storm should come and awake the deep,
What matter? I shall ride and sleep.

I love, oh, *how* I love to ride
On the fierce, foaming, bursting tide,
When every mad wave drowns the moon,
Or whistles aloft his tempest tune,
And tells how goeth the world below,
And why the sou'west blasts do blow.

I never was on the dull, tame shore,
But I loved the great sea more and more,
And backward flew to her billowy breast,
Like a bird that seeketh its mother's nest;
And a mother she *was*, and *is*, to me;
For I was born on the open sea!

The waves were white, and red the morn,
In the noisy hour when I was born;
And the whale it whistled, the porpoise rolled,
And the dolphins bared their backs of gold;
And never was heard such an outcry wild
As welcomed to life the ocean child!

I've lived since then, in calm and strife,
Full fifty summers, a sailor's life,
With wealth to spend and a power to range,
But never have sought nor sighed for change;
And Death, whenever he comes to me,
Shall come on the wild, unbounded sea!

OH, MAY I JOIN THE CHOIR INVISIBLE

BY GEORGE ELIOT

Oh, may I join the choir invisible
Of those immortal dead who live again
In minds made better by their presence: live
In pulses stirr'd to generosity,
In deeds of daring rectitude, in scorn
For miserable aims that end with self,
In thoughts sublime that pierce the night like stars,
And with their mild persistence urge man's search
To vaster issues.
So to live is heaven:
To make undying music in the world,
Breathing as beauteous order that controls
With growing sway that growing life of man.

So we inherit that sweet purity
For which we struggled, fail'd, and agonized
With widening retrospect that bred despair.
Rebellious flesh that would not be subdued,
A vicious parent shaming still its child,—
Poor anxious penitence,—is quick dissolved;
Its discords, quench'd by meeting harmonies,
Die in the large and charitable air;
And all our rarer, better, truer self,
That sobb'd, religiously in yearning song,
That watch'd to ease the burden of the world,
Laboriously tracing what must be,
And what may yet be better,—saw within
A worthier image for the sanctuary,
And shaped it forth before the multitude,
Divinely human, raising worship so
To higher reverence more mix'd with love,—
That better self shall live till human time
Shall fold its eyelids, and the human sky
Be gather'd like a scroll within the tomb
Unread forever.
This is life to me,
Which martyr'd men have made more glorious
For us who strive to follow. May I reach
That purest heaven; be to other souls
The cup of strength in some great agony,
Enkindle generous ardor; feed pure love;
Beget the smiles that have no cruelty;
Be the sweet presence of a god diffused,
And in diffusion ever more intense!
So shall I join the choir invisible
Whose music is the gladness of the world.

SELF-DEPENDENCE[1]

BY MATTHEW ARNOLD

Weary of myself, and sick of asking
What I am, and what I ought to be,
At this vessel's prow I stand, which bears me
Forward, forward, o'er the starlit sea.

And a look of passionate desire
O'er the sea and to the stars I send;
"Ye who from childhood up have calm'd me,
Calm me, ah, compose me to the end!

"Ah, once more," I cried, "ye stars, ye waters,
On my heart your mighty charm renew;
Still, still let me, as I gaze upon you,
Feel my soul becoming vast like you!"

From the intense, clear, star-sown vault of heaven,
Over the lit sea's unquiet way,
In the rustling night air came the answer—
"Wouldst thou *be* as these are? *Live* as they.

"Unaffrighted by the silence round them,
Undistracted by the sights they see,
These demand not that the things without them,
Yield them love, amusement, sympathy.

"And with joy the stars perform their shining,
And the sea its long moon-silver'd roll;

[1] By permission of The Macmillan Co.

For self-poised they live, nor pine with noting
All the fever of some differing soul.

"Bounded by themselves, and unregardful
In what state God's other works may be,
In their own tasks all their powers pouring,
These attain the mighty life we see."

O air-born voice! long since, severely clear,
A cry like thine in mine own heart I hear:
"Resolve to be thyself; and know that he
Who loses himself loses his misery!"

THINGS THAT NEVER DIE

BY CHARLES DICKENS

The pure, the bright, the beautiful,
  That stirred our hearts in youth,
The impulses to wordless prayer,
  The dreams of love and truth;
The longing after something lost,
  The spirit's yearning cry,
The strivings after better hopes—
  These things can never die.

The timid hand stretched forth to aid
  A brother in his need,
A kindly word in grief's dark hour
  That proves a friend indeed;

The plea for mercy softly breathed,
  When justice threatens high
The sorrow of a contrite heart—
  These things shall never die.

The memory of a clasping hand,
  The pressure of a kiss,
And all the trifles, sweet and frail,
  That make up love's first bliss;
If with a firm, unchanging faith,
  And holy trust and high,
Those hands have clasped, those lips have met—
  These things shall never die.

The cruel and the bitter word,
  That wounded as it fell;
The chilling want of sympathy
  We feel, but never tell;
The hard repulse that chills the heart,
  Whose hopes were bounding high,
In an unfading record kept—
  These things shall never die.

Let nothing pass, for every hand
  Must find some work to do;
Lose not a chance to waken love—
  Be firm, and just, and true:
So shall a light that can not fade
  Beam on thee from on high,
And angel voices say to thee—
  These things shall never die.

THE UNCLE

BY H. G. BELL

I had an uncle once—a man
  Of threescore years and three;—
And when my reason's dawn began,
  He'd take me on his knee;
And often talk, whole winter nights,
  Things that seemed strange to me.

He was a man of gloomy mood,
  And few his converse sought;
But, it was said, in solitude
  His conscience with him wrought,
And there, before his mental eye,
  Some hideous vision brought.

There was not one in all the house
  Who did not fear his frown,
Save I, a little careless child,
  Who gamboled up and down,
And often peeped into his room,
  And plucked him by the gown.

I was an orphan and alone,—
  My father was his brother,
And all their lives I knew that they
  Had fondly loved each other;
And in my uncle's room there hung
  The picture of my mother.

There was a curtain over it,—
  'Twas in a darkened place,
And few or none had ever looked
  Upon my mother's face,
Or seen her pale expressive smile
  Of melancholy grace.

One night—I do remember well,
  The wind was howling high,
And through the ancient corridors
  It sounded drearily—
I sat and read in that old hall;
  My uncle sat close by.

I read—but little understood
  The words upon the book;
For with a sidelong glance I marked
  My uncle's fearful look,
And saw how all his quivering frame
  In strong convulsions shook.

A silent terror o'er me stole,
  A strange, unusual dread;
His lips were white as bone—his eyes
  Sunk far down in his head;
He gazed on me, but 'twas the gaze
  Of the unconscious dead.

Then suddenly he turned him round,
  And drew aside the veil
That hung before my mother's face;

Perchance my eyes might fail
But ne'er before that face to me
Had seemed so ghastly pale.

"Come hither, boy!" my uncle said,—
I started at the sound;
'Twas choked and stifled in his throat,
And hardly utterance found:—
"Come hither, boy!" then fearfully
He cast his eyes around.

"That lady was thy mother once,
Thou wert her only child;
O God! I've seen her when she held
Thee in her arms and smiled,—
She smiled upon thy father, boy,
'Twas that which drove me wild!

"He was my brother, but his form
Was fairer far than mine;
I grudged not that;—he was the prop
Of our ancestral line,
And manly beauty was of him
A token and a sign.

"Boy! I had loved her too,—nay, more,
'Twas I who loved her first;
For months—for years—the golden thought
Within my soul was nursed;
He came—he conquered—they were wed—
My air-blown bubble burst!

"Then on my mind a shadow fell,
And evil hopes grew rife;
The damning thought stuck in my heart
And cut me like a knife,
That she, whom all my days I loved,
Should be another's wife!

"By Heaven! it was a fearful thing
To see my brother now,
And mark the placid calm that sat
Forever on his brow,
That seemed in bitter scorn to say,
I am more loved than thou!

"I left my home—I left the land—
I crost the raging sea;—
In vain—in vain—where'er I turned,
My memory went with me;—
My whole existence, night and day,
In memory seemed to be.

"I came again—I found them here—
Thou'rt like thy father, boy—
He doted on that pale face there,
I've seen them kiss and toy,—
I've seen him locked in her fond arms,
Wrapt in delirious joy!

"He disappeared—draw nearer child;—
He died—no one knew how;
The murdered body ne'er was found,

The tale is hushed up now;
But there was one who rightly guessed
The hand that struck the blow.

"It drove her mad—yet not his death—
No—not his death alone;
For she had clung to hope, when all
Knew well that there was none;—
No, boy! it was a sight she saw
That froze her into stone!

"I am thy uncle, child,—why stare
So frightfully aghast?—
The arras waves, but know'st thou not
'Tis nothing but the blast?
I, too, have had my fears like these,
But such vain fears are past.

"I'll show thee what thy mother saw,—
I feel 'twill ease my breast,
And this wild tempest-laden night
Suits with the purpose best;—
Come hither—thou hast often sought
To open this old chest.

"It has a secret spring; the touch
Is known to me alone;
Slowly the lid is raised, and now—
What see you that you groan
So heavily?—That thing is but
A bare-ribbed skeleton."

A sudden crash—the lid fell down,
  Three strides he backward gave,—
"O God! it is my brother's self
  Returned from the grave!
His grasp of lead is on my throat—
  Will no one help or save?"

That night they laid him on his bed,
  In raving madness tost;
He gnashed his teeth, and with wild oaths
  Blasphemed the Holy Ghost;
And ere the light of morning broke,
  A sinner's soul was lost.

CATO ON IMMORTALITY

BY JOSEPH ADDISON

It must be so—Plato, thou reasonest well!
Else, whence this pleasing hope, this fond desire,
This longing after immortality?
Or whence this secret dread, and inward horror,
Of falling into naught? Why shrinks the soul
Back on herself, and startles at destruction?
'Tis the divinity that stirs within us;
'Tis Heaven itself that points out a hereafter,
And intimates eternity to man.
Eternity!—thou pleasing, dreadful thought!
Through what variety of untried being,
Through what new scenes and changes must we pass!

The wide, the unbounded prospect lies before me:
But shadows, clouds, and darkness rest upon it.
Here will I hold. If there's a Power above us,—
And that there is, all Nature cries aloud
Through all her works,—He must delight in virtue;
And that which He delights in must be happy.
But when? or where? This world was made for Cæsar.
I'm weary of conjectures,—this must end them.
[*Laying his hand on his sword.*
Thus am I doubly armed. My death and life,
My bane and antidote, are both before me.
This in a moment brings me to my end;
But this informs me I shall never die.
The soul, secure in her existence, smiles
At the drawn dagger, and defies its point.
The stars shall fade away, the sun himself
Grow dim with age, and Nature sink in years;
But thou shalt flourish in immortal youth,
Unhurt amid the war of elements,
The wreck of matter, and the crush of worlds.

THE CLOUD

BY PERCY BYSSHE SHELLEY

I bring fresh showers for the thirsting flowers,
From the seas and the streams;
I bear light shade for the leaves when laid
In their noonday dreams.
From my wings are shaken the dews that waken
The sweet buds every one,

When rocked to rest on their mother's breast,
  As she dances about the sun.
I wield the flail of the lashing hail,
  And whiten the green plains under,
And then again I dissolve it in rain,
  And laugh as I pass in thunder.

I sift the snow on the mountains below,
  And their great pines groan aghast;
And all the night 't is my pillow white,
  While I sleep in the arms of the blast.
Sublime on the towers of my skyey bowers,
  Lightning my pilot sits;
In a cavern under is fettered the thunder,
  It struggles and howls at fits;
Over earth and ocean, with gentle motion,
  This pilot is guiding me,
Lured by the love of the genii that move
  In the depths of the purple sea;
Over the rills, and the crags, and the hills,
  Over the lakes and the plains,
Wherever he dream, under mountain or stream,
  The Spirit he loves remains;
And I all the while bask in heaven's blue smile,
  Whilst he is dissolving in rains.

The sanguine sunrise, with his meteor eyes,
  And his burning plumes outspread,
Leaps on the back of my sailing rack,
  When the morning star shines dead,
As on the jag of a mountain crag,
  Which an earthquake rocks and swings,

An eagle alit one moment may sit
  In the light of its golden wings.
And when sunset may breathe, from the lit sea beneath,
  Its ardors of rest and of love,
And the crimson pall of eve may fall
  From the depths of heaven above,
With wings folded I rest, on mine airy nest,
  As still as a brooding dove.

That orbed maiden with white fire laden,
  Whom mortals call the moon,
Glides glimmering o'er my fleece-like floor,
  By the midnight breezes strewn;
And wherever the beat of her unseen feet,
  Which only the angels hear,
May have broken the woof of my tent's thin roof,
  The stars peep behind her and peer;
And I laugh to see them whirl and flee,
  Like a swarm of golden bees,
When I widen the rent in my wind-built tent,
  Till the calm rivers, lakes, and seas,
Like strips of the sky fallen thro' me on high,
  Are each paved with the moon and these.

I bind the sun's throne with a burning zone,
  And the moon's with a girdle of pearl;
The volcanoes are dim, and the stars reel and swim,
  When the whirlwinds my banner unfurl.
From cape to cape with a bridge-like shape,
  Over torrent sea,
Sunbeam-proof, I hang like a roof;
  The mountains its columns be.

The triumphal arch thro' which I march
  With hurricane, fire, and snow,
When the powers of the air are chained to my chair,
  Is the million-colored bow;
The sphere-fire above its soft colors wove,
  While the moist earth was laughing below.

I am the daughter of earth and water,
  And the nursling of the sky;
I pass thro' the pores of the ocean and shores;
  I change, but I can not die.
For after the rain, when with never a stain,
  The pavilion of heaven is bare,
And the winds and sunbeams with their convex gleams,
  Build up the blue dome of air,
I silently laugh at my own cenotaph,—
  And out of the caverns of rain,
Like a child from the womb, like a ghost from the tomb,
  I arise and build it again.

THE CHAMBERED NAUTILUS[1]

BY OLIVER WENDELL HOLMES

This is the ship of pearl, which, poets feign,
    Sails the unshadowed main—
    The venturous bark that flings
On the sweet summer wind its purpled wings
In gulfs enchanted, where the Siren sings,
    And the coral reefs lie bare,
Where the cold sea-maids rise to sun their streaming hair.

[1] By permission of Houghton, Mifflin & Co.

Its webs of living gauze no more unfurl;
Wrecked is the ship of pearl!
And every chambered cell,
Where its dim, dreaming life was wont to dwell,
As the frail tenant shaped his growing shell,
Before thee lies revealed—
Its irised ceiling rent, its sunless crypt unsealed!

Year after year beheld the silent toil
That spread his lustrous coil;
Still, as the spiral grew,
He left the past year's dwelling for the new,
Stole with soft step its shining archway through,
Built up its idle door,
Stretched in its last-found home, and knew the old no more.

Thanks for the heavenly message brought by thee,
Child of the wandering sea,
Cast from her lap, forlorn!
From thy dead lips a clearer note is born
Than ever Triton blew with wreathed horn!
While on mine ear it rings,
Through the deep caves of thought I hear a voice that sings:

Build thee more stately mansions, O my soul,
As the swift seasons roll!
Leave thy low-vaulted past!
Let each new temple, nobler than the last,
Shut thee from heaven with a dome more vast,
Till thou at length art free,
Leaving thine outgrown shell by life's unresting sea!

RABBI BEN EZRA[1]

BY ROBERT BROWNING

Grow old along with me!
The best is yet to be,
The last of life, for which the first was made:
Our times are in His hand
Who saith "A whole I plann'd,
Youth shows but half; trust God: see all, nor be afraid!"

Not that, amassing flowers,
Youth sigh'd "Which rose make ours,
Which lily leave and then as best recall!"
Not that, admiring stars,
It yearn'd "Nor Jove, nor Mars;
Mine be some figured flame which blends, transcends them all!"

Not for such hopes and fears
Annulling youth's brief years,
Do I remonstrate: folly wide the mark!
Rather I prize the doubt
Low kinds exist without,
Finish'd and finite clods, untroubled by a spark.

Poor vaunt of life indeed,
Were man but form'd to feed
On joy, to solely seek and find and feast:
Such feasting ended, then
As sure an end to men;
Irks care the crop-full bird? Frets doubt the maw-cramm'd beast?

[1] By permission of The Macmillan Co.

Rejoice we are allied
To That which doth provide
And not partake, effect and not receive!
A spark disturbs our clod;
Nearer we hold of God
Who gives, than of His tribes that take, I must believe.

Then, welcome each rebuff
That turns earth's smoothness rough,
Each sting that bids nor sit nor stand but go!
Be our joys three parts pain!
Strive, and hold cheap the strain;
Learn, nor account the pang; dare, never grudge the throe!

For thence —a paradox
Which comforts while it mocks—
Shall life succeed in that it seems to fail:
What I aspired to be,
And was not, comforts me:
A brute I might have been, but would not sink i' the scale.

What is he but a brute
Whose flesh has soul to suit,
Whose spirit works lest arms and legs want play?
To man, propose this test—
Thy body at its best,
How far can that project thy soul on its lone way?

Yet gifts should prove their use:
I own the Past profuse
Of power each side, perfection every turn:

Eyes, ears took in their dole,
Brain treasured up the whole;
Should not the heart beat once "How good to live and learn"?

Not once beat "Praise be Thine!
I see the whole design,
I, who saw power, see now love perfect too:
Perfect I call Thy plan:
Thanks that I was a man!
Maker, remake, complete—I trust what Thou shalt do!"

For pleasant is this flesh;
Our soul, in its rose-mesh
Pull'd ever to the earth, still yearns for rest:
Would we some prize might hold
To match those manifold
Possessions of the brute—gain most, as we did best!

Let us not always say
"Spite of this flesh to-day
I strove, made head, gain'd ground upon the whole!"
As the bird wings and sings,
Let us cry "All good things
Are ours, nor soul helps flesh more, now, than flesh helps soul!"

Therefore I summon age
To grant youth's heritage,
Life's struggle having so far reach'd its term:
Thence shall I pass, approved
A man, for ay removed
From the develop'd brute; a God tho in the germ.

And I shall thereupon
Take rest, ere I be gone
Once more on my adventure brave and new:
Fearless and unperplex'd,
When I wage battle next,
What weapons to select, what armor to indue.

Youth ended, I shall try
My gain or loss thereby;
Leave the fire ashes, what survives is gold:
And I shall weigh the same,
Give life its praise or blame,
Young, all lay in dispute; I shall know, being old.

For note, when evening shuts,
A certain moment cuts
The deed off, calls the glory from the gray:
A whisper from the west
Shoots—"Add this to the rest,
Take it and try its worth: here dies another day."

So, still within this life,
Tho lifted o'er its strife,
Let me discern, compare, pronounce at last,
"This rage was right i' the main,
That acquiescence vain:
The Future I may face now I have proved the Past."

For more is not reserved
To man, with soul just nerved
To act to-morrow what he learns to-day:

Here, work enough to watch
The Master work, and catch
Hints of the proper craft, tricks of the tool's true play.

As it was better, youth
Should strive, thro' acts uncouth,
Toward making, than repose on aught found made:
So, better, age, exempt
From strife, should know, that tempt
Further. Thou waited age: wait death nor be afraid!

Enough now, if the Right
And Good and Infinite
Be named here, as thou callest thy hand thine own,
With knowledge absolute,
Subject to no dispute
From fools that crowded youth, nor let thee feel alone.

Be there, for once and all,
Sever'd great minds from small,
Announced to each his station in the Past!
Was I, the world arraign'd,
Were they, my soul disdain'd,
Right? Let age speak the truth and give us peace at last!

Now, who shall arbitrate?
Ten men love what I hate,
Shun what I follow, slight what I receive;
Ten, who in ears and eyes
Match me: we all surmise,
They this thing, and I that: whom shall my soul believe?

Not on the vulgar mass
Called "work," must sentence pass,
Things done, that took the eye and had the price;
O'er which, from level stand,
The low world laid its hand,
Found straightway to its mind, could value in a trice:

But all, the world's coarse thumb
And finger fail'd to plumb,
So pass'd in making up the main account;
All instincts immature,
All purposes unsure,
That weigh'd not as his work, yet swell'd the man's amount:

Thoughts hardly to be pack'd
Into a narrow act,
Fancies that broke thro' language and escaped:
All I could never be,
All, men ignored in me,
This, I was worth to God, whose wheel the pitcher shaped.

Ay, note that Potter's wheel,
That metaphor! and feel
Why time spins fast, why passive lies our clay—
Thou, to whom fools propound,
When the wine makes its round,
"Since life fleets, all is change; the Past gone, seize to-day!"

Fool! All that is, at all,
Lasts ever, past recall;
Earth changes, but thy soul and God stand sure;

What enter'd into thee,
That was, is, and shall be:
Time's wheel runs back or stops: Potter and clay endure.

He fixt thee mid this dance
Of plastic circumstance,
This Present, thou, forsooth, wouldst fain arrest:
Machinery just meant
To give thy soul its bent,
Try thee and turn thee forth, sufficiently imprest.

What tho the earlier grooves
Which ran the laughing loves
Around thy base, no longer pause and press?
What tho about thy rim,
Skull-things in order grim
Grow out, in graver mood, obey the sterner stress?

Look not thou down but up!
To uses of a cup,
The festal board, lamp's flash and trumpet's peal,
The new wine's foaming flow,
The Master's lips a-glow!
Thou, Heaven's consummate cup, what need'st thou with
earth's wheel?

But I need, now as then,
Thee, God, who moldest men!
And since, not even while the whirl was worst,
Did I—to the wheel of life
With shapes and colors rife,
Bound dizzily—mistake my end, to slake Thy thirst:

So, take and use Thy work,
Amend what flaws may lurk,
What strain o' the stuff, what warpings past the aim!
My times be in Thy hand!
Perfect the cup as plann'd!
Let age approve of youth, and death complete the same!

MY NATIVE LAND

Selection from "The Lay of the Last Minstrel"

BY SIR WALTER SCOTT

Breathes there a man, with soul so dead,
Who never to himself hath said,
  This is my own, my native land!
Whose heart hath ne'er within him burned,
As home his footsteps he hath turned
  From wandering on a foreign strand!
If such there breathe, go, mark him well;
For him no minstrel raptures swell;
High tho his titles, proud his name,
Boundless his wealth as wish can claim;
Despite those titles, power, and pelf,
The wretch, concentred all in self,
Living, shall forfeit fair renown,
And, doubly dying, shall go down,
To the vile dust, from whence he sprung,
Unwept, unhonored, and unsung.

THE THREE FISHERS

BY CHARLES KINGSLEY

Three fishers went sailing out into the west,
  Out into the west as the sun went down;
Each thought on the woman who loved him the best;
  And the children stood watching them out of the town;
For men must work, and women must weep,
And there's little to earn, and many to keep,
  Tho the harbor bar be moaning.

Three wives sat up in the lighthouse tower,
  And they trimm'd the lamps as the sun went down;
They look'd at the squall, and they look'd at the shower,
  And the night rack came rolling up ragged and brown!
But men must work, and women must weep,
Tho storms be sudden, and waters deep,
  And the harbor bar be moaning.

Three corpses lay out on the shining sands
  In the morning gleam as the tide went down,
And the women are weeping and wringing their hands
  For those who will never come back to the town;
For men must work, and women must weep,
And the sooner it's over, the sooner to sleep—
  And good-by to the bar and its moaning.

ODE ON INTIMATIONS OF IMMORTALITY

BY WILLIAM WORDSWORTH

There was a time when meadow, grove, and stream,
The earth, and every common sight
To me did seem
Apparel'd in celestial light,
The glory and the freshness of a dream.
It is now as it hath been of yore—
Turn wheresoe'er I may,
By night or day,
The things which I have seen I now can see no more.
The rainbow comes and goes,
And lovely is the rose;
The moon doth with delight
Look round her when the heavens are bare;
Waters on a starry night
Are beautiful and fair;
The sunshine is a glorious birth;
But yet I know, where'er I go,
That there hath passed away a glory from the earth.

Now, while the birds thus sing a joyous song,
And while the young lambs bound
As to the tabor's sound,
To me alone there came a thought of grief:
A timely utterance gave that thought relief,
And I again am strong.
The cataracts blow their trumpets from the steep;
No more shall grief of mine the season wrong:
I hear the Echoes through the mountains throng,

The Winds come to me from the fields of sleep,
And all the earth is gay;
Land and sea
Give themselves up to jollity,
And with the heart of May
Doth every beast keep holiday;
Thou child of joy,
Shout round me, let me hear thy shouts, thou happy Shepherd boy!

Ye blest Creatures, I have heard the call
Ye to each other make; I see
The heavens laugh with you in your jubilee;
My heart is at your festival,
My head hath its coronal,
The fulness of your bliss, I feel—I feel it all.
O evil day! if I were sullen
While Earth herself is adorning
This sweet May-morning;
And the children are culling
On every side
In a thousand valleys far and wide,
Fresh flowers; while the sun shines warm
And the babe leaps up on his mother's arm:
I hear, I hear, with joy I hear!
—But there's a tree, of many, one,
A single field which I have look'd upon,
Both of them speak of something that is gone:
The pansy at my feet
Doth the same tale repeat:
Whither is fled the visionary gleam?
Where is it now, the glory and the dream?

Our birth is but a sleep and a forgetting;
The soul that rises with us, our life's star,
Hath had elsewhere its setting,
And cometh from afar;
Not in entire forgetfulness,
And not in utter nakedness,
But trailing clouds of glory do we come
From God, who is our home:
Heaven lies about us in our infancy!
Shades of the prison-house begin to close
Upon the growing boy,
But he beholds the light, and whence it flows,
He sees it in his joy;
The youth, who daily farther from the east
Must travel, still is Nature's priest,
And by the vision splendid
Is on his way attended;
At length the man perceives it die away,
And fade into the light of common day.

Earth fills her lap with pleasures of her own;
Yearnings she hath in her own natural kind,
And, even with something of a mother's mind
And no unworthy aim,
The homely nurse doth all she can
To make her foster-child, her inmate, man,
Forget the glories he hath known.
And that imperial palace whence he came.

Behold the child among his new-born blisses,
A six years' darling of a pigmy size!
See, where 'mid work of his own hand he lies,

Of childhood, whether busy or at rest,
With new-fledged hope still fluttering in his breast:
—Not for these I raise
The song of thanks and praise;
But for those obstinate questionings
Of sense and outward things,
Fallings from us, vanishings;
Blank misgivings of a creature
Moving about in worlds not realized,
High instincts, before which our mortal nature
Did tremble like a guilty thing surprized:
But for those first affections,
Those shadowy recollections,
Which, be they what they may,
Are yet the fountain-light of all our day,
Are yet a master-light of all our seeing;
Uphold us, cherish, and have power to make
Our noisy years seem moments in the being
Of the eternal silence: truths that wake,
To perish never;
Which neither listlessness, nor mad endeavor,
Nor man nor boy
Nor all that is at enmity with joy,
Can utterly abolish or destroy!
Hence in a season of calm weather
Tho inland far we be,
Our souls have sight of that immortal sea
Which brought us hither;
Can in a moment travel thither—
And see the children sport upon the shore,
And hear the mighty waters rolling evermore.

Then, sing ye birds, sing, sing a joyous song!
And let the young lambs bound
As to the tabor's sound!
We, in thought, will join your throng,
Ye that pipe and ye that play,
Ye that through your hearts to-day
Feel the gladness of the May!
What tho the radiance which was once so bright
Be now forever taken from my sight,
Tho nothing can bring back the hour
Of splendor in the grass, of glory in the flower;
We will grieve not, rather find
Strength in what remains behind;
In the primal sympathy
Which having been must ever be;
In the soothing thoughts that spring
Out of human suffering;
In the faith that looks through death,
In years that bring the philosophic mind.

And O ye Mountains, Meadows, Hills and Groves,
Think not of any severing of our loves!
Yet in my heart of hearts I feel your might;
I only have relinquish'd one delight
To live beneath your more habitual sway:
I love the brooks which down their channels fret
Even more than when I tript lightly as they;
The innocent brightness of a new-born day
Is lovely yet;
The clouds that gather round the setting sun
Do take a sober coloring from an eye
That hath kept watch o'er man's mortality;
Another race hath been, and other palms are won.

Thanks to the human heart by which we live,
Thanks to its tenderness, its joys, and fears,
To me the meanest flower that blows can give
Thoughts that do often lie too deep for tears.

THE DAY IS DONE[1]

BY HENRY WADSWORTH LONGFELLOW

The day is done, and the darkness
  Falls from the wings of night
As a feather is wafted downward
  From an eagle in his flight.

I see the lights of the village
  Gleam through the rain and the mist,
And a feeling of sadness comes o'er me
  That my soul can not resist:

A feeling of sadness and longing,
  That is not akin to pain,
And resembles sorrow only
  As the mist resembles the rain.

Come, read to me some poem,
  Some simple and heartfelt lay,
That shall soothe this restless feeling,
  And banish the thoughts of day.

[1] By permission of Houghton, Mifflin & Co.

Not from the grand old masters,
  Not from the bards sublime,
Whose distant footsteps echo
  Through the corridors of time.

For, like the strains of martial music,
  Their mighty thoughts suggest
Life's endless toil and endeavor;
  And to-night I long for rest.

Read from some humbler poet,
  Whose songs gushed from his heart,
As shadows from the clouds of summer,
  Or tears from the eyelids start;

Who, through long days of labor,
  And nights devoid of ease,
Still heard in his soul the music
  Of wonderful melodies.

Such songs have power to quiet
  The restless pulse of care,
And come like the benediction
  That follows after prayer.

Then read from the treasured volume
  The poem of thy choice,
And lend to the rime of the poet
  The beauty of thy voice.

And the night shall be filled with music,
  And the cares, that infest the day,
Shall fold their tents, like the Arabs,
  And as silently steal away.

INCIDENT OF THE FRENCH CAMP[1]

BY ROBERT BROWNING

You know, we French storm'd Ratisbon:
  A mile or so away
On a little mound Napoleon
  Stood on our storming-day;
With neck out-thrust, you fancy how,
  Legs wide, arms lock'd behind,
As if to balance the prone brow
  Oppressive with its mind.

Just as perhaps he mused "My plans
  That soar, to earth may fall,
Let once my army leader Lannes
  Waver at yonder wall"—
Out 'twixt the battery smokes there flew
  A rider, bound on bound
Full-galloping; nor bridle drew
  Until he reach'd the mound.

Then off there flung in smiling joy,
  And held himself erect
By just his horse's mane, a boy:
  You hardly could suspect—
(So tight he kept his lips comprest
  Scarce any blood came through)
You look'd twice ere you saw his breast
  Was all but shot in two.

[1] By permission of The Macmillan Co.

"Well," cried he, "Emperor, by God's grace
  We've got you Ratisbon!
The marshal's in the market-place,
  And you'll be there anon
To see your flag-bird flap his vans
  Where I, to heart's desire,
Perch'd him!" The chief's eye flash'd; his plans
  Soar'd up again like fire.

The chief's eye flash'd; but presently
  Soften'd itself, as sheathes
A film the mother-eagle's eye
  When her bruised eaglet breathes.
"You're wounded!" "Nay," the soldier's pride
  Touch'd to the quick, he said:
"I'm kill'd, sire!" And his chief beside
  Smiling the boy fell dead.

THE CATARACT OF LODORE

BY ROBERT SOUTHEY

"How does the water come down at Lodore?"
My little boy asked me thus once on a time;
And, moreover, he tasked me to tell him in rhyme.
Anon at the word, there first came one daughter,
And then came another, to second and third
The request of their brother, and to hear how the water
Comes down at Lodore, with its rush and its roar,
As many a time they had seen it before.

So I told them in rime, for of rimes I had store;
And 'twas in my vocation for their recreation
That so I should sing, because I was laureate to them and
the king.

From its sources which well in the Tarn on the fell;
From its fountains in the mountains,
Its rills and its gills,—through moss and through brake
It runs and it creeps for awhile, till it sleeps
In its own little lake. And thence at departing,
Awaking and starting, it runs through the reeds,
And away it proceeds through meadow and glade,
In sun and in shade, and through the wood-shelter,
Among crags in its flurry, helter-skelter,
Hurry-skurry. Here it comes sparkling,
And there it lies darkling; now smoking and frothing
Its tumult and wrath in, till, in this rapid race
On which it is bent, it reaches the place
Of its steep descent.

The cataract strong then plunges along,
Striking and raging, as if a war waging
Its caverns and rocks among; rising and leaping,
Sinking and creeping, swelling and sweeping,
Showering and springing, flying and flinging,
Writhing and ringing, eddying and whisking,
Spouting and frisking, turning and twisting,
Around and around with endless rebound!
Smiting and fighting, a sight to delight in;
Confounding, astounding, dizzying, and deafening
The ear with its sound.

Collecting, projecting, receding and speeding,
And shocking and rocking, and darting and parting,
All threading and spreading, and whizzing and hissing,
And dripping and skipping, and hitting and splitting,
And shining and twining, and rattling and battling,
And shaking and quaking, and pouring and roaring,
And waving and raving, and tossing and crossing,

And flowing and going, and running and stunning,
And foaming and roaming, and dinning and spinning,
And dropping and hopping, and working and jerking,
And guggling and struggling, and heaving and cleaving,
And moaning and groaning;
And glittering and flittering, and gathering and feathering,
And whitening and brightening, and quivering and shivering,
And hurrying and skurrying, and thundering and floundering;
Dividing and gliding and sliding,
And falling and brawling and sprawling,
And driving and riving and striving,
And sprinkling and twinkling and wrinkling,
And sounding and bounding and rounding,
And bubbling and troubling and doubling,
And grumbling and rumbling and tumbling,
And clattering and battering and shattering;

Retreating and beating and meeting and sheeting,
Delaying and straying and playing and spraying,
Advancing and prancing and glancing and dancing,

Recoiling, turmoiling and toiling and boiling,
And gleaming and streaming and steaming and beaming,
And rushing and flushing and brushing and gushing,

. . . .

And flapping and rapping and clapping and slapping,
And curling and whirling and purling and twirling,
And thumping and plumping and bumping and jumping,
And dashing and flashing and splashing and clashing,
And so never ending, but always descending,
Sounds and motions forever and ever are blending,
All at once and all o'er, with a mighty uproar,—
And this way the water comes down at Lodore.

ODE ON A GRECIAN URN

BY JOHN KEATS

Thou still unravish'd bride of quietness,
    Thou foster-child of silence and slow time,
Sylvan historian, who canst thus express
    A flowery tale more sweetly than our rime:
What leaf-fringed legend haunts about thy shape
    Of deities or mortals, or of both,
        In Tempe or the dales of Arcady?
What men or gods are these? What maidens loth?
    What mad pursuit? What struggle to escape?
        What pipes and timbrels? What wild ecstasy?

Heard melodies are sweet, but those unheard
    Are sweeter; therefore, ye soft pipes, play on;
Not to the sensual ear, but, more endear'd,
    Pipe to the spirit ditties of no tone:

Fair youth, beneath the trees, thou canst not leave
Thy song, nor ever can those trees be bare;
Bold lover, never, never canst thou kiss,
Tho winning near the goal—yet, do not grieve;
She can not fade, tho thou hast not thy bliss,
For ever wilt thou love, and she be fair!

Ah, happy, happy boughs! that can not shed
Your leaves, nor ever bid the spring adieu;
And, happy melodist, unwearied,
For ever piping songs for ever new;
More happy love! more happy, happy love!
For ever warm and still to be enjoy'd,
For ever panting, and for ever young;
All breathing human passion far above,
That leaves a heart high-sorrowful and cloy'd,
A burning forehead, and a parching tongue.

Who are these coming to the sacrifice?
To what green altar, O mysterious priest,
Lead'st thou that heifer lowing at the skies,
And all her silken flanks with garlands drest?
What little town by river or sea shore,
Or mountain-built with peaceful citadel,
Is emptied of this folk, this pious morn?
And, little town, thy streets for evermore
Will silent be; and not a soul to tell
Why thou art desolate, can e'er return.

O Attic shape! Fair attitude! with brede
Of marble men and maidens overwrought,
With forest branches and the trodden weed;
Thou, silent form, dost tease us out of thought
As doth eternity: Cold pastoral!

When old age shall this generation waste,
Thou shalt remain, in midst of other wo
Than ours, a friend to man, to whom thou say'st
"Beauty is truth, truth beauty,"—that is all
Ye know on earth, and all ye need to know.

THE PASSIONS

BY WILLIAM COLLINS

When Music, heavenly maid, was young,
While yet in early Greece she sung,
The passions oft, to hear her shell,
Thronged around her magic cell,—
Exulting, trembling, raging, fainting,—
Possest beyond the Muse's painting;
By turns they felt the glowing mind
Disturbed, delighted, raised, refined:
Till once, 'tis said, when all were fired,
Filled with fury—rapt, inspired,
From the supporting myrtles round
They snatched her instruments of sound
And, as they oft had heard apart
Sweet lessons of her forceful art,
Each—for Madness ruled the hour—
Would prove his own expressive power.

First, Fear his hand, its skill to try,
Amid the chords bewildered laid;
And back recoiled, he knew not why,
E'en at the sound himself had made.—
Next, Anger rushed—his eyes on fire—
In lightnings owned his secret stings:

In one rude clash he struck the lyre,
    And swept, with hurried hands, the strings.—
With woful measures, wan Despair—
    Low sullen sounds!—his grief beguiled.
A solemn, strange, and ingled air;
    'Twas sad, by fits—by starts, 'twas wild.

But thou, O Hope! with eyes so fair—
    What was thy delighted measure?
    Still it whispered promised pleasure,
And bade the lovely scenes at distance hail!
    Still would her touch the strain prolong;
And, from the rocks, the woods, the vale,
    She called on Echo still, through all her song;
And her sweetest theme she chose,
A soft, responsive voice was heard at every close;
And Hope, enchanted, smiled, and waved her golden hair.

And longer had she sung—but, with a frown,
    Revenge impatient rose.
He threw his blood-stained sword in thunder down;
    And, with a withering look,
    The war-denouncing trumpet took,
And blew a blast so loud and dread,
    Were ne'er prophetic sounds so full of woes;
    And ever and anon, he beat
    The doubling drum with furious heat;
And tho, sometimes, each dreary pause between,
    Dejected Pity, at his side,
    Her soul-subduing voice applied.
Yet still he kept his wild unaltered mien,
While each strained ball of sight seemed bursting from his
        head.

Thy numbers, Jealousy, to naught were fixt—
Sad proof of thy distressful state!
Of differing themes the veering song was mixt;
And now it courted Love—now, raving, called on Hate

With eyes upraised, as one inspired,
Pale Melancholy sat retired;
And, from her wild, sequestered seat,
In notes, by distance made more sweet,
Poured through the mellow horn her pensive soul;
And, dashing soft from rocks around,
Bubbling runnels joined the sound;
Through glades and glooms the mingled measure stole;
Or, o'er some haunted streams, with fond delay,—
Round a holy calm diffusing,
Love of peace, and lonely musing,—
In hollow murmurs died away.

But oh! how altered was its sprightlier tone,
When Cheerfulness, a nymph of healthiest hue,
Her bow across her shoulder flung,
Her buskins gemmed with morning dew,
Blew an inspiring air, that dale and thicket rung,—
The hunter's call to Faun and Dryad known!
The oak-crowned sisters, and their chaste-eyed queen,
Satyrs, and sylvan boys, were seen,
Peeping from forth their alleys green:
Brown Exercise rejoiced to hear;
And Sport leaped up, and seized his beechen spear.

Last came Joy's ecstatic trial:—
He, with viny crown, advancing,
First to the lively pipe his hand addrest;

But soon he saw the brisk awakening viol,
Whose sweet, entrancing voice he loved the best.
They would have thought, who heard the strain,
    They saw in Tempe's vale her native maids,
Amid the festal-sounding shades,
    To some unwearied minstrel dancing;
    While, as his flying fingers kissed the strings,
Love framed with Mirth a gay fantastic round—
Loose were her tresses seen, her zone unbound—
    And he, amid his frolic play,
    As if he would the charming air repay,
Shook thousand odors from his dewy wings.

THE ENGLISH LANGUAGE

BY WILLIAM WETMORE STORY

Give me of every language, first my vigorous English,
Stored with imported wealth, rich in its natural mines—
Grand in its rhythmical cadence simple for household employment—
Worthy the poet's song, fit for the speech of a man.
Not from one metal alone the perfectest mirror is shapen,
Not from one color is built the rainbow's aerial bridge,
Instruments blending together yield the divinest of music,
Out of a myriad flowers sweetest of honey is drawn.
So unto thy close strength is welded and beaten together
Iron dug from the North, ductile gold from the South;
So unto thy broad stream the ice torrents born in the mountains
Rush, and the rivers from brimming with sun from the plains.

Thou hast the sharp clean edge and the downright blow of the Saxon,
Thou the majestical march and the stately pomp of the Latin,
Thou the euphonious swell, the rhythmical roll of the Greek;
Thine is the elegant suavity caught from the sonorous Italian,
Thine the chivalric obeisance, the courteous grace of the Norman—
Thine the Teutonic German's inborn guttural strength.
Raftered by firm-laid consonants, windowed by opening vowels,
Thou securely art built, free to the sun and the air.
Over thy feudal battlements trail the wild tendrils of fancy,
Where in the early morn warbled our earliest birds;
Science looks out from thy watch-tower, love whispers in at thy lattice,
While o'er thy bastions wit flashes its glittering sword.
Not by corruption rotted, nor slowly by ages degraded,
Have the sharp consonants gone crumbling away from our words;
Virgin and clean their edgelike granite blocks chiseled by Egypt,
Just as when Shakespeare and Milton laid them in glorious voice.
Fitted for every use, like a great majestical river,
Blending thy various streams, stately thou flowest along,
Bearing the white-winged ship of poesy over thy bosom,
Laden with spices that come out of the tropical isles,
Fancy's pleasuring yacht with its bright and fluttering pennons,
Logic's frigates of war, and the toil-worn barges of trade.

How art thou freely obedient unto the poet or speaker
When, in a happy hour, thought into speech he translates;
Caught on the word's sharp angles flash the bright hues of his fancy—
Grandly the thought rides the words, as a good horseman his steed.
Now clear, pure, hard, bright, and one by one, like to hailstones,
Short words fall from his lips fast as the first of a shower—
Now in twofold column, Spondee, Iamb, and Trochee,
Unbroke, firm set, advance, retreat trampling along—
Now with a sprightlier springless bounding in triplicate syllables,
Dance the elastic Dactylics in musical cadences on,
Now their voluminous coil, intertangling like huge anacondas,
Rolls overwhelmingly onward the sesquipedalian words.
Flexile and free in thy gait, and simple in all thy construction,
Yielding to every turn, thou bearest thy rider along;
Now like our hackney or draft-horse serving our commonest uses,
Now bearing grandly the poet Pegasus-like to the sky.
Thou art not prisoned in fixt rules, thou art no slave to a grammar,
Thou art an eagle uncaged, scorning the perch and the chain.
Hadst thou been fettered and formalized, thou hadst been tamer and weaker:
How could the poor slave walk with thy grand freedom of gait?

Let then grammarians rail and let foreigners sigh for thy sign-posts,
Wandering lost in thy maze, thy wilds of magnificent growth,
Call thee incongruous, wild, of rule and of reason defiant;
In thy wildness a grand freedom of character find.
So, with irregular outline, tower up the sky-piercing mountains,
Rearing o'er yawning chasms, lofty precipitous steeps,
Spreading o'er ledges unclimbable, meadows and slopes of green smoothness,
Bearing the flowers in their clefts, losing their peaks in the clouds.
Therefore it is that I praise thee, and never can cease from rejoicing,
Thinking that good, stout English is mine and my ancestors' tongue.
Give me its varying music, the flow of its free modulation,
I will not covet the full roll of the glorious Greek,
Luscious and feeble Italian, Latin so formal and stately,
French with its nasal lisp, nor German inverted and harsh.
Not while our organ can speak with its many and wonderful voices—
Play on the soft flute of love, blow the loud trumpet of war,
Sing with the high sesquialtro, or, drawing its full diapason,
Shake all the air with the grand storm of its pedals and stops.

THE DESTRUCTION OF SENNACHERIB

BY GEORGE GORDON, LORD BYRON

The Assyrian came down like the wolf on the fold,
And his cohorts were gleaming in purple and gold;
And the sheen of their spears was like stars on the sea,
When the blue wave rolls nightly on deep Galilee.

Like the leaves of the forest when summer is green,
That host with their banners at sunset were seen;
Like the leaves of the forest when autumn hath blown,
That host on the morrow lay withered and strown.

For the Angel of Death spread his wings on the blast,
And breathed in the face of the foe as he passed;
And the eyes of the sleepers waxed deadly and chill,
And their hearts but once heaved, and forever grew still!

And there lay the steed with his nostrils all wide,
But through them rolled not the breath of his pride:
And the foam of his gasping lay white on the turf,
And cold as the spray of the rock-beating surf.

And there lay the rider distorted and pale,
With the dew on his brow, and the rust on his mail;
And the tents were all silent, the banners alone,
The lances uplifted, the trumpet unblown.

And the widows of Ashur are loud in their wail,
And the idols are broke in the temple of Baal;
And the might of the Gentile, unsmote by the sword,
Hath melted like snow in the glance of the Lord!

CHARACTER OF THE HAPPY WARRIOR

BY WILLIAM WORDSWORTH

Who is the happy warrior? Who is he
Whom every man in arms should wish to be?
It is the generous spirit, who, when brought
Among the tasks of real life, hath wrought
Upon the plan that pleased his childish thought:
Whose high endeavors are an inward light
That make the path before him always bright;
Who, with a natural instinct to discern
What knowledge can perform, is diligent to learn;
Abides by this resolve, and stops not there,
But makes his moral being his prime care;
Who, doom'd to go in company with pain,
And fear, and bloodshed, miserable train!
Turns his necessity to glorious gain;
In face of these doth exercise a power
Which is our human nature's highest dower;
Controls them and subdues, transmutes, bereaves
Of their bad influence, and their good receives;
By objects which might force the soul to abate
Her feeling, render'd more compassionate;
Is placable—because occasions rise
So often that demand such sacrifice;
More skilful in self-knowledge, even more pure,
As tempted more; more able to endure,
As more exposed to suffering and distress;
Thence, also, more alive to tenderness.
'Tis he whose law is reason; who depends
Upon that law as on the best of friends;

Whence, in a state where men are tempted still
To evil for a guard against worse ill,
And what in quality or act is best
Doth seldom on a right foundation rest,
He fixes good on good alone, and owes
To virtue every triumph that he knows;
Who, if he rise to station of command,
Rises by open means; and there will stand
On honorable terms, or else retire,
And in himself possess his own desire;
Who comprehends his trust, and to the same
Keeps faithful with a singleness of aim;
And therefore does not stoop, nor lie in wait
For wealth, or honors, or for worldly state;
Whom they must follow; on whose head must fall,
Like showers of manna, if they come at all;
Whose powers shed round him in the common strife,
Or mild concerns of ordinary life,
A constant influence, a peculiar grace;
But who, if he be called upon to face
Some awful moment to which Heaven has join'd
Great issues, good or bad for human kind,
Is happy as a lover; and attired
With sudden brightness, like a man inspired;
And, through the heat of conflict, keeps the law
In calmness made, and sees what he foresaw;
Or if an unexpected call succeed,
Come when it will, is equal to the need:
—He who, tho thus endued as with a sense
And faculty for storm and turbulence,
Is yet a soul whose master bias leans
To homefelt pleasures and to gentle scenes;

Sweet images! which, whereso'er he be,
Are at his heart; and such fidelity
It is his darling passion to approve;
More brave for this, that he hath much to love:
'Tis, finally, the man, who, lifted high,
Conspicuous object in a nation's eye,
Or left unthought of in obscurity,—
Who, with a toward or untoward lot,
Prosperous or adverse, to his wish or not,
Plays, in the many games of life, that one
Where what he most doth value must be won;
Whom neither shape of danger can dismay,
Nor thought of tender happiness betray;
Who, not content that former worth stand fast,
Looks forward, persevering to the last,
From well to better, daily self-surpassed:
Who, whether praise of him must walk the earth
Forever, and to noble deeds give birth,
Or he must go to dust without his fame,
And leave a dead, unprofitable name,
Finds comfort in himself and in his cause;
And, while the mortal mist is gathering, draws
His breath in confidence of heaven's applause:
This is the happy warrior; this is he
Whom every man in arms should wish to be.

IN GRIEF

From "In Memoriam"

BY ALFRED TENNYSON

Strong Son of God! immortal Love,
  Whom we, that have not seen Thy face,
  By faith, and faith alone, embrace,
Believing where we can not prove!

Thine are these orbs of light and shade;
  Thou madest life in man and brute;
  Thou madest Death; and lo, Thy foot
Is on the skull which Thou hast made!

Thou wilt not leave us in the dust:
  Thou madest man, he knows not why;
  He thinks he was not made to die;
And Thou hast made him: Thou art just.

Thou seemest human and divine,
  The highest, holiest manhood, Thou:
  Our wills are ours, we know not how;
Our wills are ours to make them Thine.

Our little systems have their day;
  They have their day and cease to be;
  They are but broken lights of Thee,
And Thou, O Lord, are more than they.

We have but faith: we can not know;
  For knowledge is of things we see;
  And yet we trust it comes from Thee,
A beam in darkness: let it grow.

Let knowledge grow from more to more,
  But more of reverence in us dwell;
  That mind and soul, according well,
May make one music as before,

But vaster. We are fools and slight;
  We mock Thee when we do not fear;
  But help Thy foolish ones to bear;
Help Thy vain worlds to bear Thy light.

Forgive what seemed my sin in me;
  What seemed my worth since I began;
  For merit lives from man to man,
And from man, O Lord, to Thee.

Forgive my grief for one removed,
  Thy creature, whom I found so fair.
  I trust he lives in Thee, and there
I find him worthier to be loved.

Forgive these wild and wandering cries,
  Confusions of a wasted youth;
  Forgive them where they fail in truth,
And in Thy wisdom make me wise.

O THOU ETERNAL ONE

BY GABRIEL ROMANOVITCH DERZHAVIN

O Thou eternal One! whose presence bright
All space doth occupy, all motion guide;
Unchanged through time's all-devastating flight;
Thou only God! There is no God beside!
Being above all beings! mighty One!
Whom none can comprehend and none explore;
Who fill'st existence with *Thyself* alone;
Embracing all, supporting, ruling o'er,—
Being whom we call God, and know no more!

In its sublime research, philosophy
May measure out the ocean-deep, may count
The sands or the sun's rays; but God! for Thee
There is no weight nor measure: none can mount
Up to Thy mysteries. Reason's brightest spark,
Tho kindled by Thy light, in vain would try
To trace Thy counsels, infinite and dark;
And thought is lost ere thought can soar so high,
Even like past moments in eternity.

Thou from primeval nothingness didst call
First chaos, then existence: Lord! on Thee
Eternity had its foundation; all
Sprung forth from Thee,—of light, joy, harmony,
Sole origin: all life, all beauty Thine.
Thy word created all, and doth create;
Thy splendor fills all space with rays divine.
Thou art, and wert, and shalt be! Glorious! Great!
Light-giving, life-sustaining Potentate!

Thy chains the unmeasured universe surround,
Upheld by Thee, by Thee inspired with breath!
Thou the beginning with the end hast bound,
And beautifully mingled life and death!
As sparks mount upward from the fiery blaze,
So suns are born, so worlds spring forth from Thee,
And as the spangles in the sunny rays
Shine round the silver snow, the pageantry
Of heaven's bright army glitters in Thy praise.

A million torches lighted by Thy hand
Wander unwearied through the blue abyss:
They own Thy power, accomplish Thy command,
All gay with life, all eloquent with bliss.
What shall we call them? Piles of crystal light,
A glorious company of golden streams,
Lamps of celestial ether burning bright,
Suns lighting systems with their joyous beams?
But Thou to these art as the noon to night.

Yes! as a drop of water in the sea,
All this magnificence in Thee is lost:
What are ten thousand worlds compared to Thee?
And what am *I* then? Heaven's unnumbered host,
Tho multiplied by myriads, and arrayed
In all the glory of sublimest thought,
Is but an atom in the balance, weighed
Against Thy greatness; is a cipher brought
Against infinity! Oh, what am I then? Naught!

Naught! yet the effluence of Thy light divine,
Pervading worlds, hath reached my bosom too;
Yes! in my spirit doth Thy spirit shine,
As shines the sunbeam in a drop of dew.
Naught! yet I live, and on hope's pinions fly
Eager towards Thy presence; for in Thee
I live, and breathe, and dwell; aspiring high,
Even to the throne of Thy divinity.
I am, O God! and surely *Thou* must be!

Thou art! directing, guiding all, Thou art!
Direct my understanding, then, to Thee;
Control my spirit, guide my wandering heart:
Tho but an atom midst immensity,
Still I am something, fashioned by Thy hand!
I hold a middle rank 'twixt heaven and earth,
On the last verge of mortal being stand,
Close to the realms where angels have their birth,
Just on the boundaries of the spirit-land!

The chain of being is complete in me;
In me is matter's last gradation lost,
And the next step is spirit—Deity!
I can command the lightning, and am dust!
A monarch, and a slave; a worm, a god!
Whence came I here? and how so marvelously
Constructed and conceived? unknown! this clod
Lives surely through some higher energy;
For from itself alone it could not be!

Creator, yes! Thy wisdom and Thy word
Created me! Thou Source of life and good!
Thou Spirit of my Spirit, and my Lord!
Thy light, Thy love, in their bright plenitude
Filled me with an immortal soul, to spring
Over the abyss of death, and bade it wear
The garments of eternal day, and wing
Its heavenly flight beyond this little sphere,
Even to its source—to Thee—its Author there.

O thoughts ineffable! O visions blest!
Tho worthless our conceptions all of Thee,
Yet shall Thy shadowed image fill our breast,
And waft its homage to Thy Deity.
God! thus alone my lonely thoughts can soar;
Thus seek Thy presence, Being wise and good!
Midst Thy vast works admire, obey, adore;
And when the tongue is eloquent no more,
The soul shall speak in tears of gratitude.

PRAYER

BY CHARLES FRANCIS RICHARDSON

If, when I kneel to pray,
With eager lips I say:
"Lord give me all the things that I desire;
Health, wealth, fame, friends, brave heart, religious fire,
The power to sway my fellow men at will,
And strength for might works to banish ill";
In such a prayer as this
The blessing I must miss.

Or if I only dare
To raise this fainting prayer:
"Thou seest, Lord, that I am poor and weak,
And can not tell what things I ought to seek;
I therefore do not ask at all, but still
I trust Thy bounty all my wants to fill";
My lips shall thus grow dumb,
The blessings shall not come.

But if I lowly fall,
And thus in faith I call:
"Through Christ, O Lord, I pray Thee give to me
Not what I would, but what seems best to Thee,
Of life, of health, of service, and of strength,
Until to Thy full joy I come at length";
My prayer shall then avail,
The blessing shall not fail.

NEARER TO THEE

BY SARAH FULLER FLOWER

Nearer, my God, to Thee
Nearer to Thee!
E'en tho it be a cross
That raiseth me;
Still all my song shall be,
Nearer, my God, to Thee,
Nearer to Thee!

Tho like the wanderer,
  The sun gone down,
Darkness be over me,
  My rest a stone;
Yet in my dreams I'd be
Nearer, my God, to Thee,
  Nearer to Thee!

There let the way appear
  Steps unto heaven;
All that Thou send'st to me
  In mercy given;
Angels to beckon me
Nearer, my God, to Thee,
  Nearer to Thee!

Then, with my waking thoughts
  Bright with Thy praise,
Out of my stormy griefs
  Bethel I'll raise;
So by my woes to be
Nearer, my God, to Thee,
  Nearer to Thee!

Or if on joyful wing
  Cleaving the sky,
Sun, moon, and stars forgot,
  Upward I fly,
Still all my song shall be,
Nearer, my God, to Thee,
  Nearer to Thee!

Lesson talk. The reading aloud of sacred poetry and hymns is of great value to the student of elocution. These selections usually require a spirit of reverence and devotion, and an elevated style in which feeling and imagination play a conspicuous part. The easy grace and rhythm of the lines should be maintained without falling into sing-song or uniformity.

Poetry should not be read like prose, nor is rime, when it occurs, to be obscured, but rather slightly marked. The voice does not necessarily rise or fall at the end of each line, but is governed by a just sense of the meaning of the words. Poetry demands tone-color for its proper expression, a judicious painting of the thought with feeling, by which appeal is made to the heart rather than to the intellect of the hearer. In the reading of hymns to a congregation the minister should carefully avoid the common faults of jerkiness, intoning, lifelessness, and overemphasis. Hymns should be analyzed and practised aloud in advance of the church service, and their vocal interpretation regarded as an important part of public worship.

THE CHRISTIAN PILGRIM'S HYMN

BY WILLIAM WILLIAMS

Guide me, O Thou great Jehovah,
  Pilgrim through this barren land:
I am weak, but Thou art mighty;
  Hold me with Thy powerful hand!
    Bread of heaven! bread of heaven!
    Feed me now and evermore.

Open now the crystal fountain
  Whence the healing streams do flow;
Let the fiery, cloudy pillar
  Lead me all my journey through:
    Strong Deliverer! strong Deliverer!
    Be Thou still my strength and shield.

When I tread the verge of Jordan,
  Bid my anxious fears subside;
Death of deaths, and hell's destruction,
  Land me safe on Canaan's side.
    Songs of praises, songs of praises,
    I will ever give to Thee.

Musing on my habitation,
  Musing on my heavenly home,
Fills my soul with holy longing;
  Come, my Jesus, quickly come.
    Vanity is all I see;
    Lord, I long to be with Thee!

LIGHT SHINING OUT OF DARKNESS

BY WILLIAM COWPER

God moves in a mysterious way
  His wonders to perform;
He plants His footsteps in the sea,
  And rides upon the storm.

Deep in unfathomable mines
  Of never-failing skill
He treasures up His bright designs,
  And works His sovereign will.

Ye fearful saints, fresh courage take,
  The clouds ye so much dread
Are big with mercy, and shall break
  In blessings on your head.

Judge not the Lord by feeble sense,
  But trust Him for His grace,
Behind a frowning providence
  He hides a smiling face.

His purposes will ripen fast,
  Unfolding every hour;
The bud may have a bitter taste,
  But sweet will be the flower.

Blind unbelief is sure to err,
  And scan His work in vain;
God is His own interpreter,
  And He will make it plain.

THRICE HOLY

BY BISHOP REGINALD HEBER

Holy, Holy, Holy! Lord God Almighty!
  Early in the morning our song shall rise to Thee;
Holy, Holy, Holy! merciful and mighty!
  God in Three Persons, Blessed Trinity!

Holy, Holy, Holy! all the saints adore Thee,
  Casting down their golden crowns around the glassy sea;
Cherubim and seraphim falling down before Thee,
  Which wert, and art, and evermore shalt be!

Holy, Holy, Holy! tho the darkness hide Thee,
  Tho the eye of sinful man Thy glory may not see,
Only Thou art holy, there is none beside Thee,
  Perfect in power, in love, in purity!

Holy, Holy, Holy! Lord God Almighty!
  All Thy works shall praise Thy name, in earth and sky
    and sea:
Holy, Holy, Holy! merciful and mighty!
  God in Three Persons, Blessed Trinity!

ONWARD!

BY SABINE BARING-GOULD

Onward, Christian soldiers,
  Marching as to war,
With the cross of Jesus
  Going on before;
Christ, the royal Master,
  Leads against the foe;
Forward into battle,
  See, His banners go.
    Onward, Christian soldiers,
      Marching as to war,
    With the cross of Jesus
      Going on before!

At the sign of triumph
  Satan's host doth flee;
On, then, Christian soldiers,
  On to victory!
Hell's foundations quiver
  At the shout of praise;
Brothers, lift your voices,
  Loud your anthems raise.
    Onward, etc.

Like a mighty army
  Moves the Church of God;
Brothers, we are treading
  Where the saints have trod;
We are not divided,
  All one body we,
One in hope and doctrine,
  One in charity.
    Onward, etc.

Crowns and thrones may perish,
  Kingdoms rise and wane,
But the Church of Jesus
  Constant will remain;
Gates of hell can never
  'Gainst that Church prevail;
We have Christ's own promise,
  And that can not fail.
    Onward, etc.

Onward, then, ye people,
  Join our happy throng,
Blend with ours your voices,
  In the triumph-song;
Glory, laud, and honor,
  Unto Christ the King;
This through countless ages
  Men and angels sing.
    Onward, Christian soldiers,
      Marching as to war,
    With the cross of Jesus
      Going on before!

PRAISE TO GOD

BY JOSEPH ADDISON

When all Thy mercies, O my God,
  My rising soul surveys,
Transported with the view, I'm lost
  In wonder, love, and praise!

Oh, how shall words with equal warmth
  The gratitude declare
That glows within my ravished heart?
  But Thou canst read it there.

Thy providence my life sustained,
  And all my wants redrest,
When in the silent womb I lay,
  And hung upon the breast.

To all my weak complaints and cries
  Thy mercy lent an ear,
Ere yet my feeble thoughts had learnt
  To form themselves in prayer.

Unnumbered comforts to my soul
  Thy tender care bestowed,
Before my infant heart conceived
  From whom those comforts flowed.

When in the slippery paths of youth
  With heedless steps I ran,
Thine arm unseen conveyed me safe,
  And led me up to man.

Through hidden dangers, toils, and death,
  It gently cleared my way,
And through the pleasing snares of vice,
  More to be feared than they.

When worn with sickness, oft hast thou
  With health renewed my face;
And when in sins and sorrows sunk,
  Revived my soul with grace.

Thy bounteous hand with worldly bliss
  Has made my cup run o'er,
And in a kind and faithful friend
  Has doubled all my store.

Ten thousand thousand precious gifts
  My daily thanks employ;
Nor is the least a cheerful heart,
  That tastes those gifts with joy.

Through every period of my life
  Thy goodness I'll pursue;
And after death, in distant worlds,
  The glorious theme renew.

When nature fails, and day and night
  Divide Thy works no more,
My ever-grateful heart, O Lord,
  Thy mercy shall adore.

Through all eternity to Thee
  A joyful song I'll raise;
For oh, eternity's too short
  To utter all Thy praise!

ABIDE WITH ME

BY HENRY FRANCIS LYTE

Abide with me! Fast falls the eventide;
The darkness deepens: Lord, with me abide!
When other helpers fail, and comforts flee,
Help of the helpless, oh, abide with me!

Swift to its close ebbs out life's little day;
Earth's joys grow dim; its glories pass away:
Change and decay in all around I see;
O thou, who changest not, abide with me!

Not a brief glance I beg, a passing word,
But as thou dwell'st with thy disciples, Lord,
Familiar, condescending, patient, free—
Come, not to sojourn, but 'bide, with me!

Come not in terrors, as the King of kings;
But kind and good, with healing in Thy wings:
Tears for all woes, a heart for every plea.
Come, Friend of sinners, and thus 'bide with me!

Thou on my head in early youth didst smile,
And, tho rebellious and perverse meanwhile,
Thou hast not left me, oft as I left Thee,
On to the close, O Lord, abide with me!

I need Thy presence every passing hour.
What but Thy grace can foil the tempter's power?
Who like Thyself my guide and stay can be?
Through cloud and sunshine, oh, abide with me!

I fear no foe with Thee at hand to bless:
Ills have no weight, and tears no bitterness,
Where is death's sting, where, grave, thy victory?
I triumph still, if Thou abide with me.

Hold Thou Thy cross before my closing eyes;
Shine through the gloom, and point me to the skies:
Heaven's morning breaks, and earth's vain shadows flee.
In life and death, O Lord, abide with me!

JUST AS I AM

BY CHARLOTTE ELLIOTT

Just as I am—without one plea
But that Thy blood was shed for me,
And that Thou bid'st me come to Thee—
O Lamb of God, I come!

Just as I am—and waiting not
To rid my soul of one dark blot,
To Thee, whose blood can cleanse each spot—
O Lamb of God, I come!

Just as I am—tho tossed about,
With many a conflict, many a doubt,
Fightings and fears within, without—
O Lamb of God, I come!

Just as I am—poor, wretched, blind;
Sight, riches, healing of the mind,
Yea, all I need, in Thee to find—
O Lamb of God, I come!

Just as I am—Thou wilt receive,
Wilt welcome, pardon, cleanse, relieve,
Because Thy promise I believe—
O Lamb of God, I come!

Just as I am—Thy love unknown
Has broken every barrier down;
Now to be Thine, yea, Thine alone—
O Lamb of God, I come!

Just as I am—of that free love,
The breadth, length, depth, and height to prove,
Here for a season, then above—
O Lamb of God, I come!

NEARER HOME

BY PHOEBE CARY

One sweetly solemn thought
Comes to me o'er and o'er:
I am nearer home to-day
Than I ever have been before;

Nearer my Father's house,
Where the many mansions be;
Nearer the great white throne,
Nearer the crystal sea;

Nearer the bound of life,
Where we lay our burdens down;
Nearer leaving the cross,
Nearer gaining the crown!

But lying darkly between,
Winding down through the night,
Is the silent, unknown stream,
That leads at last to the light.

Closer and closer my steps
  Come to the dread abysm;
Closer death to my lips
  Presses the awful chrism.

Oh, if thy mortal feet
  Have almost gained the brink;
If it be I am nearer home
  Even to-day than I think;

Father, perfect my trust;
  Let my spirit feel in death,
That her feet are firmly set
  On the rock of a living faith!

THE PILGRIMS OF THE NIGHT

BY FREDERICK WILLIAM FABER

Hark! hark! my soul! Angelic songs are swelling
  O'er earth's green fields and ocean's wave-beat shore;
How sweet the truth those blessed strains are telling
  Of that new life when sin shall be no more!

Darker than night life's shadows fall around us,
  And, like benighted men, we miss our mark;
God hides himself, and grace hath scarcely found us,
  Ere death finds out his victims in the dark!

Onward we go, for still we hear them singing,
  "Come, weary souls! for Jesus bids you come!"
And through the dark, its echoes sweetly ringing,
  The music of the gospel leads us home.

Far, far away, like bells at evening pealing,
  The voice of Jesus sounds o'er land and sea,
And laden souls, by thousands meekly stealing,
  Kind Shepherd! turn their weary steps to Thee.

Rest comes at length; tho life be long and dreary,
  The day must dawn and darksome night be past;
All journeys end in welcomes to the weary,
  And heaven, the heart's true home, will come at last.

Cheer up, my soul! faith's moonbeams softly glisten
  Upon the breast of life's most troubled sea;
And it will cheer thy drooping heart to listen
  To those brave songs which angels mean for thee.

Angels! sing on, your faithful watches keeping;
  Sing us sweet fragments of the songs above;
While we toil on, and soothe ourselves with weeping,
  Till life's long night shall break in endless love.